Artificial Intelligence for .NET: Speech, Language, and Search

Building Smart Applications with Microsoft Cognitive Services APIs

Nishith Pathak

With Contributing Author as Anurag Bhandari

Artificial Intelligence for .NET: Speech, Language, and Search

Nishith Pathak
Kotdwara, Dist. Pauri Garhwal, India

ISBN-13 (pbk): 978-1-4842-2948-4   ISBN-13 (electronic): 978-1-4842-2949-1
DOI 10.1007/978-1-4842-2949-1

Library of Congress Control Number: 2017951713

Cover image designed by Freepik

Managing Director: Welmoed Spahr
Editorial Director: Todd Green
Acquisitions Editor: Gwenan Spearing
Development Editor: Laura Berendson
Technical Reviewer: Fabio Claudio Ferracchiati
Coordinating Editor: Nancy Chen
Copy Editor: Mary Behr
Artist: SPi Global

Distributed to the book trade worldwide by Springer Science+Business Media New York, 233 Spring Street, 6th Floor, New York, NY 10013. Phone 1-800-SPRINGER, fax (201) 348-4505, e-mail orders-ny@springer-sbm.com, or visit www.springeronline.com. Apress Media, LLC is a California LLC and the sole member (owner) is Springer Science + Business Media Finance Inc (SSBM Finance Inc). SSBM Finance Inc is a **Delaware** corporation.

For information on translations, please e-mail rights@apress.com, or visit www.apress.com/rights-permissions.

Apress titles may be purchased in bulk for academic, corporate, or promotional use. eBook versions and licenses are also available for most titles. For more information, reference our Print and eBook Bulk Sales web page at www.apress.com/bulk-sales.

Any source code or other supplementary material referenced by the author in this book is available to readers on GitHub via the book's product page, located at www.apress.com/9781484229484. For more detailed information, please visit www.apress.com/source-code.

To the most important person in my life, my mother, late Bina Pathak, for her guidance, sacrifices, prayers, and blessings, which made me What I am today. I miss her each day. To my father, Pankaj Pathak, for teaching me to do what I believe in. You are and will always be my role model and my hero for my entire life. To my Sadh-Gurudev, who has been an eternal guiding force and entirely changed my life. To my grandfather, the late Mahesh Chandra Pathak, for his blessings and moral values.

To my wife, Surabhi, for bearing with me, sacrificing her splendid career for our family, and always staying by my side through all the ups and downs. Getting married to you is the most beautiful thing in my life. You have given me the most precious diamond of my life, Shikhar, whom I love more than anyone else. I know this book has taken a lot of me and I haven't been able to spend enough time with you, Papa and Shikhar for the past year since I've been working tirelessly to give this pleasant surprise. Surabhi and Shikhar, this book would not have been possible without all your sacrifices.

To my lovely sister, Tanwi, and my niece, Aadhya—your smiling faces give me a lot of strength and inspiration to do better each day. To my Guruji, JP Kukreti, SS Tyagi, and Rajesh Tripathi, who have been there for me countless times and always provide me with comfort, understanding, spiritual beliefs, and lots of motivation.

Lastly, I thank God for blessing me with such wonderful people in my life.

Contents at a Glance

Contents

About the Author

Nishith Pathak is a Microsoft Most Valuable Professional (MVP), architect, speaker, AI thinker, innovator, and strategist. He is a prolific writer and contributing author and has written many books, articles, reviews, and columns for multiple electronic and print publications. Having 20+ years of experience in IT, Nishith's expertise lies in innovation, research, architecting, designing, and developing applications for Fortune 100 companies using next-generation tools and technologies. As an early adopter of Microsoft technology, he has kept pace in the certification challenges and succeeded in getting several of his certifications in the beta stage.

Nishith is a gold member and sits on the advisory board of various national and international computer science societies and organizations. He has been awarded the elite Microsoft Most Valuable Professional (MVP) a couple of times for his exemplary work and his expertise in Microsoft technologies. He is a member of various advisory groups for Microsoft. Nishith is currently working as Vice President and R&D lead for Accenture Technology Labs. He is focused on key research areas, specifically AI, ML, cognitive, bot, blockchain cloud computing, and helping companies architect solutions based on these technologies. Nishith was born, raised, and educated in a town called Kotdwara in Uttarakhand, India. Beyond that, as time permits, he spends time with family and friends, and amuses them with his interests in palmistry and astrology. You can contact him at nispathak@gmail.com.

About the Contributing Author

 **Anurag Bhandari** is a researcher, programmer, and open source evangelist. His favorite research areas include NLP, IoT, and machine learning. He specializes in developing web and mobile apps and solutions. He has extensive experience working with Fortune 500 companies, startups, and NGOs in the capacity of research and software delivery. Anurag hails from Jalandhar, Punjab, where he also completed a degree in Computer Science from the National Institute of Technology. Since his undergraduate days, he has been affiliated with or led several open source projects, such as Granular Linux and OpenMandriva. He is a proud polyglot of programming (C#, Java, JavaScript, PHP, Python) and natural (English, Hindi, Punjabi, French) languages. Being a technology enthusiast, Anurag keeps meddling with trending technologies and trying out new frameworks and platforms. In his spare time, he reads books, follows sports, drools over gadgets, watches TV shows, plays games, and collects stamps. You can find him online at http://anuragbhandari.com or drop him a note at anurag.bhd@gmail.com.

About the Technical Reviewer

Fabio Claudio Ferracchiati is a senior consultant and a senior analyst/developer using Microsoft technologies. He works at BluArancio S.p.A (www.bluarancio.com) as Senior Analyst/Developer and Microsoft Dyanmics CRM Specialist. He is a Microsoft Certified Solution Developer for .NET, a Microsoft Certified Application Developer for .NET, a Microsoft Certified Professional, and a prolific author and technical reviewer. Over the past ten years, he's written articles for Italian and international magazines and co-authored more than ten books on a variety of computer topics.

Acknowledgments

This book has been a team effort by some wonderful people. This book could not have been completed without my partner, Anurag Bhandari, who has done fantastic work in helping to complete chapters, write code, and do research. We would talk at odd hours, discussing technologies and shaping the book in the right direction. Anurag, you are the "one person" who helped me in supporting this book far beyond my expectation.

Thanks to all of the people at Apress who put their sincere efforts into publishing this book. Gwenan deserves special thanks. I exchanged a lot of emails with Gwenan before really taking on this project. Thanks to Nancy and Laura for doing a fabulous job of project management and constantly pushing me to do my best. I would also like to thank Henry Li for his tech review. I would not hesitate to say that you are all extremely talented people. Each of you helped this book immensely, and I'm looking forward to working with everyone on the next one.

Last but not least, thanks to my family, especially my wife, Surabhi, and my father, Pankaj Pathak, for being so kind and supportive, and making my dreams come true. Anything I do in my life would not be possible without you.

Now on to book number six.

Introduction

This book will introduce you to the world of artificial intelligence. Normally, developers think of AI implementation as a tough task involving writing complex algorithms and hundreds of lines of code. This book aims to remove the anxiety by creating a cognitive application with a few lines of code. There is a wide range of Cognitive Services APIs available. This book focuses on some of the most useful and powerful ways that your application can make intelligent use of Microsoft Cognitive API. Microsoft has given developers a better experience and enabled them through Microsoft Cognitive APIs.

The book covers genuine insights into AI concepts. Speech, language, and search are such deep-dive domains that each of these concepts would require a separate book. This book attempts to explain each of the concepts by first explaining *why* and *what* before delving into the *how* of any API. The book also provides extensive examples to make it easier to put the new concepts into practice. *Artificial Intelligence for .NET: Speech, Language, and Search* will show you how to start building amazing capabilities into your applications today.

This book starts by introducing you to artificial intelligence via its history, terminology, and techniques. The book then introduces you to all of the Microsoft Cognitive APIs and tools before building your first smart Cognitive application step by step using Visual Studio. The book then introduces concepts around the conversational user interface (CUI), and then you create your first bot using the Microsoft Bot Framework. The book also provides great context for understanding and best practices about planning your application using the Bot Framework.

The book also provides a deep understanding about natural language understanding (NLU) and natural language processing (NLP), which let computer programs interpret humans the way they do each other. The book goes into detail about the Microsoft Language Understanding Intelligent Service (LUIS) and its concepts, as well as on how to design, consume, and apply LUIS before creating a LUIS project from scratch. The book also provides detailed steps on testing, training, and publishing a LUIS application before deploying and using it in a Bot Framework.

Speech is the most natural form of interaction. This book provides a deep walk-through of the Speech API and how to use the API for speech recognition and speech synthesis. The book then provides a deep understanding of how to use the custom speech service previously known as CRIS and a step-by-step plan for creating your first language model, an audio model, and deploying it, and using the custom speech service. The book also provides detail into understanding speaker recognition.

The book then explains all Bing Search APIs in detail and how to leverage Bing search offerings in your applications. The book also goes in detail about the concepts behind and types of recommendations, and then uses each of them to fetch recommendations in a step-by-step approach. The book ends by giving you a glimpse into the future of AI and what to expect soon. In other words, the book can be treated as a guide to help you drive your next steps.

In this book, you will

- Explore the underpinnings of artificial intelligence through practical examples and scenarios

- Get started building an AI-based application in Visual Studio

- Build a text-based conversational interface for direct user interaction

- Use the Cognitive Services Speech API to recognize and interpret speech

- Look at different models of language, including natural language processing, and how to apply them in your Visual Studio application

- Reuse Bing search capabilities to better understand a user's intention

- Work with recommendation engines and integrate them into your apps

Who This Book Is For

Artificial intelligence is the buzzword of the current industry. People are talking about AI. With this disruption going on everywhere, developers can get confused about where and how to get started with AI. The release of the Microsoft Cognitive APIs offers a wide range of new functionality for developers. This book is targeted towards novice and intermediate readers who are curious about artificial intelligence. Developers and architects with previous experience or no experience with .NET who want to apply the new Cognitive APIs to their applications will benefit greatly from the discussion and code samples in this book. This book also serves as a great resource for application developers and architects new to AI and/or the core concepts of using some of the Cognitive APIs.

Prerequisites

To get the most out of this book, you just need the .NET Framework and an Internet connection. I recommend using Microsoft Visual Studio 2017 as the development environment to experiment with the code samples, which you can find in the Source Code section of the Apress website (www.apress.com).

Obtaining Updates for This Book

As you read through this text, you may find the occasional grammatical or code error (although I sure hope not). If this is the case, my sincere apologies. Being human, I am sure that a glitch or two may be present, regardless of my best efforts. You can obtain the current errata list from the Apress website (located once again on the home page for this book), as well as information on how to notify me of any errors you might find.

Contacting the Author

If you have any questions regarding this book's source code, are in need of clarification for a given example, simply wish to offer your thoughts regarding AI, or want to contact me for other needs, feel free to drop me a line at nispathak@gmail.com. I will do my best to get back to you in a timely fashion.

Thanks for buying this text. I hope you enjoy reading it and putting your newfound knowledge to good use.

CHAPTER 1

■ ■ ■

Getting Started with AI Basics

Imagine creating a software so smart that it will not only understand human languages but also slang and subtle variations of these languages, such that your software will know that "Hello, computer! How are you doing?" and "wassup dude?" mean the same thing.

While you're at it, why not add into your software the ability to listen to a human speak and respond appropriately?

> *User*: "Computer, what's my schedule like today?"

> *Software*: "You have quite a packed day today, with back-to-back meetings from 10 am to 1:30 pm and again from 3 pm to 7 pm."

And as if that would not make your software smart enough, why not also add the ability to have human-like conversations?

> *User*: "Computer, did I miss the match? What's the score?"

> *Software*: "It's 31 minutes into the Barcelona vs. Real Madrid football match. Your favorite team, Barcelona, has not scored yet. The score is 0-1."

> *User*: "Holy cow! Who scored from Real?"

> *Software*: "Cristiano Ronaldo scored the first goal in the 10th minute."

> *User*: "That's not looking good. What's his goals tally this season?"

> *Software*: "So far, Ronaldo has scored 42 goals for his club and 13 for his country."

> *User*: "That's impressive. I hope poor Messi catches up soon."

> *User*: "Computer, thanks for the update."

> *Software*: "You are welcome."

> *Software*: "Don't forget to check back for the score after half an hour. Based on ball possession and shots-on-target stats, there's a 73% chance of Barcelona scoring in the next 20 minutes."

Wouldn't these capabilities make your software *smart* and *intelligent*? As a .NET developer, how can *you* make your software as smart as Microsoft's Cortana, Apple's Siri, or Google's Assistant? You will see in a bit.

After completing this chapter, you will have learned the following about AI:

- Truth vs. fiction

- History and evolution

- Microsoft and AI

- Basic concepts
  - *Cognitive, machine learning, deep learning, NLP, NLU, etc.*
  - *Illustrative diagrams and references (where possible)*
- Microsoft Cognitive Services
  - *talk about all five cognitive groups*
- How you can use it in your own software
- The future and beyond

Truth vs. Fiction

What comes to your mind when you hear the term *artificial intelligence*? Scary robots? A topic of sophisticated research? Arnold Schwarzenegger in *The Terminator* movie? Counter-Strike bots?

■ **Note**   **Counter-Strike** is a first-person shooter video game by Valve. It is based on a strategic battle between terrorists, who want to blow up places with bombs, and counter-terrorists, who want to stop the terrorists from causing havoc. Although this multiplayer game is usually played among human players, it is possible for a single human player to play with and against the bots.

Bots are AI-enabled, programmed, self-thinking virtual players that can fill in for human players when they are not available. Bots are a common feature in video games, and sometimes they are just referred to as the game's AI.

Counter-Strike, or CS as it's lovingly called, is especially popular among amateur and professional gamers and is a regular at top gaming contests across the globe.

The meaning of artificial intelligence (AI) has evolved over generations of research. The basic concepts of AI have not changed, but its applications have. How AI was perceived in the 1950s is very different from how it's actually being put to use today. And it's still evolving.

Artificial intelligence is a hot topic these days. It has come a long way from the pages of popular science fiction books to becoming a commodity. And, no, AI has nothing to do with superior robots taking over the world and enslaving us humans. At least, not yet. Anything intelligent enough, from your phone's virtual assistant (Siri and Cortana) to your trusty search engine (Google and Bing) to your favorite mobile or video game, is powered by AI.

Interest in AI peaked during the 2000s, especially at the start of 2010s. Huge investments in AI research in recent times by academia and corporations have been a boon for software developers. Advances made by companies such as Microsoft, Google, Facebook, and Amazon in various fields of AI and the subsequent open-sourcing and commercialization of their products has enabled software developers to create human-like experiences in their apps with unprecedented ease. This has resulted in an explosion of smart, intelligent apps that can understand their users just as a normal human would.

Have you, as a developer, ever thought about how *you* can use AI to create insanely smart software? You probably have, but did not know where to start.

In our experience with software developers at top IT companies, a common perception that we've found among both developers and project managers is that adding even individual AI elements, such as natural language understanding, speech recognition, machine learning, etc., to their software would require a deep understanding of neural networks, fuzzy logic, and other mind-bending computer science theories. Well, let us tell you the good news. That is not the case anymore.

The intelligence that powers your favorite applications, like Google search, Bing, Cortana, and Facebook, is slowly being made accessible to developers outside of these companies: some parts for free and the others as SaaS-based commercial offerings.

History and Evolution

We believe the best way to understand something and its importance is to know about its origins—*the why of something.*

Since ancient times, humans have been fascinated by the idea of non-living things being given the power of thinking, either by the Almighty or by crazy scientists. There are countless accounts, in both ancient and modern literature, of inanimate things being suddenly endowed with consciousness and intelligence.

Greek, Chinese, and Indian philosophers believed that human reasoning could be formalized into a set of mechanical rules. Aristotle (384-322 BC) developed a formal way to solve syllogisms. Euclid (~300 BC) gave us a formal model of reasoning through his mathematical work *Elements*, which contained one of the earliest known algorithms. Leibniz (1646-1716) created a universal language of reasoning which reduced argumentation to calculation, a language that explored the possibility that all rational thought could be made as systematic as algebra or geometry. Boole's (1815-1864) work on mathematical logic provided the essential breakthrough that made artificial intelligence seem plausible.

These formal systems or "theories" have time and again been put into practice, using the technology of the time, to create machines that emulated human behavior or thoughts. Using clockworks, people created everything from elaborate cuckoo clocks to picture-drawing automatons. These were the earliest forms of the robot. In more recent times, formal reasoning principles were applied by mathematicians and scientists to create what we call the computer.

The term "artificial intelligence" was coined at a conference on the campus of Dartmouth College in the summer of 1956. The proposal for the conference included this assertion: "Every aspect of learning or any other feature of intelligence can be so precisely described that a machine can be made to simulate it." It was during this conference that the field of AI research was established, and the people who attended it became the pioneers of AI research.

During the decades that followed, there were major breakthroughs in the field of AI. Computer programs were developed to solve algebra problems, prove theorems, and speak English. Government agencies and private organizations poured in funds to fuel the research. But the road to modern AI was not easy.

The first setback to AI research came in 1974. The time between that year and 1980 is known as the first "AI Winter." During this time, a lot of promised results of the research failed to materialize. This was due to a combination of factors, the foremost one being the failure of scientists to anticipate the difficulty of the problems that AI posed. The limited computing power of the time was another major reason. As a result, a lack of progress led the major British and American agencies that were earlier supporting the research to cut off their funding.

The next seven years, 1980-87, saw a renewed interest in AI research. The development of expert systems fueled the boom. Expert systems were getting developed across organizations, and soon all big giants started investing huge amount of money in artificial intelligence. Work on neural networks laid the foundation for the development of *optical character recognition* and *speech recognition* techniques. The following years formed the second AI Winter, which lasted from 1987 to 1993. Like the previous winter, AI again suffered financial setbacks.

■ **Note** An **expert system** is a program that answers questions or solves problems about a specific domain of knowledge, using logical rules that are derived from the knowledge of experts. The earliest examples included a system to identify compounds from spectrometer readings and a system to diagnose infectious blood diseases.

Expert systems restricted themselves to a small domain of specific knowledge (thus avoiding the common sense knowledge problem) and their simple design made it relatively easy for programs to be built and then modified once they were in place. All in all, the programs proved to be useful, something that AI had not been able to achieve up to this point.

1993-2001 marked the return of AI, propelled in part by faster and cheaper computers. Moore's Law predicted the speed and memory capacity of computers to double every two years. And that's what happened. Finally, older promises of AI research were realized because of access to faster computing power, the lack of which had started the first winter. Specialized computers were created using advanced AI techniques to beat humans. Who can forget the iconic match between IBM's Deep Blue computer and the then reigning chess champion Garry Kasparov in 1997?

AI was extensively used in the field of robotics. The Japanese built robots that looked like humans, and even understood and spoke human languages. The western world wasn't far behind, and soon there was a race to build the most human-like mechanical assistant to man. Honda's ASIMO was a brilliant example of what could be achieved by combining robotics with AI: a 4-foot 3-inch tall humanoid that could walk, dance, make coffee, and even conduct orchestras.

The Current State of Affairs

AI started off as a pursuit to build human-like robots that could understand us, do our chores, and remove our loneliness. But today, the field of AI has broadened to encompass various techniques that help in creating smart, functional, and dependable software applications.

With the emergence of a new breed of technology companies, the 21st century has seen tremendous advances in artificial intelligence, sometimes behind the scenes in the research labs of Microsoft, IBM, Google, Facebook, Apple, Amazon, and more. Perhaps one of the best examples of contemporary AI is IBM's Watson, which started as a computer system designed to compete with humans on the popular American TV show *Jeopardy!* In an exhibition match in 2011, Watson beat two former winners to clinch the $1 million prize money. Propelled by Watson's success, IBM soon released the AI technologies that powered its computer system as commercial offerings. AI became a buzzword in the industry, and other large tech companies entered the market with commercial offerings of their own. Today, there are startups offering highly specialized but accurate AI-as-a-service offerings.

AI has not been limited to popular and enterprise software applications. You favorite video games, both on TV and mobile, have had AI baked for a long time. For example, when playing single player games, where you compete against the computer, your opponents make their own decisions based on your moves. In many games, it is even possible to change the difficulty level of the opponents: the harder the difficulty level, the more sophisticated the "AI" of the game, and the more human-like your opponents will be.

Commoditization of AI

During recent years, there has been an explosion of data, almost at an exponential rate. With storage space getting cheaper every day, large corporations and small startups alike have stopped throwing away their extraneous and archive-worthy data in order to analyze it at some point to derive meaningful information that could help their business. This trend has been supported in a large portion by the cloud revolution. The cloud revolution itself is fueled by faster computers and cheaper storage. Cloud computing and storage available from popular vendors, such as Amazon AWS and Microsoft Azure, is so cheap that it's no longer a good idea to throw away even decades-old log data generated by servers and enterprise software.

As a result, companies are generating mind-boggling amounts of data every day and every hour. We call this large amount of data as **big data**. Big data has applications in almost all economic sectors, such as banking, retail, IT, social networking, healthcare, science, sports, and so on.

■ **Note**   To imagine the scale of big data, consider the following stats.

As of August 2017, Google was handling roughly 100 billion searches per month. That's more than 1.2 trillion per year! Google analyzes its search data to identify search trends among geographies and demographics.

Facebook handles 300+ million photos per day from its user base. Facebook analyzes its data, posts, and photos to serve more accurate ads to its users.

Walmart handles more than 1 million customer transactions every hour. Walmart analyzes this data to see what products are performing better than the others, what products are being sold together, and more such retail analytics.

Traditional data techniques were no longer viable due to the complexity of data and the time it would take to analyze all of it. In order to analyze this huge amount of data, a radically new approach was needed. As it turned out, the machine learning techniques used to train sophisticated AI systems could also be used with big data. As a result, AI today is no longer a dominion of large private and public research institutes. AI and its various techniques are used to build and maintain software solutions for all sorts of businesses.

Microsoft and AI

Microsoft has had a rich history in artificial intelligence. When Bill Gates created Microsoft Research in 1991, he had a vision that computers would one day see, hear, and understand human beings. Twenty-six years hence, AI has come closer to realizing that vision. During these years, Microsoft hasn't been announcing humanoid robots or building all-knowing mainframes. Its progress in AI has not been "visible" to the common public per se. It has been silently integrating human-like thinking into its existing products.

Take Microsoft Bing, for example, the popular search engine from Microsoft. Not only can Bing perform keyword-based searches, it can also search the Web based on the intended meaning of your search phrase. So doing a simple keyword search like "Taylor Swift" will give you the official website, Wikipedia page, social media accounts, recent news stories, and some photos of the popular American singer-songwriter. Doing a more complex search like "Who is the president of Uganda?" will give you the exact name in a large font and top web results for that person. It's like asking a question of another human, who knows you do not mean to get all web pages that contain the phrase "Who is the president of Uganda," just the name of the person in question.

In both examples (Taylor Swift and President of Uganda), Bing will also show, on the left, some quick facts about the person: date of birth, spouse, children, etc. And depending on the type of person searched, Bing will also show other relevant details, such as education, timeline, and quotes for a politician, and net worth, compositions, and romances for a singer. How is Bing able to show you so much about a person? Have Bing's developers created a mega database of quick facts for all the famous people in the world (current and past)? Not quite.

Although it is not humanly impossible to create such a database, the cost of maintaining it would be huge. Our big, big world, with so many countries and territories, will keep on producing famous people. So there's a definite scalability problem with this database.

The technique Microsoft used to solve this problem is called *machine learning*. We will have a look at machine learning and its elder brother, deep learning in a bit. Similarly, the thing that enables Bing to understand the meaning of a search phrase is *natural language understanding*. You can ask the same question of Bing in a dozen different ways and Bing will still arrive at the same meaning every time. NLU makes it smart enough to interpret human languages in ways humans do subconsciously. NLU also helps detect spelling errors in search phrases: "Who is the preisident of Uganda" will automatically be corrected to "Who is the president of Uganda" by Bing.

Basic Concepts

Before you can start building smart apps using artificial intelligence, it would be helpful to familiarize yourself with the basics. In this section, we'll cover the basic terminology and what goes on behind the scenes in each to give you an idea about how AI works. Figure 1-1 shows a glimpse of the future when a human is teaching a machine and the machine is taking notes.

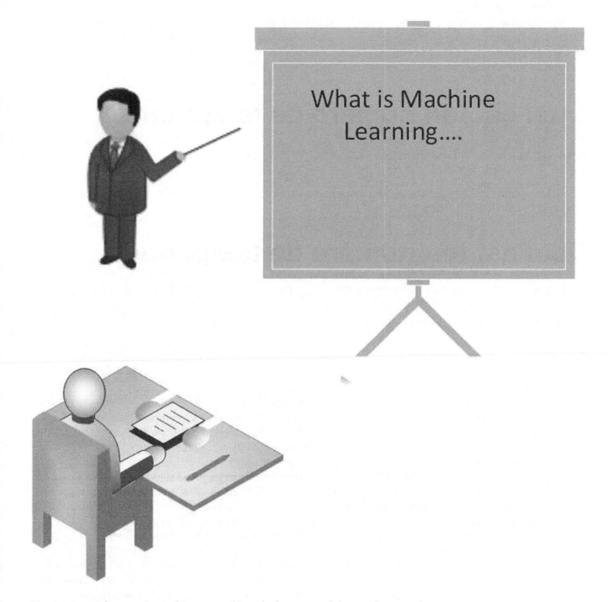

Figure 1-1. *A human is teaching a machine the basics, and the machine is taking notes*

But before we can dive into details of the various forms of AI, it is important to understand the thing that powers all of them. That thing is *machine learning* (Figure 1-1).

The term *machine learning* was coined by Arthur Samuel in his 1959 paper "Some Studies in Machine Learning." As per Samuel, machine learning is what "gives computers the ability to learn without being explicitly programmed." We all know a computer as a machine that performs certain operations by following instructions supplied by humans in the form of programs. So how is it possible for a machine to learn something by itself? And what would such a machine do with the knowledge gained from such learning?

To understand machine learning better, let's take for instance the popular language translation tool Google Translate, a tool that can easily translate a foreign language, say, French, into English and vice versa. Have you ever wondered how it works?

Consider the following sentence written in French (Figure 1-2).

Quel est ton numéro de téléphone?

Figure 1-2. *A sentence in French*

The simplest translation system would translate a sentence from one language to another by using a word-to-word dictionary (Figure 1-3).

Quel est ton numéro de téléphone?
which   is   your   number   of   telephone

Figure 1-3. *A literal translation into English*

What in French means "what's your phone number" literally translates to "which is your number of telephone" in English. Clearly, such a simplistic translation completely ignores language-specific grammar rules.

This can be fixed by feeding the translation system the grammar rules for both languages. But here's the problem: rules of grammar work with an assumption that the input sentence is grammatically correct. In the real world, this is not always true. Besides, there may be several different correct variations of the output sentence. Such a rule-based translation system would become too complicated to maintain.

An ideal translation system is one that can learn to translate by itself just by looking at the training data. After having gone through thousands and thousands of training sentences, it will start to see *patterns* and thus automatically figure out the rules of the language. This self-learning is what machine learning is about.

Google Translate supports not 10, not 20, but 100+ languages, including some rare and obscure ones, with more languages being added regularly. Of course, it's humanly impossible to *hard code* translations for all possible phrases and sentences. Machine learning is what powers Google Translate's ability to understand and translate languages.

Although not flawless, the translations provided by Google Translate are fairly reasonable. It learns not only from the training data that Google gives it but also from its millions of users. In the case of an incorrect translation, users have an option to manually submit the correct one. Google Translate learns from its mistakes, just like a human, and improves its understanding of languages for future translations. That's machine learning for you!

■ **Note**   Very recently, Google Translate switched from using machine learning algorithms to deep learning ones.

Machine Learning (ML) vs. Deep Learning (DL)

If you have been following the news, you have probably heard the term *deep learning* in association with artificial intelligence. Deep learning is a recent development, and people who are apparently not familiar with its exact meaning confuse is as the successor to machine learning. This is so untrue.

While machine learning is a way to achieve artificial intelligence, deep learning is a machine learning technique. In other words, deep learning is NOT an alternative to machine learning but part of machine learning itself.

A common technique used in machine learning has traditionally been artificial neural networks. ANNs are extremely CPU intensive and usually end up producing subhuman results. The recent AI revolution has been made possible because of deep learning, a breakthrough technique that makes machine learning much faster and more accurate. Deep learning algorithms make use of parallel programming and rely on various layers of neural networks and, not hundreds or thousands, but millions of instances of training data to achieve a goal (image recognition, language translation, etc.). Such "deep" learning was unthinkable with previous ML techniques.

Companies have internally developed their own deep learning tools to come up with AI-powered cloud services. Google open sourced its deep learning framework, Tensorflow, in late 2015. Head over to www.tensorflow.org to see what this framework can do and how you can use it.

Machine Learning

Machine learning is the very fundamental concept of artificial intelligence. ML explores the study and construction of algorithms that can learn from data and make predictions based on their learning. ML is what powers an intelligent machine; it is what *generates* artificial intelligence.

A regular, non-ML language translation algorithm has static program instructions to detect which language a sentence is written in: words used, grammatical structure, etc. Similarly, a non-ML face detection algorithm has a hard-coded definition of a face: something round, skin colored, having two small dark regions near the top (eyes), etc. An ML algorithm, on the other hand, doesn't have such hard-coding; it learns by examples. If you train it with lots of sentences that are written in French and some more that are not written in French, it will learn to identify French sentences when it sees them.

A lot of real-world problems are nonlinear, such as language translation, weather prediction, email spam filtering, predicting the next president of the United States, classification problems (such as telling apart species of birds through images), and so on. ML is an ideal solution for such nonlinear problems where designing and programming explicit algorithms using static program instructions is simply not feasible.

We hope the language translation example in the previous section gave you a fair understanding of how machine learning works. It was just the tip of the iceberg. ML is much more elaborate, but you now know the basic concept. ML is a subfield of computer science which encompasses several topics, especially ones related to mathematics and statistics. Although it will take more than just one book to cover all of ML, let's have a look at the common terms associated with it (Figures 1-4 and 1-5).

Figure 1-4. *A machine learning algorithm, such as a neural network, "learns" the basics about a topic from training data. The output of such learning is a trained model.*

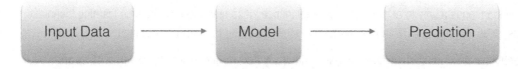

Figure 1-5. *The trained model can then take in new or familiar data to make informed predictions*

Before a machine learning system can start to intelligently answer questions about a topic, it has to first learn about that topic. For that, ML relies heavily on an initial set of data about the topic. This initial data is called *training data*. The more the training data, the more patterns our machine is able to recognize, and the more accurately it can answer questions—new and familiar—about that topic. To get reliable results, a few hundred or even thousands of records of training data are usually insufficient.

Really accurate, human-like machines have been trained using millions of records or several gigabytes of data over a period of days, months, or even years. And we are not even slightly exaggerating. A personal computer with good processing power and a high-end graphics card will take more than a month of continuous running time to train a language translation algorithm with more than 1GB data for a single pair of languages [see `https://github.com/tensorflow/tensorflow/issues/600#issuecomment-226333266`].

The quality of the training data and the way the model is designed are equally important. The data used must be accurate, sanitized, and procured through reliable means. The model needs to be designed with real-life scenarios. So the next time your image recognition application incorrectly recognize the object being captured or your favorite language translation app produces a laughable translation, blame the quality of training data or the model they have used. Also, it's important to note that learning is not just an initial process: it's a continuous process. Initially, a machine learns from training data; later it does from its users.

AI research has led to the development of several approaches to implementing machine learning. An artificial neural network is one of the most popular approaches. An ANN, or simply a *neural network*, is a learning algorithm that is inspired by the structure and functional aspects of biological neural networks. Computations are structured in terms of an interconnected group of artificial neurons, processing information using a connectionist approach to computation. They are used to model complex relationships between inputs and outputs, to find patterns in data. Other popular approaches are *deep learning*, *rules-based*, *decision tree*, and *Bayesian networks*.

So when enough training data has been supplied to neural networks, we get what is called a trained *model*. Models are mathematical and statistical functions that can make a *prediction* (an informed guess) for a given input. For example, based on weather information (training data) from the last 10 years a machine learning model can learn to predict the weather for the next few days.

Types of Machine Learning

Supervised learning is when the training data is labeled. For a language detection algorithm, learning would be supervised if the sentences we supply to the algorithm are explicitly labeled with the language they are written in: sentences written in French and ones not in French; sentences written in Spanish and ones not in Spanish; and so on. As prior labeling is done by humans, it increases the work effort and cost of maintaining such algorithms.

Unsupervised learning is when the training data is not labeled. Due to a lack of labels, an algorithm cannot, of course, learn to magically tell the exact language of a sentence, but it can differentiate one language from another. That is, through unsupervised learning, an ML algorithm can learn to see that French sentences are different from Spanish ones, which are different from Hindi ones, and so on.

Reinforcement learning is when a machine is not explicitly supplied training data. It must interact with the environment in order to achieve a goal. Due to a lack of training data, it must learn by itself from scratch and rely on a hit-and-trial technique to make decisions and discover its own correct paths. For each action the machine takes, there's a consequence, and for each consequence, it is given a numerical reward. So if an action produces a desirable result, it receives "good" remarks. And if the result is disastrous, it receives "very, very bad" remarks. Like humans, the machine strives to maximize its total numerical reward—that is, to get as many "good" and "very good" remarks as possible by not repeating its mistakes. This technique of machine learning is especially useful when the machine has to deal with very dynamic environments, where creating and supplying training data is just not feasible. For example, driving a car (Figure 1-6), playing a video game, and so on.

Figure 1-6. *Self-driving cars, vehicles that do not require a human to operate them, use reinforcement learning to learn from the dynamic and challenging environment (roads and traffic) to improve their driving skills over time*

Language

Humans interact with one another in one of three ways: verbal, written, and gestures. The one thing common among all three ways is "language." A language is a set of rules for communication that is the same for every individual. Although the same language can be used for written and spoken communication, there are usually subtle and visible variations, with written being the more formal of the two. And sign language, the language of gestures, is totally different.

The most effort spent in AI research has been to enable machines to understand humans as naturally as humans do themselves. As it is easier for machines to understand written text than speech, we'll start our discussion with the basics of language as in written language.

Natural Language Understanding

NLU is the ability of a machine to understand humans through human languages. A computer is inherently designed to understand bits and bytes, code and logic, programs and instructions, rather than human languages. That is, a computer is adept at dealing with structured rather than unstructured data.

A human language is governed by some rules (grammar), but those rules are not always observed during day-to-day and informal communication. As a result, humans can effortlessly understand faulty written or verbal sentences with poor grammar, mispronunciations, colloquialisms, abbreviations, and so on. It's safe to say that human languages are governed by flexible rules.

NLU converts unstructured inputs (Figure 1-7), governed by flexible and poorly defined rules, into structured data that a machine can understand. If you've been wondering, this is what makes Microsoft's Cortana, Apple's Siri and Amazon's Alexa so human-like.

how is the weather going to be in Delhi tomorrow

| intent | city | day |

Figure 1-7. NLU analyzes each sentence for two things: <u>intent</u> (the meaning or intended action) and <u>entities</u>. In this example, retrieving **weather** info is the detected intent and **city** (Delhi) and **day** (tomorrow) are the entities. A user may ask the same question in a hundred different ways, yet a good NLU system will always be able to extract the correct intent and entities out of the user's sentence. The software can then use this extracted information to query an online weather API and show the user their requested weather info.

Natural Language Processing

Of course, there's much more to human-machine interaction than just understanding the meaning of a given sentence. NLP encompasses all the things that have to do with a human-machine interaction in a human language. NLU is just one task in the larger set that is NLP. Other tasks in natural language processing include

- **Machine translation:** Converting text from one language to another.

- **Natural language generation:** The reverse of NLU; converting structured data (usually from databases) into human-readable textual sentences. For example, by comparing two rows of weather info in a database, a sentence like this can be formed, "Today's weather in Delhi is 26 degrees centigrade, which is a drop of 2 degrees from yesterday."

- **Sentiment analysis:** Scan a piece of text (a tweet, a Facebook update, reviews, comments, etc.) relating to a product, person, event, or place in order to determine the overall sentiment (negative or positive) toward the concerned entity.

- **Named entity recognition:** For some text, determining which items in the text map to proper names, such as people or places, and the type of each such name (e.g. person, location, organization).

- **Relationship extraction:** Extracting relationships between the entities involved in a piece of text, such as who is the brother of whom, causes and symptoms, etc.

NLP is much wider than the few tasks mentioned above, with each task being under independent research.

Speech

Besides intelligently analyzing text, AI can help machines with a listening device, such as a microphone, understand what is being spoken. Speech is represented as a set of audio signals, and acoustic modeling is used to find relationships between an audio signal and the phonemes (linguistic units that make up speech).

Speech Recognition

Speech recognition is the recognition and translation of spoken language into text by computers. When you ask a question of Siri or Google (search by voice), it uses speech recognition to convert your voice into text. The converted text is then used to perform the search. Modern SR techniques can handle variations in accents and similar sounding words and phrases based on the context.

Applications of speech recognition range from designing accessible systems (like software for the blind) to voice-based search engines to hands-free dictation.

Voice Recognition

The terms *voice recognition* or *speaker identification* refer to identifying the speaker, rather than what they are saying. Recognizing the speaker can simplify the task of translating speech in systems that have been trained on a specific person's voice or can be used to authenticate or verify the identity of a speaker as part of a security process.

TTS and STT

Text-to-speech (TTS) and speech-to-text (STT) are interrelated but different technologies.

TTS, also known as *speech synthesis*, is the ability of a machine to "speak" a piece of written text. Synthesized speech can be created by concatenating pieces of recorded speech (a recording each for a word) that are stored in a database. Alternatively, a synthesizer can incorporate a model of the vocal tract and other human voice characteristics to create a completely "synthetic" voice output.

STT, on the other hand, is the next step in speech recognition. Once speech has been broken down into audio signals and then into phonemes, machines can then convert the phonemes into text. It may be possible to construct multiple textual sentences using the same set and sequence of phonemes, so the machine intelligently assigns each construction a confidence score, with more sensical sentences getting a higher score.

Computer Vision

We have finally arrived at the section where we discuss AI techniques that apply to visual data: images and videos. The broader term for such techniques is called *computer vision*, the ability of a computer to "see." As with speech, computers cannot inherently deal with images as well as they can with text. Image processing techniques combined with intelligent AI algorithms enable machines to see images and to identify and recognize objects and people.

Object Detection

A scene in a photo may comprise dozens or even hundreds of objects. Most of the time, we are concerned with only a small number of objects in a scene. Let's call such objects "interesting" objects. Object detection refers to the ability of a machine to detect interesting objects in a scene. Interesting objects may vary from context to context. Examples include

- A speeding car on a road (traffic control) (Figure 1-8)

Figure 1-8. *A car being detected on the road*

- A planet-like object in a vast solar system or galaxy (astronomy)
- A burglar trespassing through the backyard (home security)
- A bunch of people entering a mall (counting the footfall)

Image Recognition

Detection is commonly succeeded by recognition. It is the ability to recognize as well as label the exact *type* of detected objects and actions (Figure 1-9). For example,

- Recognizing a boat, two humans, water, and sun in a scene

- Recognizing the exact species of animals in a photo

Figure 1-9. *A group of riders on a dirty road*

Image recognition is also known as object *classification* or *matching*. Among other systems, it is common for augmented reality apps, such as Google Goggles.

The accuracy of an image recognition system, like everything else in AI, depends heavily on the training data. Using machine learning techniques, as seen in the machine translation section earlier, a system is trained with hundreds of images to recognize objects of the specific class. So we could first train the system to generally recognize a dog using hundreds of images that have one or more dogs in it. Once the system is able to recognize dogs, it could then be trained to recognize a German Shepherd or a Doberman or even a Chihuahua.

Face Recognition

Detecting and recognizing faces are subtasks of image recognition (Figure 1-10). Using the same techniques, it is possible to detect faces in a photo and their related attributes (age, gender, smile, etc.). And if the system is pretrained on the face of a specific person, it can do matching to recognize that person's face in a photo. Face recognition could be used as a security authentication mechanism or to detect a dangerous criminal in a public place using CCTV cameras.

Figure 1-10. *Faces being identified in an image*

Optical Character Recognition

OCR is a method used to convert handwritten, typed, or printed text into data that can be edited on a computer. An OCR system looks at the scanned images of paper documents and compares the shapes of the letters with stored images of letters. It is thus able to create a text file that can be edited with a normal text editor. Text detected using OCR can then be fed to text-to-speech (TTS) software to speak it out loud to a blind person who could not otherwise see the document.

OCR is commonly used by online bookstores to create soft copies of printed books. It is also used by some language translation tools to help translate directly off a foreign language signboard using a mobile camera. Figure 1-11 shows how Google uses OCR to make your phone a real-time translator.

Figure 1-11. Google allows your phone to be a real-time translator

Microsoft's Cognitive Services

Cognitive Services is a set of software-as-a-service (SaaS) commercial offerings from Microsoft related to artificial intelligence. Cognitive Services is the product of Microsoft's years of research into cognitive computing and artificial intelligence, and many of these services are being used by some of Microsoft's own popular products, such as Bing (search, maps), Translator, Bot Framework, etc.

Microsoft has made these services available as easy-to-use REST APIs, directly consumable in a web or a mobile application. As of writing this book, there are 29 available cognitive services, broadly divided into five categories (Table 1-1).

Table 1-1. Cognitive Services by Microsoft

Vision
- Computer Vision API
- Content Moderator API
- Emotion API
- Face API
- Video API
- Custom Vision Service
- Video Indexer

Speech
- Bing Speech API
- Custom Speech Service
- Speaker Recognition API
- Translator Speech API

Language
- Bing Spell Check API
- Language Understanding Intelligent Service
- Linguistic Analysis API
- Text Analytics API
- Translator API
- WebLM API

Knowledge
- Academic Knowledge API
- Entity Linking Intelligent Service
- Knowledge Exploration API
- QnA Maker API
- Recommendations API
- Custom Decision service

(*continued*)

Table 1-1. (*continued*)

Search
- Bing Autosuggest API
- Bing Image Search API
- Bing News Search API
- Bing Video Search API
- Bing Web Search API
- Bing Custom Search API

Vision

Vison services deal with visual information, mostly in the form of images and videos.

- **Computer Vision API**: Extracts rich information from an image about its contents: an intelligent textual description of the image, detected faces (with age and gender), and dominant colors in the image, and whether the image has adult content.

- **Content Moderation**: Evaluates text, images, and videos for offensive and unwanted content.

- **Emotion API**: Analyze faces to detect a range of feelings, such as anger, happiness, sadness, fear, surprise, etc.

- **Face API**: Detects human faces and compares similar ones (face detection), organizes people into groups according to visual similarity (face grouping), and identifies previously tagged people in images (face verification).

- **Video API**: Intelligent video processing for face detection, motion detection (useful in CCTV security systems), generating thumbnails, and near real-time video analysis (textual description for each frame).

- **Custom Vision Service:** When you need to perform image recognition on things other than scene, face, and emotions, this lets you create custom image classifiers, usually focused on a specific domain. You can train this service to, say, identify different species of birds, and then use its REST API in a mobile app for bird watching enthusiasts.

- **Video Indexer**: Extracts insights from a video, such as face recognition (names of people), speech sentiment analysis (positive, negative, neutral) for each person, and keywords.

Speech

These services deal with human speech in the form of audio.

- **Bing Speech API**: Converts speech to text, understands its intent, and converts text back to speech. Covered in detail in Chapter 7.

- **Custom Speech Service**: Lets you build custom language models of the speech recognizer by tailoring it to the vocabulary of the application and the speaking style of your users. Covered in detail in Chapter 7.

- **Speaker Recognition API**: Identifies the speaker in a recorded or live speech audio. Speaker recognition can be reliably used as an authentication mechanism.

- **Translator Speech API**: Translates speech from one language to another in real time across nine supported languages.

Language

These services deal with natural language understanding, translation, analysis and more.

- **Bing Spell Check API**: Corrects spelling errors in sentences. Apart from dictionary words, takes into account word breaks, slang, persons, and brand names. Covered in detail in Chapter 5.

- **Language Understanding Intelligent Service (LUIS)**: The natural language understanding (NLU) service. Covered in detail in Chapters 4 and 6.

- **Linguistic Analysis API**: Parses text for a granular linguistic analysis, such as sentence separation and tokenization (breaking the text into sentences and tokens) and part-of-speech tagging (labeling tokens as nouns, verbs, etc.). Covered in detail in Chapter 5.

- **Text Analytics API**: Detects sentiment (positive or negative), keyphrases, topics, and language from your text. Covered in detail in Chapter 5.

- **Translator API**: Translates text from one language to another and detects the language of a given text. Covered in detail in Chapter 5.

- **Web Language Model API**: Provides a variety of natural language processing tasks not covered under other Language APIs: word breaking (inserting spaces into a string of words lacking spaces), joint probabilities (calculating how often a particular sequence of words appear together), conditional probabilities (calculating how often a particular word tends to follow another), and next word completions (getting the list of words most likely to follow). Covered in detail in Chapter 5.

Knowledge

These services deal with searching large knowledge bases to identify entities, provide search suggestions, and give product recommendations.

- **Academic Knowledge API**: Allows you to retrieve information from Microsoft Academic Graph, a proprietary knowledge base of scientific/scholarly research papers and their entities. Using this API, you can easily find papers by authors, institutes, events, etc. It is also possible to find similar papers, check plagiarism, and retrieve citation stats.

- **Entity Linking Intelligence Service**: Finds keywords (named entities, events, locations, etc.) in a text based on context.

- **Knowledge Exploration Service**: Adds support for natural language queries, auto-completion search suggestions, and more to your own data.

- **QnA Maker**: Magically creates FAQ-style questions and answers from the provided data. QnA Maker offers a combination of a website and an API. Use the website to create a knowledge base using your existing FAQs website, pdf, doc, or txt file. QnA Maker will automatically extract questions and answers from your document(s) and train itself to answer natural language user queries based on your data. You can think of it as an automated version of LUIS. You do not have to train the system, but you do get an option to do custom retraining. QnA Maker's API is the endpoint that accepts user queries and sends answers for your knowledge base. Optionally, QnA Maker can be paired with Microsoft's Bot Framework to create out-of-the-box bots for Facebook, Skype, Slack, and more.

- **Recommendations API**: This is particularly useful to retail stores, both online and offline, in helping them increase sales by offering their customers recommendations, such as items that are frequently bought together, personalized item recommendations for a user based on their transaction history, etc. Like QnA Maker, you have the Recommendations UI website use your existing data to create product catalog and usage data in its system.

- **Custom Decision Service**: Uses given textual information to derive context, upon which it can rank supplied options and make a decision based on that ranking. Uses a feedback-based reinforcement learning ML technique to improve over time.

Search

These services help you leverage the searching power of the second most popular search engine, Bing.

- **Bing Autosuggest API**: Provides your application's search form, intelligent type-ahead, and search suggestions, directly from Bing search, when a user is parallel typing inside the search box.

- **Bing Image Search API**: Uses Bing's image search to return images based on filters such as keywords, color, country, size, license, etc.

- **Bing News Search API**: Returns the latest news results based on filters such as keywords, freshness, country, etc.

- **Bing Video Search API**: Returns video search results based on filters such as keywords, resolution, video length, country, and pricing (free or paid).

- **Bing Web Search API**: Returns web search results based on various filters. It is also possible to get a list of related searches for a keyword or a phrase.

- **Bing Custom Search**: Focused Bing search based on custom intents and topics. So instead of searching the entire web, Bing will search websites based on topic(s). It can also be used to implement a site-specific search on a single or a specified set of websites.

All Cognitive Services APIs are available in free and pay-as-you-go pricing tiers. You can choose a tier based on your application's usage volume.

Although we would love to cover each of these APIs in great detail, we are limited by the scope of this book. We will cover enough services from speech, language, and search categories to launch you into building really smart applications in little time.

You can learn more about these services (and possibly more that may have been added recently) by visiting www.microsoft.com/cognitive-services/en-us/apis.

Recap

This chapter served as an introduction to artificial intelligence, its history, basic terminology, and techniques. You also learned about Microsoft's endeavors in artificial intelligence research and got a quick overview of the various commercial AI offerings by Microsoft in the form of their Cognitive Services REST APIs.

To recap, you learned

- What people normally think of AI: what's real vs, what's fiction

- The history and evolution of artificial intelligence

- How and where AI is being used today

- About machine learning, which is really the backbone of any intelligent system

- About Microsoft's Cognitive Services, which are enterprise-ready REST APIs that can be used to create intelligent software applications

In the **next chapter**, you will learn how to install all the prerequisites for building AI-enabled software and then you will build your first smart application using Visual Studio.

CHAPTER 2

■ ■ ■

Creating an AI-Based Application in Visual Studio

The entire suite of Microsoft Cognitive Services is available as a set of REST APIs. The good thing about a REST API is that it does not need a special SDK or library for use in a programming language. A REST API has an HTTP URL endpoint that can accept input in JSON or XML format and give output in the same formats. Because of this, REST APIs are directly consumable in all major programming languages, such as C#, Java, PHP, Ruby, Python, JavaScript, and so on. As this book targets .NET developers, we will restrict ourselves to using C# throughout the book. But, really, the fundamentals of using Cognitive Services remain the same for any language.

Before you can start using Cognitive Services, you will need a subscription key for each service you want to use in your application, which in turn requires you to have a Microsoft Azure account. At the time of writing, most APIs in the Cognitive Services suite have a free-to-use and a paid model (some only have a paid model). The free-to-use model, the free tier, allows you to use an API without paying anything to Microsoft, but it usually comes with restrictions that make this tier fit for only personal and low-volume applications. The pay-as-you-go tier, on the other hand, allows you to use the API without restrictions on a pay-per-use model. A subscription key is required for both the free and pay-as-you-go tiers.

■ **Note** Azure is one of the leading cloud computing platforms for enterprise and personal use. It provides SaaS (software as a service), PaaS (platform as a service), and IaaS (infrastructure as a service) services and supports many different programming languages, tools, and frameworks, including both Microsoft-specific and third-party software and systems. Among the many cloud services that Azure provides are Cognitive Services.

Other services available include Windows- and Linux-based virtual machines (virtual private servers for hosting web sites and applications), databases, storage, cache, and content delivery networks (CDNs).

After completing this chapter, you will have learned

- What the prerequisites are for using Cognitive Services

- How to get a subscription key for a Cognitive Services API from Azure

- How to test a Cognitive Services API

- How to create your first AI-enabled application using Visual Studio and C#

© Nishith Pathak 2017

N. Pathak, *Artificial Intelligence for .NET: Speech, Language, and Search*, DOI 10.1007/978-1-4842-2949-1_2

Prerequisites for Using Cognitive Services

As we said before, using REST APIs is pretty straightforward. All you need is your favorite programming language, a code editor, and the API's documentation to reference the input and output formats. This is true for most REST APIs. For Cognitive Services, you also need a subscription key to be able to make calls to the desired API. Without a valid subscription key, your program will not be granted access to use that API.

Here is a list of things you will need to create your AI-based application:

- Visual Studio
- An Azure subscription key
- Your enthusiasm

In this chapter, we will help you create your first AI-based application. You will use the **Computer Vision API** to create your AI-based application. Computer vision is the ability of a machine to "see" an image, just like humans, and label the various objects, features, and people that make up that image.

Setting Up the Development Environment

Visual Studio (VS) is one of the most powerful integrated development editors in the world, and the de facto editor for .NET developers. VS is practically the only thing you need to have installed on your computer to be able to start building intelligent (and regular) applications. VS comes bundled with the latest version of .NET Framework, which includes compilers for all languages supported by the framework, including C#.

The latest stable, production-ready version of VS, as of this writing, is version 2017. VS 2017 is available in several editions (Community, Professional, Enterprise, and Test Professional), all of which are paid except Community.

Throughout this book, we will be using VS 2017 Professional as our choice of IDE. But you are welcome to use VS 2017 Community or any of the other editions of VS 2015. VS Professional and Community editions are pretty much the same, apart from a few enterprise features that are available in Professional and not in Community.

If you already have VS installed on your computer, you do not need to do any additional installation or configuration. You are all set! However, if you do not have VS yet, we highly recommend you head to www.visualstudio.com and download the latest version of Visual Studio Community for free.

■ **Note**   It is worth noting that Visual Studio Code is not the same as Visual Studio. The latter is a fully-featured IDE for building desktop, web, and mobile applications, and the former is a specialized IDE for building web and hybrid mobile applications. VS Code is not an edition of Visual Studio; rather it's an independent, free, and open-source code editor for web development.

Getting an Azure Subscription Key for Cognitive Services

You will need a separate subscription key for each of the 22 Cognitive Services APIs in order to use them in your application. Let's go through all the steps you need to follow to get your own subscription key for the Computer Vision API.

Step 1: Set Up an Azure Account

If you already have an Azure account, feel free to skip this section. Signing up for an Azure account is easy, but requires you to have a Microsoft account. Get it free at signup.live.com if you don't already have one. You have two options to sign up for an Azure account: get a pay-as-you-go subscription or start with a 30-day free trial.

With a pay-as-you-go subscription, you pay monthly charges for services that you use, as per you use them. The subscription is a no-commitment one, meaning it does not require you to pay any additional initial or fixed monthly charges. For example, if the only service you are availing is a VM that costs $20/month, then that's all you pay monthly, for as long as you use it. Likewise, if you have activated the free tier of a Cognitive Services API, you pay $0 or nothing if you stay within the bounds imposed by the free tier.

The 30-day free trial is your safest bet and is highly recommended if you are a first-time user. With the trial, you get a complimentary $200 credit in your Azure account. You can use this credit however you like. Once you have exhausted your free credits, which is usually an unlikely scenario, you will be asked to pay for the additional paid services. After the 30 days of the trial period are over, you will be given an option to switch to pay-as-you-go subscription. If you don't, you will lose access to the services you set up during the trial period. Your Azure Portal access, however, will remain intact. But unlike how trials go usually, Azure does not automatically upgrade you to a paid plan after your trial expires. So there is zero risk of your credit/debit card getting involuntarily charged.

It is worth mentioning that Visual Studio Professional and Enterprise subscribers get complimentary Azure credits every month: $50 for Professional and $150 for Enterprise subscribers. This amount is automatically credited every month to the Microsoft account linked to a Visual Studio subscription.

Assuming that you do not have an existing Azure account, sign up for the free trial. With a Microsoft account, head over to azure.microsoft.com/en-us/free and click the "Start free" button. You may be asked to log in using your Microsoft account at this point. Figure 2-1 shows the screen you will see if you don't have an account yet. Once you do, you will receive a message about your account having no existing subscriptions.

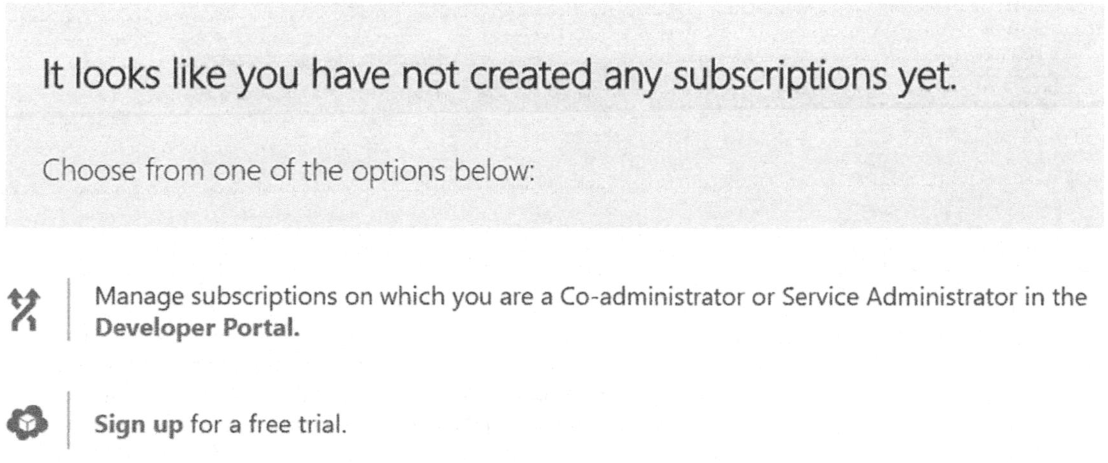

It looks like you have not created any subscriptions yet.

Choose from one of the options below:

Manage subscriptions on which you are a Co-administrator or Service Administrator in the **Developer Portal.**

Sign up for a free trial.

Figure 2-1. The Azure landing page when you do not have a subscription

Click the "sign up for a free trial" link. This will bring up a sign up form where you will need to supply basic information about yourself, as shown in Figure 2-2.

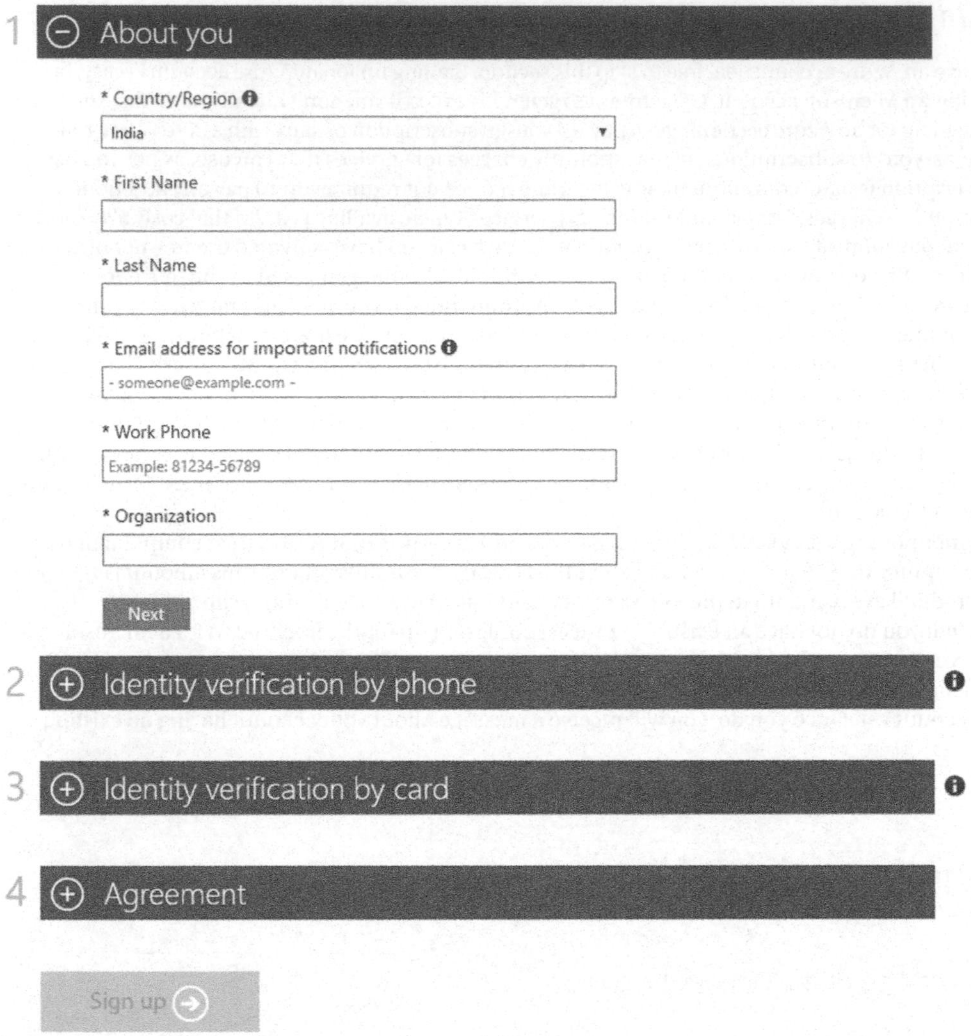

Figure 2-2. *Azure trial sign up form*

Next, you will be asked to enter some additional information for identity verification purpose. This includes your mobile number and credit card details. Please note that credit card details are required only for verification. You may be charged a minor phony amount during signup, but that transaction will be instantly reversed. As stated by Microsoft on its website, *one of the ways we keep prices low is to verify that account holders are real people, not bots or anonymous trouble makers. We use credit card information for identity verification.*

Once your identity is verified, you will need to accept the subscription agreement to complete your application. At this point, it's a good idea to spend a few minutes quickly scanning through the agreement terms and offer details, links to both of which are given in the Agreement section of the application form. Once you've accepted the agreement and clicked the "Sign up" button, you will be redirected to the subscriber's page. Here, click the "Start managing my service" button to go to Azure Portal.

Step 2: Create a New Cognitive Services Account

It's now time to create your first resource in Azure: a Cognitive Services account. Azure Portal gives you a wizard-like interface that helps you easily create new resources in a step-by-step, self-explanatory fashion, as shown in Figure 2-3.

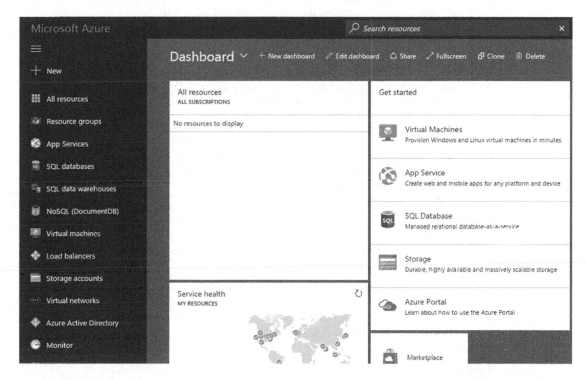

Figure 2-3. *Azure Portal is your go-to place for creating and managing resources, including VMs, databases, and Cognitive Services APIs*

Each step in the wizard is called a blade. Let's create an account for the Computer Vision API.

1. In the Portal's left side menu, click the "New" button. The new resource blade appears.

2. You have two options:

    - Use the search textbox to find "cognitive services."

    - From the Marketplace menu, choose Intelligence + Analytics ➤ Cognitive Services APIs.

27

3. In the "Create Cognitive Services account" blade, fill in fields as below.

- **Account name:** A name that uniquely identifies your API account. This name must be globally unique in Azure. Our recommended naming scheme for an account name is <myname-cs-apitype>. For example, I selected anuragbhd-cs-computervision, which was globally unique until I reserved it. If you specify a name that has already been taken, the wizard form will warn you.

- **Subscription:** You will need to change this only when you have more than one subscriptions applied on your Azure account. For free trial users, "Free Trial" will be auto-selected.

- **API Type:** Clicking this field will present you with a list of all Cognitive Services APIs supported by Azure. From this list, select "Computer Vision API."

- **Location:** Azure resources are generally available in over 32 locations or regions in the US, Canada, Europe, Asia, and Australia. It's a good idea to pick a location closest to your target audience. For example, one should select a location in India if their smart app will target only the Indian population. As of this writing, the Computer Vision API is available only in West US.

- **Pricing tier:** Each Cognitive Services API comes with its own set of pricing options. Most have a free as well as a paid tier. Free tiers usually come with restrictions that suit only small-scale and personal applications. For the purpose of learning, select the free tier from this list.

- **Resource group:** A resource group allows you to keep your Azure resources logically grouped together. For example, all resources that go along with one application (VM, database, cache, APIs) should be put under the same resource group. That is, all resources in a group share the same lifecycle: you deploy, update, and delete them together. Select the "Create new" option and specify a globally unique name.

- **Legal terms:** This is the last field in the form. Review the legal terms associated with using Microsoft Cognitive Services, and click the "I Agree" button.

4. Once all the fields are filled in, click the "Create" button, as shown in Figure 2-4. It will take a few seconds to a minute for your new account to be created and deployed to the selected resource group. You can track the deployment status in the alerts menu in the top-right corner of the Portal.

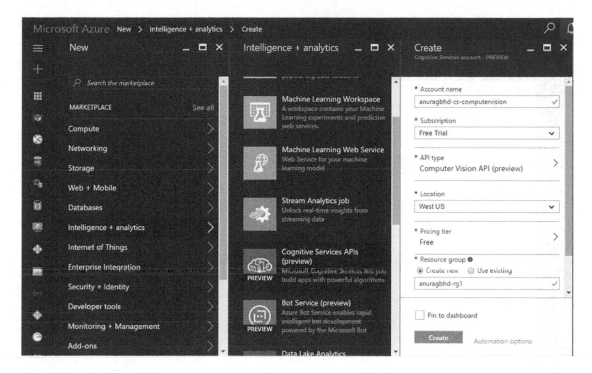

Figure 2-4. *Creating a new Cognitive Services account*

5. Once your shiny new Cognitive Services account is ready, it will be time to get the subscription key you need to start using the Computer Vision API.

Step 3: Get the Subscription Key(s)

You should have received an alert notification upon successful deployment of your new Cognitive Services account. This success notification signals that the new account is ready for use.

In the left-side menu, click the "All resources" link. You will find your newly created account on the list. Click the account entry to open the resource details blade.

The details blade opens, by default, with the Overview section, as shown in Figure 2-5. Scroll down a bit to find the Keys option under Resource Management. Clicking this option will reveal two subscription keys created especially for you. Copy any one of the two keys and keep it handy. You are going to need it pretty soon.

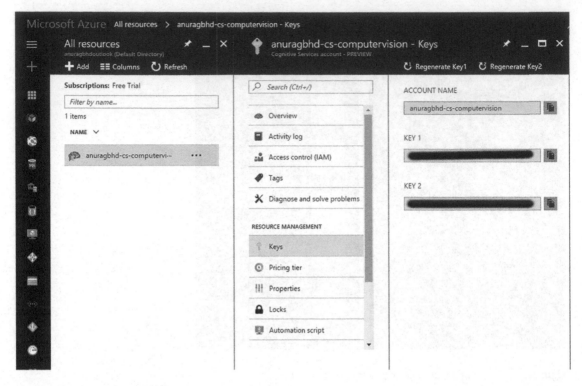

Figure 2-5. *Getting the subscription key from the portal*

***

■ **Note**   *Free subscriptions that are not used for 90 days consecutively may expire. However, if your subscription expires, you can request new keys.*

***

Testing the API

Before taking the API out on the road, it's always a good idea to first take it for a test drive. Doing so has two key benefits:

- You get a clear picture of the HTTP request data format (and headers) that the API expects. Similarly, you get first-hand exposure to the HTTP response that is sent out by the API.

- You get to check whether your subscription key is working fine. In some cases, you may get an "invalid subscription key" error, in which case you should try using the second of the two keys. If both fail, you should try regenerating the keys from the Cognitive Services account details blade in the portal.

These benefits apply to RESTful APIs in general, especially the first one. That's why we have such wonderful GUI API testing tools, such as Postman. There are many other API testing tools available either as standalone applications or Chrome/Firefox extensions. We have found Postman to be both feature-rich and reliable in all our testing.

Simply put, Postman lets you make an HTTP request to and read the response from a REST API, something you would normally do using a programming language. It provides you with a powerful graphical interface to construct your request, however complex, using a simple interface. It gives you the ability to save your requests for later use, such that you will be able to replicate an API call through the saved request data and headers. Postman is available free of cost for all major desktop platforms, including Windows, Linux, and macOS. To download your copy, go to `www.getpostman.com`.

What You Want To Do

As mentioned previously, computer vision is the ability of a machine to "see" pictures (just like a human would) and give details about it. For example, what's the picture about, are there any people in it, how old do they look, and are they smiling?

The Computer Vision API is a bundle of several functions, such as analyzing the image, describing the image, OCR, etc. What you want to do is use the Vision API's `DescribeImage` function to provide a brief caption for a picture you supply it.

Before playing around with the computer vision API in Postman, spend some time reading the API's documentation to learn in advance the request and response formats. Microsoft has made available a well-written API documentation for Cognitive Services at `go.microsoft.com/fwlink/?LinkID=761228`. Check the "API Reference" page under the Computer Vision API section. Your function of interest for this exercise is describe image.

How To Do It

Open Postman to test the Computer Vision API. Its tabbed interface, by default, will have one tab open for you. In the address bar, select POST as the HTTP method and enter this URL (as is mentioned in the API documentation):

`https://api.projectoxford.ai/vision/v1.0/describe`

Next, specify your subscription key in the request header. To do this, open the Headers tab, below the address bar, and enter the following details:

Key: Ocp-Apim-Subscription-Key

Value: *Your subscription key*

You will NOT be able to use this API without a valid subscription key.

Now, it's time to specify the image you want to send to the API. You do this in the request body. Click the Body tab just beside the Header tab. The Computer Vision API's `DescribeImage` function accepts image in two formats: an online image URL (`application/json`) and binary image data (`multipart/form-data`). You'll go with the latter.

In the Body tab, ensure that the "form-data" option is selected. Enter the following key-value data:

Key: image

Value: *Click the "Choose Files" button to pick the image file (jpg/png) from your hard drive*

Type: *Choose File from the dropdown*

Figure 2-6 shows how your Postman should look at this point.

Figure 2-6. *The Postman interface with request parameters set*

You are all set to make a call to the API now. Click the "Send" button beside the address bar to do this. Postman will make an HTTP POST request to the DescribeImage function of Vision API, along with your subscription key and raw image data of the photo that you selected (Figure 2-7). It may take a few seconds for response to come back from the API. Postman will display the JSON response in the Response section below.

Figure 2-7. *The image that we used in our API testing*

The JSON response we received for this image went like this:

```
{"description":{"tags":["dog","grass","outdoor","white","sitting","small","laying","wooden",
"table","top","water","black","beach","mouth","frisbee","board"],"captions":[{"text":"a white
dog laying on the ground","confidence":0.82710220507003307}]},"requestId":"10f3cde1-8de1-4d7c-
b3f3-6a34371f505d","metadata":{"width":1280,"height":853,"format":"Jpeg"}}
```

The text caption as returned by the API was, "a white dog laying on the ground." Pretty accurate!

You have successfully tested the API. Now that you have a good understanding of the request and response formats of this API, it's time to use it to create your first AI-enabled application.

Creating Your First AI-based Application

Time to take out your hard hat and fire up Visual Studio (Figure 2-8). Open Visual Studio and create a new project by going to File ➤ New ➤ Project. In the New Project dialog, select Console Application under Visual C# ➤ Windows. Give your new project a relevant name, such as CognitiveServicesVisionApp, and click the OK button to create the project.

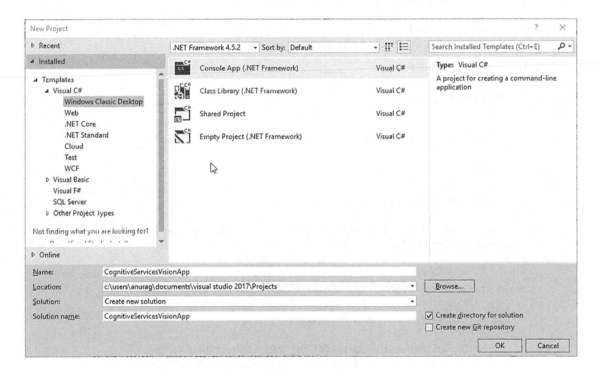

Figure 2-8. *Creating a new console application in Visual Studio 2017*

■ **Note**   A *console application* is one that runs entirely in the console (command prompt). It does not have a graphical look, like a desktop or a web app. It's the most basic app that you can create using .NET.

By default, Visual Studio creates a new console application with only one file: `Program.cs`. This file contains the class that has the entry point method `Main`. All your executable code must go inside the `Main` method because this method is what will be called by the C# compiler when your application starts.

Visual Studio creates a new console application project with default files and folders. Once VS is ready with the new application, open `Program.cs` by double-clicking the file in the Solution Explorer pane on the right. If Solution Explorer isn't open for you, go to View ➤ Solution Explorer or press Ctrl+Alt+L to make it appear.

At this point, your `Program.cs` will be a barebones file with just one class, `Program`, and one method, `static void Main`.

The Code

Modify `Program.cs` so it looks like the code written in Listing 2-1.

Listing 2-1. Program.cs Modified

```
using System;
using System.Configuration;
using System.Net.Http;
using System.Threading.Tasks;
using System.Web;

namespace CognitiveServicesVisionApp
{
    class Program
    {
        static void Main(string[] args)
        {
            Task<string> result = DescribeImage(@"C:\Users\anurag\Downloads\photo.jpg");
            Console.WriteLine(result.Result);
        }

        public static async Task<string> DescribeImage(string imageFilePath)
        {
            using (HttpClient hc = new HttpClient())
            {
                hc.DefaultRequestHeaders.Add("Ocp-Apim-Subscription-Key",
                ConfigurationManager.AppSettings["AzureSubscriptionKeyVision"]);
```

```
using (MultipartFormDataContent reqContent = new MultipartFormDataContent())
{
    var queryString = HttpUtility.ParseQueryString(string.Empty);
    queryString["maxCandidates"] = "1";
    var uri = "https://api.projectoxford.ai/vision/v1.0/describe?" + queryString;

    try
    {
        var imgContent = new ByteArrayContent(System.IO.File.
        ReadAllBytes(imageFilePath));
        reqContent.Add(imgContent);

        HttpResponseMessage resp = await hc.PostAsync(uri, reqContent);
        string respJson = await resp.Content.ReadAsStringAsync();
        return respJson;
    }
    catch(System.IO.FileNotFoundException ex)
    {
        return "The specified image file path is invalid.";
    }
    catch(ArgumentException ex)
    {
        return "The HTTP request object does not seem to be correctly formed.";
    }
}
            }
        }
    }
}
```

You will need to add references to the following assemblies for this code to work:

- System.Web
- System.Configuration
- System.Net.Http

To do this, right-click the References node in Solution Explorer and select Add Reference. From the resulting dialog, select the above three assemblies, as seen in Figure 2-9.

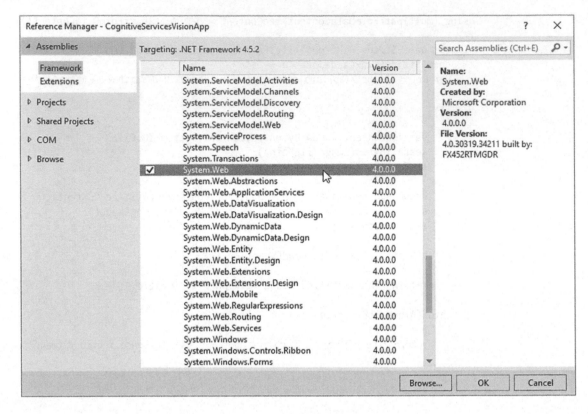

Figure 2-9. *Adding references to your application in Visual Studio 2017*

Let's breakdown this largish piece of code and analyze it line-by-line to see what's going on.

The Walkthrough

As a seasoned programmer, you will immediately notice that the meat of the code is in the DescribeImage() method. On a high level, the code in DescribeImage() calls the Computer Vision API by sending it an image and gets back a one-line (intelligently guessed) description of the image.

The steps for how it's done, followed by a line-by-line analysis, goes like this:

- Create an HTTP client object to be able to make API calls.

- Build the HTTP request object with the required header (subscription key) and request parameters and API URL.

- Read the image file as multipart form data, and add it to the HTTP request object.

- Call the Computer Vision API by supplying it your HTTP request object.

- Display the HTTP response from the API as a string.

```
public static async Task<string> DescribeImage(string imageFilePath)
```

You start by creating a method to do all the work for you. You must make it static to be able to call it from Main, which is also static. It takes in the absolute file path of the target image as a string, and returns the response received from the API as a string. Here, you make use of C#'s async programming while calling the API to make the user experience smoother and more responsive, hence the words "async" and "Task." More on these later.

Best Practice: Using async and await whenever you can for a non-blocking, snappy user experience.

Bad Practice: Making synchronous HTTP calls or using async and await incorrectly.

```
using (HttpClient hc = new HttpClient())
```

Next is an instance of HttpClient, a class that provides the methods to make get, post, put and delete HTTP calls. Creating an instance inside a using block automatically disposes the object at the end of the block. Disposing of I/O intensive objects appropriately is important because the system resources they use aren't kept reserved and are immediately made available to other programs. An alternative to using the using block is to call HttpClient's dispose() method at the end.

Best practice: Always calling the dispose() or close() methods of objects that implement the IDisposable interface.

Bad practice: Not caring about resource-intensive objects may lead to memory leaks and inconsistencies with other system/user programs that depend on the resources being reserved by your program.

```
hc.DefaultRequestHeaders.Add("Ocp-Apim-Subscription-Key", ConfigurationManager.AppSettings
["AzureSubscriptionKeyVision"]);
```

An HTTP request is made up of two things:

- Headers
- Content

Here you set your API subscription key in HttpClient's request header, as mentioned in the documentation.

Best practice: Storing volatile data in and reading it from a configuration file. A subscription is something that is liable to change after some time. It's best to store it in Web.config.

Bad practice: Using your key as a string directly in the code. In the event of a key change, you will need to recompile your code and possibly redeploy it for the app to use the new key.

```
using (MultipartFormDataContent reqContent = new MultipartFormDataContent())
```

The Computer Vision API requires you to send the request as multipart form data content. So you must create your HTTP request's content in the required format. Fortunately, there's a class in .NET designed just for that purpose. It's optional to use the using block here, but a best practice to do so.

```
var queryString = HttpUtility.ParseQueryString(string.Empty);
queryString["maxCandidates"] = "1";
var uri = "https://api.projectoxford.ai/vision/v1.0/describe?" + queryString;
```

Next, you specify the API's URL and its query string parameters. Query string parameters are different for each Cognitive Service API and are 100% optional. If you do not specify them, the API will assume default values for them. The Describe Image API can return multiple descriptions for the same image with varying levels of confidence score. You want to restrict it to return only one with the maximum score. You do that by specifying the maxCandidates parameter's value as 1 (the default is 1 anyway, but you can increase this value for more matches to be returned).

Best practice: Using .NET's built-in helper function `ParseQueryString()` to create the query string. This function encodes your parameters and their values in URL-safe format. For example, a valid URL may not contain whitespaces and special (non-Latin) characters. Such characters must be converted to a URL-safe format before making an HTTP request. A space is represented by %20. Another best practice is using use `string.Empty` instead of the empty string literal "".

Bad practice: Specifying the query string, along with the URL string, yourself, such as `var uri = "https://api.projectoxford.ai/vision/v1.0/describe?maxCandidates=1"`. Doing so may involuntary lead to specifying an invalid URL that may not work as expected.

```
var imgContent = new ByteArrayContent(System.IO.File.ReadAllBytes(imageFilePath));
reqContent.Add(imgContent);
```

Your HTTP request is all built up except for one crucial thing: the image itself. There are two ways to supply an image to the API: the URL of an existing image on the Web and contents of the image file stored on your local hard drive. We chose the latter way. The way to send an image's content along with HTTP request is to send its byte sequence. The `File.ReadAllBytes()` method takes in the absolute path of a file and returns its byte sequence. You use the `ByteArrayContent` to wrap the byte sequence into an HTTP-safe format, and add it to the multipart form data content object you created earlier.

Best practice: I/O functions usually perform "dangerous" operations and so they are liable to throw exceptions. A good developer will always wrap such dangerous code inside a `try` block and catch as many specific exceptions as she can.

Bad practice: Not using `try-catch` for exception handling or not catching specific exceptions by using the all-catching `Exception` class.

```
HttpResponseMessage resp = await hc.PostAsync(uri, reqContent);
string respJson = await resp.Content.ReadAsStringAsync();
return respJson;
```

You finally make an HTTP POST request to the API, sending it an appropriately constructed request object. This is an asynchronous operation, meaning that execution will not wait for the result to arrive from the API before moving to the next statement. Blocking operations, especially ones related to networking, in C# must execute asynchronously to avoid "hanging" the user interface of the application. While it seems like a logical thing from a user's perspective, the developer may find herself in trouble if the code that immediately follows the async operation is dependent on the operation's result. This is where the `await` keyword comes into play. `await` internally registers a callback function that will execute the post-operation code after the result is successfully received, making it appear as if the execution has actually paused for an async operation to complete. All async operations should be awaited, and a method that has awaited operations must be marked as `async`, like you did in your `DescribeImage()` method's signature. The return type of such methods must either be void or `Task<T>` (where `T` is the return type of the async operation's result).

The Result

In Visual Studio, pressing F5 or Ctrl+F5 will run your program. Your program, being part of a console application, will open and run inside the command prompt.

Figure 2-10 shows the result we received against the dog image we used in our Postman example.

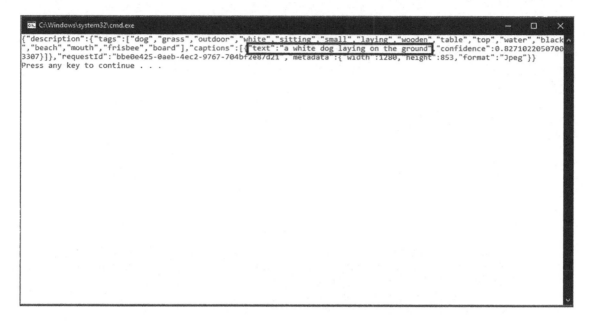

Figure 2-10. *The highlighted text is the caption we received in the API's result*

Making Your Application More Interesting

So you've developed your first AI-based application using the Computer Vision API's DescribeImage method. But why stop there? The Vision API has six more methods that can do six more smart things with an image. You can use your existing subscription key to call any of the seven methods this API comes with.

Extracting Text Out of Images

One of the Vision API's seven methods is OCR. Optical character recognition, OCR for short, is a technique to detect and extract visible text out of images. OCR has so many applications that listing out even a couple of examples will help you imagine a dozen more:

- Extracting text out of scanned, written, or printed documents

- Translating text off foreign-language sign boards

- Automatic vehicle number plate recognition

- Converting handwriting in real time to control a computer

Although OCR is not new or something that Microsoft pioneered, the character recognition offered by Cognitive Services is powerful, capable of extracting both printed and handwritten text and even auto-detecting the language of extracted text.

The Code

You'll use your existing console application and add some code to the Program.cs file. You'll create a new method called ExtractText(), which is essentially the same as the DescribeImage() method, differing only in the API URL and the request query string parameters.

Modify Program.cs so that it looks like Listing 2-2.

Listing 2-2. Program.cs Modified Again

```
using System;
using System.Configuration;
using System.Net.Http;
using System.Threading.Tasks;
using System.Web;

namespace CognitiveServicesVisionApp
{
    class Program
    {
        static void Main(string[] args)
        {
            Task<string> resultDescribe = DescribeImage(@"C:\Users\anurag\Downloads\photo.jpg");
            Task<string> resultText = ExtractText(@"C:\Users\anurag\Downloads\another-photo.jpg");
            Console.WriteLine(resultDescribe.Result);
            Console.WriteLine(Environment.NewLine);
            Console.WriteLine(resultText.Result);
        }

        public static async Task<string> DescribeImage(string imageFilePath)
        {
            using (HttpClient hc = new HttpClient())
            {
                hc.DefaultRequestHeaders.Add("Ocp-Apim-Subscription-Key",
                ConfigurationManager.AppSettings["AzureSubscriptionKeyVision"]);

                using (MultipartFormDataContent reqContent = new MultipartFormDataContent())
                {
                    var queryString = HttpUtility.ParseQueryString(string.Empty);
                    queryString["maxCandidates"] = "1";
                    var uri = "https://api.projectoxford.ai/vision/v1.0/describe?" + queryString;

                    try
                    {
                        var imgContent = new ByteArrayContent(System.IO.File.
                        ReadAllBytes(imageFilePath));
                        reqContent.Add(imgContent);

                        HttpResponseMessage resp = await hc.PostAsync(uri, reqContent);
                        string respJson = await resp.Content.ReadAsStringAsync();
                        return respJson;
                    }
                    catch(System.IO.FileNotFoundException ex)
                    {
                        return "The specified image file path is invalid.";
                    }
                    catch(ArgumentException ex)
                    {
```

```
                    return "The HTTP request object does not seem to be correctly formed.";
                }
            }
        }
    }

    public static async Task<string> ExtractText(string imageFilePath)
    {
        using (HttpClient hc = new HttpClient())
        {
            hc.DefaultRequestHeaders.Add("Ocp-Apim-Subscription-Key",
            ConfigurationManager.AppSettings["AzureSubscriptionKeyVision"]);

            using (MultipartFormDataContent reqContent = new MultipartFormDataContent())
            {
                var uri = "https://westus.api.cognitive.microsoft.com/vision/v1.0/ocr";

                try
                {
                    var imgContent = new ByteArrayContent(System.IO.File.
                    ReadAllBytes(imageFilePath));
                    reqContent.Add(imgContent);

                    HttpResponseMessage resp = await hc.PostAsync(uri, reqContent);
                    string respJson = await resp.Content.ReadAsStringAsync();
                    return respJson;
                }
                catch (System.IO.FileNotFoundException ex)
                {
                    return "The specified image file path is invalid.";
                }
                catch (ArgumentException ex)
                {
                    return "The HTTP request object does not seem to be correctly formed.";
                }
            }
        }
    }
}
```

The Walkthrough

There is no need for an entire walkthrough of the new code (Figure 2-11).

You have created a new method called ExtractText() in the same class as DescribeImage(). ExtractImage also accepts a string parameter for the absolute file path of the image you want to analyze. It returns the JSON result received from the API as text, and you display that text in the console.

```
Task<string> resultText = ExtractText(@"C:\Users\anurag\Downloads\another-photo.jpg");
Console.WriteLine(resultText.Result);
```

Figure 2-11. *The image used to test the OCR API*

The Result

The output we received in our console upon running our updated app is shown in Figure 2-12 (detected text pieces are highlighted).

```
C:\Windows\system32\cmd.exe
{"description":{"tags":["dog","grass","outdoor","white","sitting","small","laying","wooden","table","top","water","black
","beach","mouth","frisbee","board"],"captions":[{"text":"a white dog laying on the ground","confidence":0.8271022050700
3307}]},"requestId":"f26c1464-c4ed-4289-9fd7-32d78b341b62","metadata":{"width":1280,"height":853,"format":"Jpeg"}}


{"language":"en","textAngle":1.4999999999999629,"orientation":"Up","regions":[{"boundingBox":"280,328,664,210","lines":[
{"boundingBox":"514,328,189,63","words":[{"boundingBox":"514,328,189,63","text":"Next"}]},{"boundingBox":"280,410,664,12
8","words":[{"boundingBox":"280,422,209,116","text":"BIG"},{"boundingBox":"528,410,416,120","text":"THING"}]}]}]}
Press any key to continue . . . _
```

Figure 2-12. *The highlighted pieces represent the text detected by the API*

Isn't it magical? The Vision API could even honor the lowercase and uppercase for each character. That's the incredible power of AI now in your hands.

Recap

In this chapter, you learned about all of the tools you need to build your first AI-based application. You saw how Visual Studio is pretty much the only development environment you need. You also learned how to get your own Azure subscription key for using Cognitive Services APIs. After setting up your environment, you followed a step-by-step, methodical approach to creating your AI-based application that could intelligently suggest a brief textual description for your images. On the way, you learned the best and bad practices for each major piece of code. And, finally, you successfully extended your first AI-based application to do something even more interesting: extracting text out of images.

To recap, you learned about

- Setting up Visual Studio 2017 as your development environment

- Getting your own Azure subscription key, which is the most important prerequisite for using Cognitive Services

- Using Postman to test run the Computer Vision API's DescribeImage method to gain a better understanding of its request and response formats

- Creating your first AI-based console application in Visual Studio

- Understanding the code and best practices

- Extending your application to do even more

In the **next chapter**, you will learn about an emerging trend in user interface design called *conversational user interfaces*, something that allows us to interact with a computer via human-like conversations rather than purely graphical or textual interactions.

CHAPTER 3

■ ■ ■

Building a Conversational User Interface with Microsoft Technologies

Flip the pages back to Chapter 1. In the first pages, you see what it would be like to have a conversation with an intelligent computer regarding a live football (soccer) match. Let's take it a step further: it's pretty reasonable to order food while watching your favorite team in action.

Consider the last time you ordered food online. Of course, if you already knew what you wanted to order, you might have called the restaurant directly. Otherwise, you went to their website, checked their menu, selected the items, specified quantities and finally made the order. The whole process probably took 5-10 minutes, depending on the order.

Now imagine placing an order via one simple WhatsApp message (Figure 3-1). No clicking 20 times to place one order. No talking to mostly irritated shop assistants who always seem to be in a hurry.

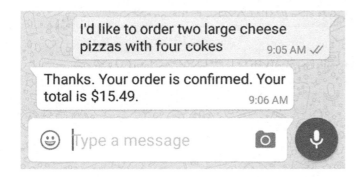

Figure 3-1. *Placing a order via WhatsApp*

And why just WhatsApp? Facebook Messenger, Slack, Google Talk, and even good ol' SMS would work just fine.

One simple message on your favorite messaging platform, and boom! Your order is confirmed. That's way easier and much more time saving. If clarifications are needed, the vendor may ask you a question or two, as shown in Figure 3-2.

© Nishith Pathak 2017

N. Pathak, *Artificial Intelligence for .NET: Speech, Language, and Search*, DOI 10.1007/978-1-4842-2949-1_3

Figure 3-2. *The chat-based pizza ordering system may ask for more details from the user about the order*

Using simple, text-based conversations to interact with a company's products or services is what the *conversational user interface (CUI)* is about. There is no graphical interface involved in the traditional sense: there are no pages to go through, no forms to fill, no buttons to click. Just plain text! It's like talking to a friend in an informal tone. An ideal CUI would give you an effortless interface to interact with due to the lack of formal rules, thus resulting in easy-going conversations.

After completing this chapter, you will have learned the following about CUI:

- What the conversational user interface is

- A brief history

- CUI vs. GUI (what it can do, what it cannot do)

- Real-world examples

- Design principles

- Creating a CUI application using the Microsoft Bot Framework

- Understanding the code

- Running, debugging, and testing your CUI application

What Is a Conversational User Interface?

You have seen via an example what it is like to interact with a conversational user interface. Is that all of what CUI is about, or is there more to it? Of course there's more to it; otherwise we wouldn't have a complete chapter on it. Let's start with the following question.

In the food ordering example above, who's talking at the other end? For all you know, it could be a real person or some sort of kickass automated system. The thing with a real person is that such a person would burn her fingers typing at the speed of light when flooded with dozens of orders per minute. Plus, there's a good chance she would confuse items across orders or, worse, miss an order altogether.

So although it's possible, and sometimes desirable, to have a real person texting at the other end, most of the time it makes more sense to have automated software listening and replying to users. Software can easily handle multiple users at the same time, limited only by the resources of the computer it is hosted on. Such an automated software is commonly called a **bot**. You have probably talked to more bots than you realize: a product's support account on Twitter, IM chat for sales inquiries, Alexa on Amazon Echo, Cortana on Windows, and Siri on iOS.

To interact with a bot, you don't need any special graphical elements, such as buttons or a mouse, just the messaging platform itself. The messaging platform could be WhatsApp, Twitter, Facebook, or a custom webpage. It doesn't matter. What matters is that the only thing that you need to talk to a bot, and get things done, is a keyboard. What do we call such an interface where all interactions are via text? Surely, calling it a graphical user interface or GUI would be unfair. So a wise person named it after the only visible thing in the interaction: the conversation. Thus the name *conversational user interface*.

A Brief History

The story of why and how conversational user interfaces came into being cannot be understood without first knowing the history of the user interface itself. But what is a user interface?

The user interface (UI) is your window to interact with a computer. It is what you use to instruct a computer to do things for you. Conversely, a UI is what a computer presents to its users to make human-computer interaction possible. Without a UI, you would have no control over a computer other than to fiddle with its hardware directly, which is not very helpful.

In the Very Beginning: the Command-Line Interface (CLI)

The earliest computers used the command line as their sole user interface. Users would enter a command in a purely textual, non-graphical interface, and the computer would execute that command and display the results. Figure 3-3 shows the result of a command to view the running processes, similar to what we see in Task Manager in Windows.

```
Processes: 210 total, 2 running, 9 stuck, 199 sleeping, 901 threads     23:30:03
Load Avg: 1.40, 1.75, 1.00  CPU usage: 4.15% user, 4.40% sys, 91.44% idle
SharedLibs: 1648K resident, 0B data, 0B linkedit.
MemRegions: 31278 total, 1892M resident, 117M private, 564M shared.
PhysMem: 5893M used (1191M wired), 10G unused.
VM: 523G vsize, 1026M framework vsize, 0(0) swapins, 0(0) swapouts.
Networks: packets: 12105/8925K in, 11907/1964K out.
Disks: 80156/2205M read, 21235/425M written.

PID   COMMAND      %CPU TIME      #TH   #WQ  #PORT MEM     PURG    CMPR PGRP PPID
592   screencaptur 0.0  00:00.02 7     5    55+   1952K+  20K+    0B   262  262
590   mdworker     0.0  00:00.01 3     0    44    2032K   0B      0B   590  1
589   mdworker     0.0  00:00.01 3     0    44    1572K   0B      0B   589  1
588   top          1.7  00:00.51 1/1   0    22+   2860K   0B      0B   588  584
584   bash         0.0  00:00.00 1     0    15    588K    0B      0B   584  583
583   login        0.0  00:00.01 3     1    28    1228K   0B      0B   583  482
574   auditd       0.0  00:00.00 2     0    25    560K    0B      0B   574  1
567   System Prefe 0.0  00:03.23 3     0    270   39M     8364K   0B   567  1
561   systemstatsd 0.0  00:00.01 2     1    19    1040K   0B      0B   561  1
560   com.apple.We 0.0  00:01.42 9     0    229   25M     0B      0B   560  1
558   com.apple.We 0.0  00:05.07 15    3    224   151M    1716K   0B   558  1
555   bash         0.0  00:00.00 1     0    15    604K    0B      0B   555  554
554   login        0.0  00:00.01 3     1    28    1176K   0B      0B   554  482
550   bash         0.0  00:00.00 1     0    15    608K    0B      0B   550  549█
```

Figure 3-3. Interfaces like this were common in the 1970s and 1980s. They were not just limited to stereotypical "hacker" groups, but were used by all computer users alike.

The CLI offered different commands for performing various operations on a computer. Although the basic operations across different computers and operating systems remained the same, the commands varied. MS-DOS was the direct predecessor of Micrsoft Windows OSes. It featured a command line interface to let users control the computer. Some popular commands for MS-DOS were

- dir: List contents of a directory.

- cd: Change current working directory.

- md: Create a new directory.

- copy: Copy a file to the specified destination.

- at: Schedule a time to execute commands or programs.

Each command had its set of options to tweak its behavior. For example, the command dir would return name of files and folders along with last modified date-time for each (Figure 3-4). The command dir /B would return only the names, without the dates and times.

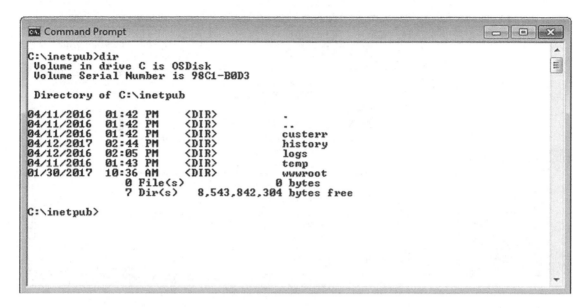

Figure 3-4. The dir command returns the list of all files and folders inside a directory

CLI was fast because it required few system resources as compared to graphical interfaces. And it was easier to automate via scripting.

While it was great for expert users, who had full control over the machine, CLI was very unfriendly to beginners. It came with a steep learning curve and required months or years of practice to get used to it. It was unintuitive, with commands not being obvious to a new user.

Despite its demerits, CLI is still offered as an alternative UI in operating systems as a means for expert/power users to get stuff done quickly. You might have used it in one of these forms: command prompt in Windows or terminal in macOS and UNIX/Linux.

And Then Came the Graphical User Interface

The graphical user interface or GUI is informally pronounced "goo-ee." Most of us were born in the GUI era. We are so accustomed to using buttons, menus, textboxes, and two dozen other graphical elements that make up the GUI that we cannot imagine interacting with our computers any other way. GUI just feels natural. Do you know what started the GUI revolution?

It all started with Douglas Engelbart's pioneering work on human-computer interaction in late 1960s. His research led to the development of a precursor to GUIs, which in turn led to the invention of the mouse. Engelbart's primitive GUI was then perfected at Xerox PARC, where the Xerox Alto computer was created. Alto was the first computer with a WIMP (windows, icons, menus, pointer) graphical interface, the sort of GUI that we use today (Figure 3-5).

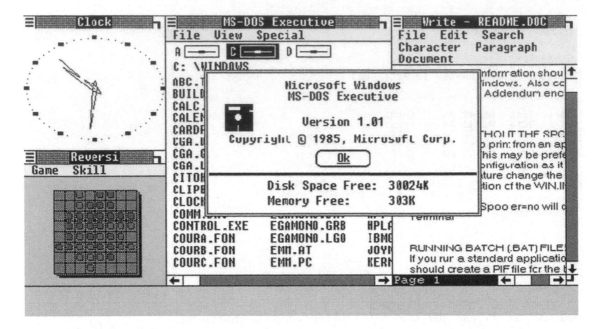

Figure 3-5. *A screenshot of Windows 1.01 operating system, one of the earliest commercially successful GUIs. In the screenshot, you can see a clock, a game, a file manager, and a document editor.*

■ **Note** Although Xerox practically invented the GUI as we know it today, it had little market impact. Xerox was slow to appreciate the value of the technology that had been developed at its PARC research center, and, as a result, failed to properly commercialize it when the time was ripe. Xerox did develop Alto into a commercial offering, Xerox Star, but couldn't make good on it due to the prohibitively high price of the Star and a lack of proper advertising. Xerox realized its blunderous mistake only after Apple's Macintosh had revolutionized the PC market, but it was too late by then.

GUIs completely changed the personal computing landscape through the beginner-friendly design. For the very first time, people who were not researchers, scientists, or enthusiasts could actually use computers. They could execute commands not by typing but by clicking buttons, they could "see" their files and folders, they could play games, and much, much more. Apple and Microsoft capitalized on Xerox's failure and thus started the PC revolution. While the Apple Macintosh was the first cheap commercial PC with a GUI operating system, Microsoft eventually won over the business and personal users through its Windows operating system, which was not tied to a specific hardware or machine and could be installed on a PC from vendors other than IBM.

Graphical interfaces have come a long way since their launch. From operating systems to web and mobile applications, the visual design is focused on being simple, elegant, and functional. The GUI has evolved from being simple in the 1980s and 1990s to eye candy in 2000s to flat and functional in 2010s.

The smartphone revolution has contributed as much to the evolution of GUI as PCs did early on. While the early smartphones had menu-driven operating systems (Nokia S60), our contemporary phones have OSes much like their desktop counterparts. Still, GUIs on screens smaller than PC monitors had to be reinvented for touch-friendly usage. This gave birth to new UI elements, such as sliding side menu, swipe actions, the "three dots" context menu, toggle/switch, notifications, share menu, etc. New design languages were written from scratch for all major platforms: Material Design (Android), Human Interface (iOS), and Metro Design (Windows). The recent UI elements are both pleasing to the eye and very functional. There has been cross-pollination of design ideas not just among mobile OSes but also from mobile to desktop.

And UI Evolved Yet Again: Conversational User Interface

The current technological landscape is dominated by mobiles. The GUI has been reinvented for these small screen devices and lets its users do the same things faster on a mobile than on a PC. But if we could simply talk to our mobile, just like we talk to a friend, it would be even easier to get things done. Advances in artificial intelligence have made it easier than ever to create such interfaces that allow you to talk to devices, both via speech and text.

There is a big difference between talking to a device through commands and talking to it in a more natural, informal way. Talking through commands is what CLI is all about. Such an approach results in a one-sided and strict communication. The device then appears to be a dumb machine that can only understand certain keywords, and is so rigid about the keywords that if you say anything out of its dictionary it would simply refuse to oblige. Consider this command-based conversation:

> *User*: I want to order a pizza.

> *Bot*: Sorry, I couldn't understand.

> *User suddenly remembers that this machine can only understand commands.*

> *User*: order pizza 1 large margarita

> *Bot*: Thanks, your order has been placed. Do you want to order more? (Y/n)

> *User*: No.

> *Bot*: Sorry, I couldn't understand.

> *User pulls her hair.*

A more natural conversation would go like this:

> *User*: I want to order a pizza.

> *Bot*: Great. What type of pizza would you like?

> *User*: Umm... I think Id like a Margarita. Wait, I think I'll go with Pepperoni.

> *Bot*: Is it a Margarita or a Pepperoni?

> *User*: Pepperoni. And make it large.

> *Bot*: Good. Would you like any sides?

> *User*: Nope, I'm good without them.

> *Bot*: Cool. Your order for 1 Pepperoni pizza has been placed successfully.

> *Bot*: I'll let you know when you order is dispatched.

> *Bot*: Is there anything else I can help you with?

> *User*: Nope, thank you.

> *Bot*: Thanks for ordering. Have a good day.

What's peculiar about the above conversation? Ok, let me help you out:

- It's much more informal than the strict command-based conversation you saw earlier, thus making it easy and fun for the user.

- The user DID NOT need to know in advance how to talk to the bot; the ideal bot will understand any abberations in the user query because each user may have their own way of asking questions.

■ **Note**   It is worth pointing out that CUI is not limited to text. Speech-based conversations are usually offered by most CUIs. Internally, speech is first converted to text, the result is obtained in text, and it's presented as such as well as via text-to-speech.

Messaging applications have played a big role in the evolution of GUI to CUI. Twitter popularized microblogging (expressing one's thoughts and opinions in short sentences of up to 140 characters). If you have ever used Twitter or seen tweets referenced on a news website, you know that Twitter allows for a very conversational flow wherein a user can send a tweet as a reply to a tweet posted by another user and someone can reply in response to another reply. It has not only been used by individual people to express themselves but also by organizations to provide support to their followers.

The same thing happened with WhatsApp. What was introduced as fast personal chatting app evolved into a much larger messaging platform with support for rich content (audio, video, documents, contacts, etc.). As with Twitter, organizations started offering support on WhatsApp to connect at a more personal level with their followers.

A lot of businesses today depend solely on messaging platforms to interact with their customers, freeing themselves from with the expensive responsibility of developing apps for their services. This is especially true of e-commerce. Apps such as WeChat, QQ, and Alipay are extremely popular among Chinese small and big e-sellers. This is how it works:

- A seller uses an e-commerce platform, such as Alibaba, to post items for sale.

- A potential customer looking to buy one of their items then connects with the seller via WeChat to place their order.

- Later, a real human connects with the customer with order fullfulment details and payment options. There may be a few additional exchanges for bargaining.

- The customer pays the amount via bank transfer or PayPal.

- The seller ships the item to the specified address.

Unlike traditional e-commerce websites, there is no "Buy" or "Add to cart" button on such e-commerce websites. The seller earns the full amount paid by the customer and the e-commerce website earns through item posting fees. But how does the customer gain? For a customer, this type of transaction is especially helpful when dealing with less popular or unknown sellers. Directly connecting with a seller's representative via a messaging platform gives the customer more buying confidence by getting to know the seller better.

People are so used to messaging that most find it easier to type a quick message rather than clicking/tapping buttons and filling out forms. As a result, businesses are turning to messaging platforms for selling their products and services. This has two benefits: (1) it's more convenient for the users and (2) it saves the company, especially small ones and startups, the additional cost of developing a dedicated app. We hope our point about the need for CUI is better explained now.

But what good is a messaging platform for a business if they must have real people talking to their customers on the other end? In that case, the cost spent on human operators would be equal to or more than the cost saved from app development. That's where AI-based chat bots are so invaluable.

AI's Role in CUI

Artificial intelligence techniques, such as natural language understanding (NLU), help in determining the meaning of a user's sentence. No matter how a user expresses a particular intention to get or do something, a good NLU back end will be able to determine that intention.

For example, say you are developing a bot to which "Hey," "Hi," "Hello," and "What's up" all mean the same thing. You, the developer, can train your NLU back end to recognize all these phrases as the same intention, say HelloGreeting. So when a user sends a message to your bot, it will be routed to the NLU back end. In return, the back end will return a single word name (intent) that represents the intention of the user. If one of the above phrases is detected in the message, the returned intention will be HelloGreeting. In your bot's logic code, you can put a condition like that in Listing 3-1 to send back an appropriate response.

Listing 3-1. Pseudocode That Uses an NLU Back End to Determine the User's Intention from Their Message in Order to Send Out an Appropriate Response Message Back to the User

```
string intent = NLUBackend.getIntent(userMessage);
if (intent == "HelloGreeting")
{
        sendReply("Hi there! I am Pizza Bot. Say something like 'I want to order a pizza' to
        get started.'");
}
```

It is worth noting that NLU is smarter than simply being able to return an intent for phrases that the intent has been trained against. A good NLU system will return the correct intent even for phrases it has never seen before (not trained with). For example, based on the above phrases for HelloGreeting, an NLU back end can determine that "hi there" and "hello buddy" might also mean the same thing, and so will return the HelloGreeting intent for these new phrases with high confidence.

And it gets smarter and smarter with training. The more, and better, the training, the better the intent determination of the NLU back end. You will learn detailed NLU concepts in Chapter 4. In Chapter 6, you will gain hands-on experience in using Microsoft's NLU framework LUIS.

Evidently, NLU has made creating smart bots easier than ever before. From single words to phrases to full sentences, a properly trained NLU back end will determine intents for all of these simple and complex user messages. While designing a chat box, you no longer have to worry about the two dozen variations users may use to order pizza through your bot.

"I want to order a pizza"

- User A

"Could you help me order a pizza?"

- User B

"Dude, note down my order"

- User C

"Hey, I want a large pepperoni with garlic bread and a dip."

- User D

All of the above user messages essentially mean the same thing. The way these messages are written are different but the intention of placing an order is the same. With enough training, an NLU back end will return the same intent for all of these and other similar messages.

Pitfalls of CUI

The world of conversational interfaces has a great promise. But it's not all rosy.

Chat bots are limited by today's AI technologies. NLU is an AI-hard problem, one of the most difficult problems in the field of artificial intelligence. It has come a long way and, with a lot of training, can handle specialized use cases well. But despite independent research on NLU by AI scientists across the globe, it has room for improvement.

Bots powered by NLU can make mistakes, from silly and harmless to downright blunderous (Figures 3-6 and 3-7). Bots that offer command-based conversations operate with certainty because they respond only to commands and completely ignore words that are not commands. NLU bots, on the other hand, come with the side effect of uncertainty. Even the developers who have trained the bot's NLU back end sometimes do not know how it's going to respond to unfamiliar phrases.

Figure 3-6. *A Facebook Messenger bot, Poncho, isn't able to understand the difference between a location and a non-location message. A silly, but harmless, mistake.*

Figure 3-7. Tay was an artificial intelligence Twitter chat bot, created by Microsoft's Technology and Research division. Tay was designed to mimic the language patterns of a 19-year-old American girl, and to learn from interacting with human users of Twitter. It caused major controversy when a group of pranksters taught Tay inflammatory messages. Within 24 hours, Tay started tweeting racist and sexually-charged messages in response to other Twitter users. It was subsequently taken down by Microsoft. Tay remains a good example of an AI experiment gone horribly wrong.

The best bots learn from their mistakes. It's a good idea to maintain logs of user messages and the bot's response to those messages. Developers can regularly look for user messages that went unanswered or were wrongly replied to, and use that information to further train their NLU back end.

CUIs are not just limited by their NLU back ends. Some things are still easier done with a GUI. For example, in our pizza ordering example, the bot should be able to show a menu (with prices) to users who do not know their food options beforehand. A menu with pictures of each item is 10 times better than a text-only menu. The bot can make things even more convenient for the user by giving them an "Add to card" button below each menu item's image. The user then wouldn't have to type the full name of the item that they want.

As CUI stands today, it would be imprudent for an organization to leave its business to a bot. It's a good idea to have complex conversations rerouted to a human operator who can deal with such conversations better.

A Hybrid UI (CUI+GUI) May Be the Future

Until CUI is advanced enough to handle every type of conversation and user messages by itself, an ideal UI will combine a CUI with some elements of a GUI. This greatly improves the user experience of the app by making it many times easier for the user to use it. Figure 3-8 demonstrates our point through a Skype-based travel bot.

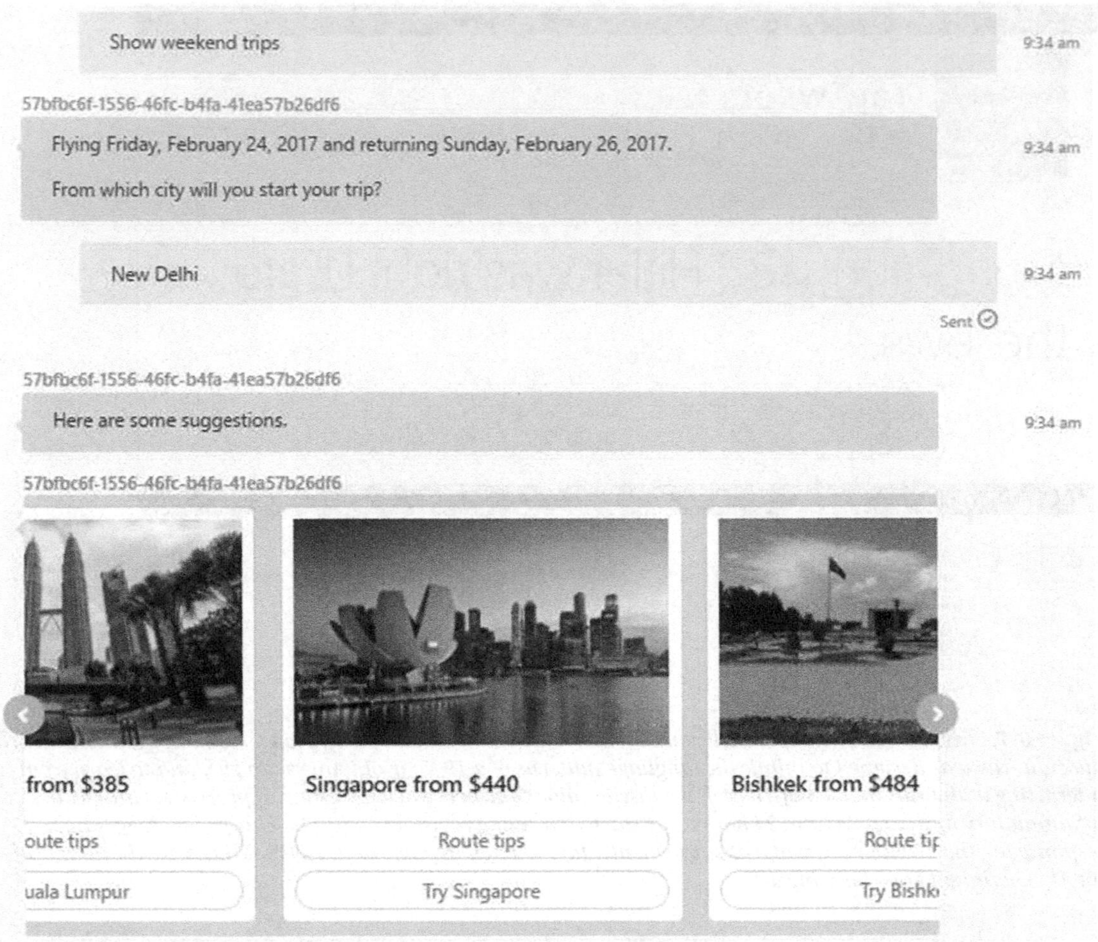

Figure 3-8. *Booking an air ticket through a Skype bot, Skyscanner. The trip suggestions have images and buttons.*

A user doesn't have to pick a suggestion by typing its name or id. Instead, they can just click/tap a button to get started. Clicking a button continues the conversation by sending the corresponding text message on the user's behalf. Some of the further messages from the bot also contain GUI elements (Figure 3-9).

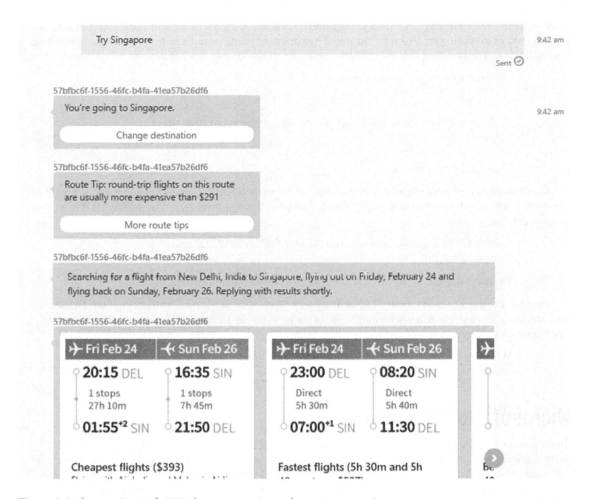

Figure 3-9. *Interacting with GUI elements continues the text conversation*

Design Principles

The most important rule, the holy grail, you must remember when designing conversational interfaces is that your users will not have a what-you-see-is-what-you-get (WYSISYG) interface. All they will be able to do is talk to your bot. Naturally, it is your duty to make this experience as intuitive as possible.

The thing with CUIs is that unlike GUIs, there can be no "Getting Started" or "FAQs" pages to guide a user. There is just text and occasional links and buttons. Keep the following things in mind and you'll be on the right track.

Introduction: In 99% of all cases, it will be the user who starts a conversation. It could be a one-word greeting or a straight-to-the-point question. Your bot should use this opportunity to let the user know what all it can do and how it can do it. Give your bot a human name to make the conversation more natural.

> Hello! I am Ted. How can I help you today? I can help you book a movie or sports ticket. You can start by saying, "book a ticket."

Progress: Your CUI may not have a visual interface, such as a loader, to indicate that your bot is actively fetching data or executing an action for the user. Give frequent progress hints so that the user doesn't think that the bot is not responding. You may program your bot to ignore user messages received during this time.

> I am still looking for the best deals.
>
> ...
>
> I am sorry it is taking so much time. Good things take time, don't they?
>
> ...
>
> I have not forgotten you.

Confirmation and next steps: When your bot is done with the task the user asked it to do, send out a nice confirmation with possible next steps. You may also use this opportunity to give hints about what else your bot can do.

> Your ticket to Singapore has been booked for Feb 14, 2017 2:30am.
> Have a safe flight!
>
> Do you want me to remind you about your travel 12 hrs before departure?

Humor: Be funny at times. Instead of having your bot respond in a formal and boring tone all the time, program it to reply with witty messages. Quote famous books, movies, TV series, etc. to make user's experience more interesting.

> While I fetch available seats... have you seen the latest Star Wars flick? I have heard rave reviews about it.

Microsoft Bot Framework

The Microsoft Bot Framework is a collection of open source SDKs for building enterprise-grade bots easily and quickly. Through its several built-in constructors, the framework speeds up the development of CUI applications. These may be simple applications designed to handle user messages independently or contextual applications that can adapt as per previous user messages to send more customized messages.

Using Bot Framework, it is easy to write the logic of a bot and then publish it to one or more messaging platforms supported by the framework, such as Skype, Facebook Messenger, and so on. By leveraging a channel's capabilities, bots can use hybrid interfaces to make user interaction more engaging.

The framework is not part of the Cognitive Services package, but it can be seamlessly integrated with several of its APIs to give your bots a more human feel through natural language understanding, computer vision, and speech recognition.

At the time of writing, the Bot Framework was in still in the preview phase. We encourage you to visit `https://dev.botframework.com` to get a glimpse of its capablities. The website also has a bot directory, which is a list of bots created using the framework that are publically listed by their developers. Try one of the featured bots through a supported channel of your choice and see for yourself what a CUI application feels like.

Creating a CUI Application Using Bot Framework

A bot in the context of the Bot Framework is essentially a combination of three components. Refer to Figure 3-10 to see how these components work together.

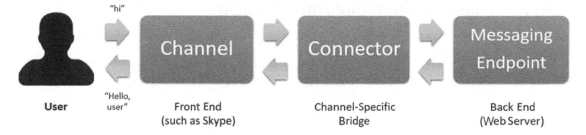

Figure 3-10. Architecture diagram of a Bot Framework CUI application

- **Messaging Endpoint**: This is a web service/API created using the Bot Framework. It is the main thing, the place where all the bot's logic resides. When you say you're creating a bot, you're essentially creating its back-end web service. Bot Framework currently officially supports only C# (ASP.NET MVC) and Node.js for web service creation.

- **Channel**: The messaging platform your bot uses. Your bot may be configured to use more than one channel. Currently, Bot Framework supported channels include Skype, Telegram, Facebook Messenger, Slack, GroupMe, Kik, SMS, and Office 365 Email.

- **Connector**: A software component, part of the Bot Framework, that connects your endpoint with one or more channels and takes care of message routing between them. It is the Connector that gives your endpoint the ability to be reused by multiple channels at the same time.

With an understanding of the underlying architecture for a Bot Framework application, you are going to create a simple Health Checkup bot that helps in scheduling appointment with a doctor.

Step 0: Prep Your Development Environment

Visual Studio is the only thing you need to create your bot. The main thing that you need to create for your bot is the messaging endpoint. The endpoint must be a RESTful web service, hosted on a web server such that Bot Framework's connectors can easily find it to connect it with one or more channels.

In .NET, the recommended way to create a RESTful web service is using ASP.NET MVC. In VS 2017, it's easy to create an ASP.NET-based web service. VS comes preinstalled with a lot of templates so you don't have to start from scratch when creating specific types of applications. In Chapter 2, you created a Console Application using a VS 2017 template. Similarly, there is a template for creating ASP.NET MVC applications. On choosing this template, Visual Studio creates a new MVC application, adds all dependencies (reference DLLs, NuGet packages, JavaScript libraries, etc.), and adds sample code for you to get started.

■ **Note** If you are new to ASP.NET MVC or web services in general, we recommend reading an Apress book titled *ASP.NET Web API 2: Building a REST Service from Start to Finish* by Jamie Kurtz and Brian Wortman.

Bot Framework's documentation has a lot of examples to help you create your ASP.NET MVC-based messaging endpoint. Additionally, the framework provides an even better way to create an endpoint: a dedicated Visual Studio template just for the purpose. Head to `http://aka.ms/bf-bc-vstemplate` to download this template. Save the zip file to your Visual Studio 2017 `templates` directory which is traditionally in `%USERPROFILE%\Documents\Visual Studio 2017\Templates\ProjectTemplates\Visual C#\`.

Step 1: Create a New Bot Application Project

You will create a simple health checkup bot. The sole purpose of the bot is to help a user book an appointment with a doctor.

Open Visual Studio 2017 and create a new project by going to File ➤ New ➤ Project. Select the **Bot Application** template under Visual C#, as shown in Figure 3-11. This will create an ASP.NET MVC application customized according to the Bot Framework.

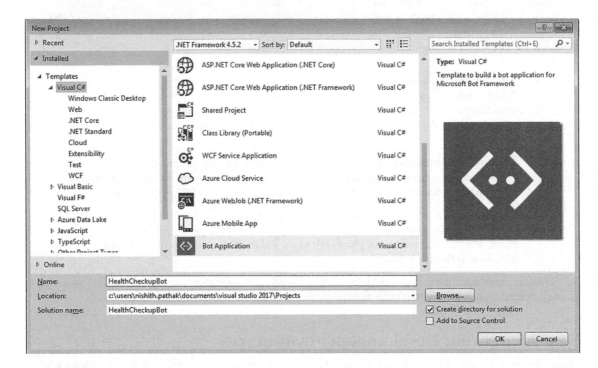

Figure 3-11. *Creating a new Bot Application in Visual Studio 2017*

Step 2: First and Default Messages

Your newly created Bot Application should have only one controller. From Solution Explorer, open Controllers ➤ MessagesController.cs to start editing it.

Your main method here is Post(). This is where all the logic of your bot will go. User messages are captured here and this is where appropriate responses are sent out. Currently, it is configured to send back the same message that it receives from a user, along with the character length of that message.

Let's modify your code to return greeting and default messages. See Listing 3-2.

Listing 3-2. New Code

```
[BotAuthentication]
    public class MessagesController : ApiController
    {
        string[] greetingPhrases = new string[] { "hi", "hello", "howdy", "how are you",
        "good morning", "good afternoon" };
```

```
/// <summary>
/// POST: api/Messages
/// Receive a message from a user and reply to it
/// </summary>
public async Task<HttpResponseMessage> Post([FromBody]Activity activity)
{
    if (activity.Type == ActivityTypes.Message)
    {
        ConnectorClient connector = new ConnectorClient(new Uri(activity.ServiceUrl));
        string userText = activity.Text.ToLower();
        string replyText = "";
        if(this.greetingPhrases.Contains(userText))
        {
            replyText = "Hi! I am Health Checkup Bot. I will be glad to help you
            schedule a meeting with a doctor. Say, 'schedule a meeting.'";
        }
        else
        {
            replyText = "Sorry, I did not understand that.";
        }

        Activity reply = activity.CreateReply(replyText);
        await connector.Conversations.ReplyToActivityAsync(reply);
    }
    else
    {
        HandleSystemMessage(activity);
    }
    var response = Request.CreateResponse(HttpStatusCode.OK);
    return response;
}

private Activity HandleSystemMessage(Activity message) {...}
}
```

A breakdown of this code is as follows:

```
public async Task<HttpResponseMessage> Post([FromBody]Activity activity)
```

A piece of communication between bot and user is called an *activity*. You receive an activity object from an HTTP POST call made to your messaging endpoint web service. The Bot Framework supports several types of activities, some of which you'll see in a bit. Right now you are concerned with the type message. A message activity represents a text message and some information about it, such as

- The text string
- Sender
- Receiver
- Timestamp

```
if (activity.Type == ActivityTypes.Message)
{
    ConnectorClient connector = new ConnectorClient(new Uri(activity.ServiceUrl));
    string userText = activity.Text.ToLower();
```

If the activity that your endpoint has received is a message type, you convert the message text into lowercase (for easy comparison) and create an instance of connector. This instance of connector is what you will use to send a reply back to the user. activity.ServiceUrl signifies to the URL where the bot's reply will be posted. Every channel has its own service URL to listen to replies.

```
if(this.greetingPhrases.Contains(userText))
{
    replyText = "Hi! I am Health Checkup Bot. I will be glad to help you schedule a meeting
    with a doctor. Say, 'schedule a meeting.'";
}
else
{
    replyText = "Sorry, I did not understand that.";
}
```

Next, you check whether the user's message matches one of the phrases specified in the in greetPhrases string array. If it does, you set your reply to a nice introduction message. Otherwise, you send out a default message to let the user know you don't know an appropriate response to their message.

```
Activity reply = activity.CreateReply(replyText);
await connector.Conversations.ReplyToActivityAsync(reply);
```

You use the received activity's CreateReply() method to create a new activity for your response message. You then send your reply through the connector object.

```
var response = Request.CreateResponse(HttpStatusCode.OK);
return response;
```

Once your reply has been posted, you return out a simple HTTP 200 status code from your web service's Post method to signal the successful completion of this operation.

Step 3: Running, Testing, and Debugging Your Bot

Time to run your application to see how it responds to user messages. Visual Studio comes bundled with a lightweight web server software, IIS Express, to run web applications and services. IIS Express is the stripped-down version of its full fledged brother, IIS.

To run your messaging endpoint, select the option called Start Debugging from the Debug menu. Alternatively, press F5. This will start the application in debug mode and open a new tab in your default browser with the endpoint's URL. Bot Framework applications are configured by default to run on port 3979. You should see the default page at http://localhost:3979 in your browser, as shown in Figure 3-12.

HealthCheckupBot

Describe your bot here and your terms of use etc.

Visit <u>Bot Framework</u> to register your bot. When you register it, remember to set your bot's endpoint to

```
https://your_bots_hostname/api/messages
```

Figure 3-12. *The default page of the messaging endpoint. If you see this, things are working well*

The default page does not give you a way to test your bot. It's a static web page that you may use to describe your bot. To test your application, you can make use of Postman, as you did with the Cognitive Services RESTful APIs in Chapter 2, given you know the HTTP header and body format for the API. But we have a better option.

Bot Framework Emulator is free software that is specifically designed to test Bot Framework applications locally or remotely. Download the emulator from `https://aka.ms/bf-bc-emulator`.

Once downloaded, open the emulator and specify the following URL in the address bar.

```
http://localhost:3979/api/messages
```

Leave the Microsoft App Id and Password fields empty and press the Connect button.

If you had placed a debugger breakpoint in your code, your VS might look like what you see in Figure 3-13. You may use Visual Studio's rich debugging options to navigate through the code. Try using the F10 (Step Over), F11 (Step Into), and F5 (Continue) options.

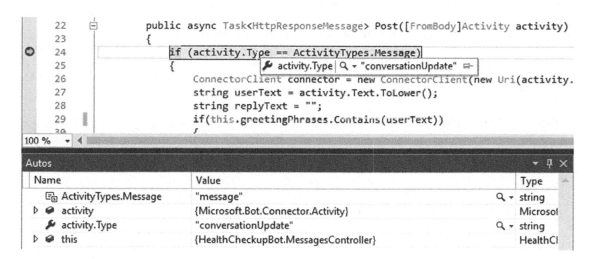

Figure 3-13. *Visual Studio shows an active breakpoint that has been hit due to an incoming message from the emulator*

Press F5 in Visual Studio to finish debugging, if you have active breakpoints. Now open the emulator again and start a conversation with your bot. Send "hi" to begin.

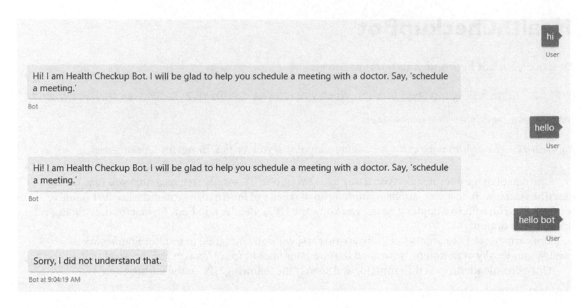

Figure 3-14. *Starting a conversation with the bot in the emulator*

As you can see in Figure 3-14, the bot responded as expected to your "hi" and "hello" messages. It did not, however, understand "hello bot" and returned the default message. You can quickly fix this by adding the following method to the MessagesController class:

```
private bool MessageHasPhrase(string message, string[] phraseList)
{
    foreach (string phrase in phraseList)
    {
        if (message.Contains(phrase))
        {
            return true;
        }
    }
    return false;
}
```

Next, replace your phrase-checking if condition with this:

```
if(this.MessageHasPhrase(userText, greetingPhrases))
{
    replyText = "Hi! I am Health Check Bot. I will be glad to help you schedule a meeting
    with a doctor. Say, 'schedule a meeting.'";
}
else
{
    replyText = "Sorry, I did not understand that.";
}
```

The result can be seen in Figure 3-15.

64

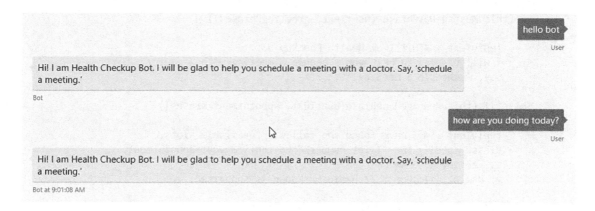

Figure 3-15. *Your bot can now recognize phrases that are not an exact match in your phrase list*

At this point, your bot is a bit more intelligent because it can recognize similar phrases. It cannot, however, recognize other similar phrases whose fragments are not present in your phrase list:

- "hey bot, what's up"
- "good evening"
- "what can you do"

So what do you do? Update your phrase list with all possible words/phrases a user may send? Of course not. This is where natural language understanding can help. You will use LUIS, Microsoft's NLU service, in Chapter 6 to add language understanding capability to your bot so that you don't have to manually hardcode all possible phrases and can rely on the trusty LUIS service to take care of new and familiar phrases.

Step 3: Appointment Scheduling

Now to the main part: scheduling an appointment with the doctor. Let's add the logic that will recognize a user's appointment request, offer them available slots to pick from, and confirm the appointment. Ideally, a bot will check the doctor's calendar or some sort of database to extract free slots. In your simple bot, you will hardcode the slots.

Update your code as shown in Listing 3-3. There are two new phrase arrays and else if conditions.

Listing 3-3. Updated Code

```
string[] greetingPhrases = new string[] { "hi", "hello", "howdy", "how are you", "good
morning", "good afternoon" };
string[] appointmentPhrases = new string[] { "appointment", "schedule", "meeting" };
string[] slotPhrases = new string[] { "1", "2", "3", "4", "5", "first", "second", "third",
"one", "two", "three" };

public async Task<HttpResponseMessage> Post([FromBody]Activity activity)
{
    if (activity.Type == ActivityTypes.Message)
    {
        ConnectorClient connector = new ConnectorClient(new Uri(activity.ServiceUrl));
        string userText = activity.Text.ToLower();
        string replyText = "";
```

```
        if(this.MessageHasPhrase (userText, greetingPhrases))
        {
            replyText = @"Hi! I am Health Checkup Bot.
            I will be glad to help you schedule a meeting with a doctor.
            Say, 'schedule a meeting.'";
        }
        else if (this.MessageHasPhrase(userText, appointmentPhrases))
        {
            replyText = @"I have found the following available slots.
            Please specify the **slot number** to confirm your appointment.
            1. Feb 26, 9:00 am
            2. Mar 02, 12:30pm"; // basic markdown is supported
        }
        else if (this.MessageHasPhrase(userText, slotPhrases))
        {
            replyText = "Your appointment is confirmed with Dr. John Doe. See you soon.";
        }
        else
        {
            replyText = "Sorry, I did not understand that.";
        }

        Activity reply = activity.CreateReply(replyText);
        await connector.Conversations.ReplyToActivityAsync(reply);
    }
    else
    {
        HandleSystemMessage(activity);
    }
    var response = Request.CreateResponse(HttpStatusCode.OK);
    return response;
}
```

Figure 3-16 shows an appointment request conversation with the updated bot.

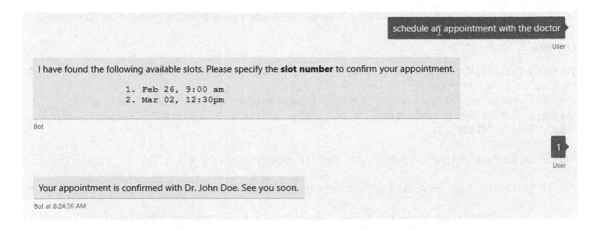

Figure 3-16. *Showing the confirmation with Dr. John via the health checkup bot*

This completes the conversational flow of your very simple bot. The bot is now capable of introducing itself and scheduling appointments. But there is a lot that is wrong with the bot.

It cannot recognize the date and time in an appointment request. Even if these are present in user's message, your bot will conveniently ignore them. So something like "schedule an appointment for 9 am on Feb 27" would result in the same hardcoded message. Ideally, the bot should take into account the user's requested time and check the calendar accordingly.

Furthermore, different users may have different styles of specifying date/time info. A bot should be able to understand all of the following and more:

- 02/27/17 9:00

- Feb 27, 9 am

- 27 feb at 9 in the morning

- 9 am tomorrow

This can be achieved using natural language understanding support, as you will see in Chapter 6 on LUIS.

Also, your bot has absolutely no memory of a user's previous messages. All it knows and cares about is the current user message. Consider Figure 3-17 for an example.

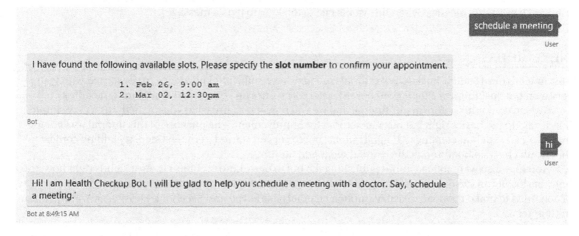

Figure 3-17. *While scheduling a meeting, if the user intentionally or unintentionally sends another type of message that the bot supports, it immediately "drops" the previous context and responds with an entirely new and unrelated message. Ideally, the bot should have complained that the user's message didn't look like a valid slot.*

This is a problem of **context**. Your bot doesn't know the context of the ongoing conversation and thus treats each message as independent. This problem can be fixed through the use of **dialogs**. The Bot Framework comes with powerful dialog support for creating **contextual** CUI applications. You will see a limited use of dialogs in Chapter 6. We recommend you check the Bot Framework's official C# documentation on this subject for a better understanding.

Step 4: Handling System Messages

System messages are messages or signals not sent by the user but by their channel. Not all system messages are supported by all channels, but here'a a general list of messages supported by the Bot Framework:

- **ConversationUpdate**: Conversation state changes, like members being added and removed.

- **DeleteUserData**: User requests for conversation or profile deletion. Some countries make it mandatory for messaging platforms to provide this option to protect the privacy of users.

- **ContactRelationUpdate**: Bot has been added or removed from a user's contact list.

- **Typing**: A signal that indicates that the user is typing something. Some channels may send it more frequently than others.

- **Ping**: Tests whether security has been implemented correctly in a bot.

In `MessagesController.cs`, there is a `HandleSystemMessage()` method that Visual Studio added while creating the application. All the above system message types are covered in that method. You can add your custom code to handle each message type. You may either log a system message or send a response to the user (such as a witty message when the user is taking too long to type a message).

Next Steps

This finishes our Health Checkup Bot tutorial. You now have sufficient knowledge to get started with your very own bot. Just think of a topic your bot will cater to, and fire up your Visual Studio to start coding.

We have said this before in our tutorial and we will repeat it again: what you created was a very simple bot. It can do the basics right but has much room for improvement. The purpose of this tutorial was not to make you an expert at creating CUI applications, but to get you started. As a next step, try adding context to the health checkup bot through the use of dialogs and prompts.

You may also want to read about publishing the bot to one or more channels. As it stands right now, the bot runs locally on the developer's computer and can only be connected to via the emulator. The final goal, of course, is to make the bot accessible through channels like Skype and Facebook Messenger. You will do so in Chapter 6.

EXERCISE: FORMFLOW

Re-create the Health Checkup Bot Using FormFlow

FormFlow is a feature in the Bot Framework that can automatically convert a C# class into a form-based conversation through the use of dialogs. This feature is especially helpful in situations where the bot's purpose is to have the user fill out a form through text-based conversations.

Head to `docs.botframework.com` to read more about FormFlow. By following the examples mentioned on that page, re-create the health checkup bot using FormFlow. Hint: Add more things to the conversation, such as asking the user about their symptoms before scheduling an appointment with a doctor with an appropriate speciality.

Recap

In this chapter, you learned

- A brief history of the evolution of user interfaces
- What conversation interfaces are and why they are important
- What a CUI can do and what it cannot do (yet)
- How to create a CUI app (bot) using Microsoft's Bot Framework

In the **next chapter**, you will learn in detail about natural language understanding, its underlying concepts, and where to use it.

CHAPTER 4

■ ■ ■

Using Natural Language Understanding

Natural language understanding or NLU: you have been hearing this term since Chapter 1. You have seen with examples what it's about and what it can do. By now you know that this is the thing that lends an application a human-like ability to understand a user's natural language sentences. In this chapter, you will learn about NLU in detail and understand concepts related to LUIS, the NLU component in Cognitive Services.

■ **Note** Although you can think of a *natural language* as being the direct opposite of an *artificial language* (such as a programming language), it does not always have the same meaning as a *human language*. All natural languages are human languages but not all human languages are natural. A natural language is one that has been in use by humans for a long time, and has evolved naturally from generation to generation. English, French, Hindi, Latin, Arabic, etc. are natural languages.

There is another class of human languages called *constructed languages*, which have been artificially created by one person or group with a formal set of unchanging grammar. The most popular constructed language is Esperanto which, according to some estimates, is spoken by about 2 million people across the globe.

The supreme goal of artificial intelligence has always been to serve humanity in ways unthinkable with traditional machines. In order to serve humans, AI must be able to understand them the way humans do each other. For a human, getting something done from AI should be as effortless as asking a fellow human for help. Unsurprisingly, a major part of overall research on AI has been concentrated on processing and understanding natural languages, the languages of humans.

NLU is one of the several tasks of the wider AI field of natural language processing (NLP). But unlike most other NLP tasks, NLU is an AI-hard problem. AI-hard problems, AI-complete as they are otherwise known, are the most difficult problems of AI and they deal with making a machine as intelligent as a human. These problems cannot be solved using one specially designed algorithm like the other AI problems but may require a combination of several complex algorithms that work together on different parts of the same problem to achieve the same goal. NLU along with computer vision and machine translation are the main AI-hard problems.

The ability to understand human languages and interpret the meaning of sentences is an indispensable quality of an intelligent system. As a result, NLU has wide variety of commercial, academic, and personal applications: personal robots that understand our needs, CUI applications that provide medical advice by listening to our symptoms, and content-analysis systems that can extract key details from huge amounts of text and voice communication between terrorist groups, proactively preventing attacks.

© Nishith Pathak 2017

N. Pathak, *Artificial Intelligence for .NET: Speech, Language, and Search*, DOI 10.1007/978-1-4842-2949-1_4

After reading this chapter, you will have learned the following about natural language understanding:

- What NLU is

- A brief history

- Why natural language is difficult for machines to understand

- Microsoft Language Understanding Intelligent Service (LUIS)

- The architecture of a LUIS-enabled application

- How to get a subscription key for LUIS from Azure

- How to make a demo of a working LUIS-based web app

What Is NLU?

By now, you no doubt have this etched in your brain that NLU is the ability of a machine to understand human languages. More specifically, it is the process of converting natural language text into a form that computers can understand. In Chapter 1, you saw how an NLU program determines the meaning of a sentence by breaking it down into intents and entities. Not all NLU implementations work with intents and entities, but they are something you will find across major open-source and proprietary NLU frameworks.

A given piece of text can be represented by one intent and one or multiple entities. Using this information, a program can decide

- What action to perform based on the intent

- How to perform the action based on the entities

Let's use Chapter 1's example to illustrate this point. Consider this sentence again:

"How is the weather going to be in Delhi tomorrow?"

To us humans, it is immediately clear that the above sentence is a person's way of inquiring about the weather at a place. To a computer that does not know the rules of grammar, this sentence could just as well be gibberish because it would not know the parts of speech (nouns, verbs, adjectives, prepositions, etc.) and thus could not make sense of the meaning by putting all of them together. Would the computer be able to correctly understand the above sentence if it knew all the rules of grammar? No doubt. But then what would it make of these questions/requests:

"How's weather gonna be at Delhi tomorrow?"

"Delhi weather tmrow"

A computer that always goes by the rules wouldn't be able to understand these grammatically incorrect, slang-ridden sentences. Of course, it is impossible to expect users to always type grammatically correct sentences: (a) native and non-native speakers alike are susceptible to making grammatical mistakes and (b) most people don't have the time to type full words or sentences.

The trick in achieving accurate language understanding is not to teach a computer all the rules, slang, common mistakes, etc., but to train it with hundreds of thousands or millions of sentences and let it figure out on its own the formal and informal rules of a language through some sort of pattern recognition. This has been made possible by machine learning techniques, especially deep learning.

A commercial NLU offering is usually a cloud service that has been through this initial training. Now that it knows the basics of a language, developers can train it to recognize more specific use cases, like "get weather info." They can train the service so that it knows that "weather," "what's the weather," "how's the weather," "tell me the weather," etc. all mean the same thing: get weather info. The developers do not have to train the service with all 1,000 ways of asking the same thing. Using its basic understanding of a language, the service can make smart guesses when it encounters a similar but unknown user query. So when a user asks about the weather in any one the aforementioned (or other similar) ways, their intention is to get weather info. In other, more technical words, we say that the **intent** of their sentence is to get weather info.

In a similar fashion, developers can train the service to recognize certain keywords in a sentence that complements the intent. Weather info is usually associated with a place and a time. Developers can train the service with the names of several cities, states, and countries and with different ways of expressing the day/date. The city and date would then be the **entities**. Entities may or may not be optional, depending on the intent. In case of weather, if neither city nor date is specified, it can be implicitly assumed that the user wants to know *today's* weather in their *current* location.

Figure 4-1 illustrates the breakdown of a sentence by an NLU service.

how is the weather going to be in Delhi tomorrow
intent   city   date

Figure 4-1. A natural language sentence with intent and entities highlighted

This breakdown of a sentence into intent and entities is something that the developers' program can understand to perform an action.

```
if (intent == "getWeatherInfo")
{
        result = getWeatherInfo(entities.City, entities.Date); // returns "21 degrees
        celsius with low chance of rain"
        print "The weather in " + entities.City + " on " + entities.Date + " is going to be
        " + result;
}
```

Figure 4-2 shows the intent-entities breakdown of flight ticket booking example.

book a ticket to new york for 2 adults for march 12
intent   destination   ticket count   departure date

Figure 4-2. A computer program can make use of the extracted intent and entities data to make an actual booking for a user

■ **Note** The reverse of language understanding is language generation. *NLG (natural language generation)* is the process of converting data in a format that computers can understand (such as numeric data stored in database) into natural language text.

For example, a comparison between the weather data of two consecutive days for a city may result in the following auto-generated text:

The weather in New Delhi today is moderately hot, which is an increase of 3 degrees Celsius from yesterday. Although no rain is expected, it may feel a little humid during the afternoon.

Unlike NLU, NLG is not an AI-hard problem due to the fact that language generation is a controlled process where synthesizing sentences is governed by a fixed set of formal grammatical rules. That is, there is zero uncertainty in the rules of the game.

History of Natural Language Understanding

The history of NLU is almost as old as the field of artificial intelligence itself. In 1964, PhD student Daniel Bobrow of MIT created a computer program named STUDENT for his doctoral thesis. The program was written in the Lisp programming language, and was designed to solve high school algebra problems. STUDENT is considered to be one of the earliest known attempts at natural language understanding.

> *The question naturally arises, "What do you mean by having a computer understand natural language?" I have adopted the following operational definition of understanding. A computer understands a subset of English if it will accept input sentences which are members of this subset, and correctly answer questions based on information contained in these sentences. The ability must extend to deductions based on implicit information contained in several sentences. It is desirable that the answers also be in English to facilitate communication between the computer and a person.*
>
> — "Natural Language Input for a Computer Problem Solving System," Daniel Bobrow, 1964

STUDENT could solve algebra questions expressed as English sentences and provide answers in English. So something like, "The sum of two numbers of 96, and one of the numbers is 16 larger than the other number. Find the two numbers." would result in an answer like, "One of the numbers is 56. The other number is 40."

Perhaps the most famous example of NLU is the computer program ELIZA, created by Joseph Weizenbaum between 1965-66 at the MIT Artificial Intelligence Laboratory. ELIZA was an interactive chat bot that could be programmed to converse with a user on any topic in English. The most popular topic was psychotherapy, implemented through a script called DOCTOR, a psychotherapist simulator. Figure 4-3 shows conversation between ELIZA and a user.

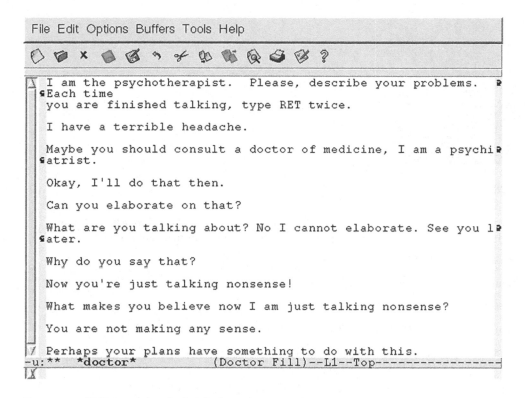

File Edit Options Buffers Tools Help

I am the psychotherapist. Please, describe your problems.
Each time
you are finished talking, type RET twice.

I have a terrible headache.

Maybe you should consult a doctor of medicine, I am a psychi
atrist.

Okay, I'll do that then.

Can you elaborate on that?

What are you talking about? No I cannot elaborate. See you l
ater.

Why do you say that?

Now you're just talking nonsense!

What makes you believe now I am just talking nonsense?

You are not making any sense.

Perhaps your plans have something to do with this.
-u:** *doctor*   (Doctor Fill)--L1--Top-------------

Figure 4-3. *ELIZA running the DOCTOR script*

ELIZA used substitution and pattern matching techniques to give an illusion of understanding. Although Weizenbaum created ELIZA to demonstrate the artificiality of communication between a human and a machine, it had the exact opposite effect on its many users who felt it exhibited a human-like understanding of their problems. At one point when Weizenbaum was away, his secretary used the opportunity to secretly talk to ELIZA. When Weizenbaum came back, he found his secretary leaving the office crying. Later when he told her that it was just a computer program and that it didn't truly understood her feelings, she refused to believe that the "friend" she talked to was not more than a programmed machine.

Another wildly successful demonstration of natural language understanding, and artificial intelligence in general, was Terry Winograd's SHRDLU. Professor Winograd created the program in 1970 at Massachusetts Institute of Technology (MIT). SHRDLU (pronounced sher-duh-loo) was a natural language parser whose scope was restricted to a world of blocks. That is, it could understand interactive English dialog to answer questions and execute commands pertaining to a virtual world full of geometric block figures, such as cuboids, cubes, cones, etc. For example, a human could ask the program to move a block from one place to another in casual, conversation-like English and the program would respond by performing the requested action using a virtual robotic arm. Figure 4-4 is an illustration of SHRDLU's perceived block world.

Figure 4-4. *SHRDLU's "block world"*

Excerpts from the dialog that was used during Winograd's demo go as follows. Notice how human SHRDLU sounds with its simulated understanding of syntax, semantics, grammar, and context.

Person: PICK UP A BIG RED BLOCK.

Computer: OK. (does it)

Person: GRASP THE PYRAMID.

Computer: I DON'T UNDERSTAND WHICH PYRAMID YOU MEAN.

Person: FIND A BLOCK WHICH IS TALLER THAN THE ONE YOU ARE HOLDING AND PUT IT INTO THE BOX.

Computer: BY "IT," I ASSUME YOU MEAN THE BLOCK WHICH IS TALLER THAN THE ONE I AM HOLDING.

Computer: OK. (does it)

Person: WHAT DOES THE BOX CONTAIN?

Computer: THE BLUE PYRAMID AND THE BLUE BLOCK.

...

Person: CALL THE BIGGEST BLOCK "SUPERBLOCK."

Computer: OK.

Person: HAVE YOU PICKED SUPERBLOCK UP SINCE WE BEGAN?

Computer: YES.

Person: WHY DID YOU DROP IT?

Computer: BY "IT," I ASSUME YOU MEAN THE SUPERBLOCK.

 I CAN'T EXPLAIN A NON-EXISTENT EVENT.

Person: IS THERE ANYTHING TO THE RIGHT OF THE RED PYRAMID?

Computer: YES, FOUR THINGS: THE BOX, THE RED CUBE, THE BLUE PYRAMID, AND THE BLOCK NAMED SUPERBLOCK.

Person: THANK YOU.

Computer: YOU'RE WELCOME!

SHRDLU, however seemingly intelligent, was a simple program with a lot of constraints. In its time, it was one of the most advanced AI programs ever written. It inspired further research in the field of NLU, which eventually proved much more complicated than previously thought. Professor Winograd moved to Stanford shortly thereafter, where he created the Human-Computer Interaction Group and advised several high-profile companies started by his students, including Google.

Commercial interest in NLU picked up during the 1980s, when Gary Hendrix formed Symantec Corporation in 1982 to develop a natural language interface for database queries. If you're wondering, Symantec is the same company that makes popular anti-virus and security software today. Symantec is a portmanteau of the words syntax, semantics, and technology.

In the early 2000s, IBM's Watson was one of the first cognitive supercomputers to exhibit advanced language understanding capabilities. But it was not until very recently that we have had breakthroughs in NLU, thanks to deep learning techniques, because of which we have major tech companies offering cloud services for integrating NLU capabilities in any software application. Microsoft LUIS is one such cloud service. There are ones from Google and Facebook as well.

Why Natural Language Is Difficult for Machines to Understand

This section is optional. Feel free to skip if you cannot wait to apply NLU in your application. But we encourage you to go through the "Complexities in Natural Language" subsection because it may give you indicators when your NLU training isn't working as expected.

Complexities in Natural Language

An ideal analysis of a natural language sentence would involve checking its syntax (grammar), semantics (meaning), and pragmatics (context). Chances are you might be aware of syntax and semantics but not pragmatics. Let's explain with the help of examples.

Syntax refers to the grammatical structure of a sentence, such as subject-verb-object: "The boy is playing with a ball." It is not difficult to build a program using the rules of a language's grammar to break down the structure of a sentence, that is, identify subject, verb, and object. In the real world, people don't always write or speak 100% grammatically correct sentences. The more we train an NLU program using real-world sentences, the better it is able to identify even the grammatically incorrect structures.

> Incorrect syntax: The best items we tried in the restaurant was pasta and ravioli.

> Correct syntax: The best items we tried in the restaurant were pasta and ravioli.

Semantics refers to the meaning of words and phrases in a sentence, and how they are related to each other. Language is a tool to communicate ideas or express emotions. Think of syntax as being the universal rules to use language to talk to another person: the correct sequence of words to use such that the other person can clearly understand you. Now think of semantics as being the meaning of your words, the actual idea you want to convey. The other person may be able to understand your idea even if your sequence of words is not 100% as per the universally accepted standards, but you will have failed to convey your message if the meaning of your words cannot be clearly interpreted by the other person.

For example, an apple is a round and red edible thing whereas a mango is an oval-shaped, yellowish, sweet-smelling edible thing. If you want to convey the message that you are eating an apple, the same can be done in ten different ways, all of which can be syntactically correct. But choosing the wrong words to convey your message completely changes the meaning of your message. Eating a mango is NOT the same as eating an apple, not to you, not to the other person, not for anyone else in the world.

A: I am fond of apples.

B: I love eating apples.

Sentences A and B have the same meaning.

A: I like apples.

B: I like mangoes.

Sentences A and B have different meanings.

We humans know that many words may mean the same thing: good, nice, great, wonderful, etc. We call them synonyms. Similarly, we have antonyms, homonyms, hypernyms, etc. Semantics covers all these as they directly affect the meaning of a sentence. An ideal NLU program can flawlessly understand the semantics of a sentence. This, however, is not a trivial problem to solve in artificial intelligence.

Pragmatics refer to the ways in which context contributes to meaning. Context may be based on the speaker, the listener, or the world around. It is not unusual for the other person to convey a message indirectly, such that its true meaning can only be inferred rather than interpreted directly. Imagine yourself at a busy train station with a friend, having the following conversation.

You: Hey look, someone has dropped their wallet on the floor.

Friend: That man right there seems to be looking for something.

From this conversation, it is not difficult for humans to make out that the person your friend is pointing to might be the one who has dropped his wallet, despite your friend never explicitly saying that. In such conversations, the meaning of a sentence—your friend's, in this case—is implied through contextual information. As a standalone sentence, what your friend said doesn't mean much. But with context, it gets a whole new meaning. The ideal NLU program would have to not only understand the meaning of standalone sentences but also consider the context around them to interpret meanings more accurately.

The complexities do not end with syntax, semantics, and pragmatics. A non-exhaustive list of other things that your ideal NLU program needs to worry about are

- Words that have multiple meanings ("you are *right'* vs "take a *right* turn")

- Sentences that require an understanding of the world ("pick up the second block" - second to what?)

- Vague sentences ("I was late for the meeting" - how late?)

- Sentences that can be interpreted in more than one way ("I saw a man on a hill with a telescope." - is it a man, on a hill, whom I saw with my telescope OR did I see a man, who was on a hill and carrying a telescope?)

And then there is a considerable difference in written and spoken language. People tend to be formal and grammatically correct while writing emails, essays, articles, stories, etc. However, when talking to each other, they tend to be informal and less constrained by the rules. "I am going to complete this by day after tomorrow." vs. "I'm gonna do this by day after." Plus there is the matter of dialects (localized variations of a language) and slang (informal words) to include. The English language alone has dozens of dialects, the major ones being British English, American English, and Australian English.

We hope you now better appreciate the challenges in designing the ideal NLU program.

Statistical Models as a Solution Are Insufficient

The earliest attempts at natural language understanding, especially SHRDLU, were pretty accurate at understanding. They were built using the linguistics rules of syntax and semantics. Those are not the only things that lent them a deep understanding. These early systems focused on limited, small worlds, and could thus understand commands pertaining to specific domains. ELIZA was only good at psychotherapy. SHRDLU's whole world was one full of geometric blocks. Simple logic based on substitution and pattern-matching was enough to seemingly give them an ability to understand their users. Such simple logic, however, could not be scaled to design more generic NLU systems.

The 1990s saw a revolution in NLP. Researchers were able to use statistics as a better way to understand natural languages. Before the statistical revolution, techniques like decision trees were commonly used in machine learning. Such systems resulted in complicated if-then rules that were difficult to maintain and troubleshoot. The turn of the 21st century saw the emergence of complicated statistical models that could analyze large amounts of textual content and produce fairly accurate results.

This gave rise to statistical machine learning techniques that could be used to understand natural language more generically. The heavy computational power that such statistical models required was now available, thanks in part to Moore's Law. Initially, the training textual data (corpus) was manually created by hand. Later, the public records of governmental proceedings in European Union countries were used as corpora for training NLU systems.

In Chapter 1, you learned about two main approaches to machine learning: supervised and unsupervised. Supervised learning is where a machine learns to understand text, speech, or images through labels (or annotations) handmade by humans. With unsupervised learning, a machine learns by itself through tons and tons of training data. As of now, supervised learning results in more accurate results as compared to unsupervised learning. Despite all the advancements that have been made in the field of AI, purely statistical machine learning has room for improvement even if it is supervised.

Statistical models try to solve the NLP problem through *dependency parsing* or *word vectors*. In dependency parsing, parts of speech (nouns, verbs, adjectives, prepositions, etc.) are identified in a sentence and grammatical relationships between them are established. This is not the same as end-to-end understanding of the meaning of a sentence. Figure 4-5 shows dependency parsing of a sentence.

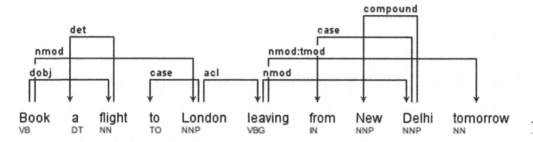

Figure 4-5. *Dependency parsing of a sentence generated using Stanford Parser*

Another approach to solving this problem is word vectors, wherein weighted vectors of words in a sentence are generated. Percy Liang, Assistant Professor of Computer Science at Stanford University, argues that "although word vectors get some aspects of semantics right, they still present an incomplete picture."

■ **Note** In case you are thinking about the efficiency of deep learning models in language understanding, let us remind you that most deep learning techniques are inherently statistical. The recursive neural network (RNN) is a popular deep learning model that is especially effective in machine translation applications. RNNs can be used to build NLU models, but require huge computational power and incredibly large amounts of training data to produce fairly accurate results, resources that are generally available only with large corporations. Check out the Google Tensorflow implementation of the word2vec algorithm and Facebook's fastText (which is based on shallow neural networks), both of which work by generating word vectors.

A Promising Future

We have seen the trade-offs in both the early NLU systems of the 1980s and the statistical models of the 1990s and 2000s. Research is vigorously trying to achieve a balance: the accuracy (depth) of early systems and the generality (breadth) of current statistical systems.

Pat.ai is a work-in-progress that claims to be that balanced NLU solution. John Ball, Cognitive Scientist and founder of Pat Inc., in his paper "The Science of NLU" writes that while most NLU solutions today rely on statistical analysis of word order and frequency, Pat.ai combines Patom Theory (modeled after human brain function) and Role and Reference Grammar (based on language models developed from analysis of diverse languages). He claims that this combination of brain theory and linguistics (rather than statistics) is that potent mixture that has allowed them to interpret true end-to-end meaning of sentences. He distinguishes Pat.ai from existing NLU solutions by labeling it a *meaning matcher*. Ball argues that while existing NLU solutions may not understand a missive such as "Call Beth, No John," Pat.ai won't.

It has been claimed in the white paper that Pat.ai can solve the Winograd Schema Challenge, a multiple-choice test of machine intelligence proposed by Hector Levesque (University of Toronto) and named after Terry Winograd (he's our beloved SHRDLU's creator, remember?). For example, Pat.ai can tell what "they" in the ambiguous sentence "The city councilmen refused the demonstrators a permit because they feared violence." refers to.

As of writing this book, Pat.ai is in a preview stage, access to which can only be obtained by signing up on a private waitlist.

Language Understanding Intelligent Service (LUIS)

LUIS is Microsoft's natural language understanding cloud service and a part of the Cognitive Services suite. It uses the intent-entities scheme and provides several other building blocks to allow for creating rich NLU applications. Through a simple website, you can create a LUIS application and teach it to understand all use cases for how users will interact with your application. A LUIS application is NOT the actual software application that you want to make available to your users. Rather, it's just the language-understanding part of your software application that is accessed as a cloud service. Your software application may be a website, a chat bot, a mobile app, or a desktop app, developed as usual, which may use an online API that a LUIS application exposes.

At the time of writing this book, LUIS supports NLU in nine language cultures: English, Chinese, French, Spanish, Italian, German, Japanese, Brazilian Portuguese, and Korean. It is not possible to use multiple cultures in the same LUIS application. The culture selected at the time of creating a LUIS application cannot be changed later. There are some differences in the way LUIS breaks down utterances across cultures. Chinese and Korean utterances are broken down into character-wise tokens, whereas utterances in any other culture are broken down into word-wise tokens.

Not only can LUIS be used in text-based conversation, it can also be used for use cases involving speech recognition. LUIS integrates seamlessly with Microsoft's Speech API in the Cognitive Services suite. So instead of requiring your users to type their messages, you can, with the help of the Speech API, have them speak to your app and let LUIS do the understanding. Internally, speech is converted to text before being passed to LUIS but the integration with the Speech API makes this pretty seamless. Speech is covered in Chapter 7.

As we said a little earlier, each LUIS application offers an HTTP API endpoint as a means to allow your software applications to implement NLU. This API accepts an utterance and returns its intent-entities breakdown. LUIS offers another API to programmatically manage a LUIS application. This RESTful API can be used to programmatically list, add, edit, and delete intents and entities, label and train utterances, publish the application, and so on. This is useful in scenarios where you want to create custom LUIS training interfaces or do not want give direct access to your LUIS account.

Architecture of a LUIS-Based Software Application

A LUIS application is seldom created as an all-understanding AI. Rather, a LUIS application's design revolves around the problem(s) that your software is trying to solve. For example, if your application assists in ordering food, your LUIS application must be trained to understand only utterances pertaining to food orders and not, say, flight bookings. Every LUIS application comes with a prebuilt intent, none that can be used to handle irrelevant utterances.

Let's take the example of DefinitionApp, an application whose sole purpose is to provide the definition of a word or a phrase. Even such a simple application will require NLU capabilities to correctly understand the one thousand ways in which users may put forth their queries.

> "what is the definition of ___"
>
> "define ___"
>
> "tell me what is ___"
>
> "dude, could help me understand the definition for ___?"

The list goes on and on. All of the above utterances are different in structure but similar in meaning, which is the users' intention to learn the definition of something. That something, the blank, the dash, is the key; let's call it a "phrase."

The following are the minimum steps one would take to create a LUIS application for DefinitionApp:

1. Create a new application in LUIS, perhaps with the same name as your software application's name.

2. Add a new intent called GetDefinition in the LUIS application.

3. Add a new entity called Phrase.

4. Under the GetDefinition intent, add as many different variations of utterances that can be interpreted as asking for the definition of something.

5. In each utterance, highlight the Phrase entity. In the case of "define sumptuous," the word *sumptuous* would be marked as the Phrase entity.

6. Click the Train button to start the training.

Once your LUIS application has been trained to break down relevant utterances into intents and entities, you can publish it as an HTTP endpoint (API) that will then accept utterance strings from your software and send back intent-entity breakdowns as JSON data that looks something like the following:

```json
{
  "query": "define sumptuous",
  "topScoringIntent": {
    "intent": "GetDefinition",
    "score": 0.9820167
  },
  "intents": [
    {
      "intent": "GetDefinition",
      "score": 0.9820167
    },
    {
      "intent": "None",
      "score": 0.03545451
    },
    {
      "intent": "Hello",
      "score": 0.00300396071
    }
  ],
  "entities": [
    {
      "entity": "sumptuous",
      "type": "Phrase",
      "startIndex": 7,
      "endIndex": 15,
      "score": 0.851388454
    }
  ]
}
```

This JSON is pretty much self-explanatory. One point we'd like to highlight here is that the more we train, the higher the confidence score. Keep this point in mind. We're going to repeat this several times anyway.

Figure 4-6 is a screenshot of LUIS' web interface. Figure 4-7 is an architecture diagram of a LUIS-based software application.

DefinitionApp

Dashboard
Intents
Entities
Features
Train & Test
Publish App

← Back to App list

GetDefinition

Here you are in full control of this intent; you can manage its utterances, used entities and suggested utterances ... Learn more

Utterances (3)   Entities in use (1)   Suggested utterances

| Type a new utterance & press Enter ... | × |

🖫 Save   ✕ Discard   🗑 Delete

Reassign Intent ∨

Labels view (Ctrl+E): Entities ⬍

Search in utterances 🔎 ▽

☐	Utterance text	Predicted Intent
☐	what does [$Phrase] mean	**0.69** GetDefinition
☐	what is the definition of [$Phrase] ?	**0.81** GetDefinition
☐	define [$Phrase]	**0.69** GetDefinition

Figure 4-6. A LUIS application called DefinitionApp that fetches the definition of a word or phrase. The GetDefinition intent currently has three labelled utterances, but you can add as many as you want. For accurate results, utterances labelled under an intent should be similar or have the same meaning. $Phrase is an entity that represents the word or phrase for which a definition must be fetched.

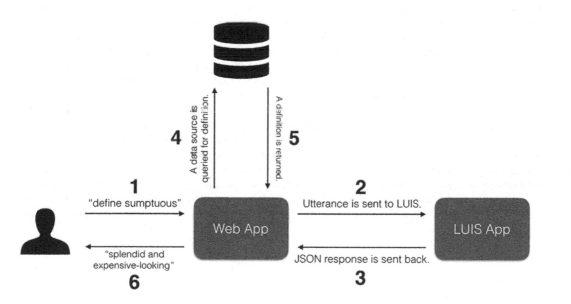

Figure 4-7. A sequential architecture diagram that illustrates the interaction between a user and a LUIS-enabled web application that returns a definition of a word or phrase

The workflow of your web app can be described in the following steps:

1. The user sends a message "define sumptuous" to the web app.

2. The web app passes the message as an utterance to its corresponding LUIS app.

3. LUIS performs its NLU analysis and returns its predictions for intent and entity. The result is return as JSON.

4. The web app checks for the top scoring intent in the returned JSON. If it is `GetDefinition`, it looks for the value `Phrase` entity in JSON. In the above example, this value is "sumptuous." Using this information, the app now knows what to do. It must reach out to a data source to retrieve the definition for "sumptuous." The data source could be a database especially created for the app or an online API (such as a dictionary or Wikipedia).

5. The data source sends back to the web app a brief definition of the target word/phrase.

6. The web app presents the obtained definition to the user, thus completing its utility.

Behind the Scenes

By now, you have no doubt inferred that LUIS uses supervised learning as it requires you to label utterances with intents and entities before it can determine intents and entities for previously seen and unseen utterances. LUIS internally uses *logistic regression classifiers* (LRCs) to determine intents and *conditional random fields* (CRFs) to determine entities. As a developer, you do not need to know this. But an idea about the internals might give you an insight a technology's pros and cons. LRC and CRF are statistical models: the more a LUIS application is trained with labelled utterances, the more optimized these models become. Better optimized models lead to better predictions, which in turn lead to improved confidence scores for intents and entities.

Logistic regression (LR) is a modeling technique used for making predictions using previously known data, such as the prediction of tomorrow's weather based on the weather data of the past seven days or the prediction of infant mortality rate in a region based on infant deaths recorded in previous years and current conditions. LR can also be used as a classifier to predict the category of given data based on previously known categorized data. That's exactly what LRCs do with utterances: they predict an intent based on our labelled utterances.

CRFs are a type of sequence modeling in which words are categorized or tagged after taking into account the neighboring words. So, a sequence of words in a sentence is important while training a CRF model. You saw earlier in the section "Complexities in Natural Language" that a word's meaning may vary depending on the context. CRF, by considering neighboring words, helps in understanding the context. CRFs are generally used in part-of-speech (POS) tagging and named-entity recognition (NEM), two important tasks in NLP.

In POS tagging, a sentence is broken down into syntactical units. For example,

"Mike is playing football at the nearby stadium" becomes

"Mike [NOUN] is playing [VERB] football [NOUN] at [PREPOSITION] the [ARTICLE] nearby [ADJECTIVE] stadium [NOUN]"

In NEM, entities are extracted from a sentence based on previously labelled entities. For example,

"Microsoft was co-founded in 1975 by Bill Gates" becomes

"Microsoft [COMPANY] was co-founded in 1975 [TIME] by Bill Gates [PERSON]"

Extensive Training Is the Key

It may require considerable amount of training to get LUIS to the level of understanding you'd expect from your app, depending on the use cases. We saw in the JSON output earlier that for one utterance multiple competing intents may be returned with varying levels of confidence. This is despite the exact utterance being trained against only one intent. LUIS is based on statistical models and such models are probabilistic.

If your application must deal with multiple similar use cases, there's a good chance LUIS will get confused in the lack of sufficient training for each of the similar use cases. Consider the following two utterances that are labelled against two different intents:

BookFlight: "book me a flight from [$Origin] to [$Destination] leaving today."

BookReturnFlight: "book me a return flight [$Origin] to [$Destination]."

The utterances have only subtle differences in structure and meaning. With insufficient training, LUIS may return BookFlight intent for the second utterance and vice versa. As a solution, you should either handle both utterances with one intent (ideal solution) or supply enough training data to remove LUIS' ambiguity.

LUIS cannot be right 100% of the time, although with enough training its precision can be increased. LUIS uses something called "active learning" to improve itself over time. It keeps track of all utterances for which it was unable to predict an intent with high confidence. You will find such utterances under the Suggested Utterances section on an intent's page. Use this option to appropriately label utterances and confirm to LUIS whether it was right or wrong.

The overview/dashboard page in a LUIS application displays several key statistics and graphs related to its training and usage over time. This information is useful in tweaking the application as per how users are using it (utterances from which intent are they sending the most) and how uniform your training is (what percentage of labelled utterances have gone into each intent). Figure 4-8 shows dashboards for the DefinitionApp. For a live, in-production application, the stats will be much denser.

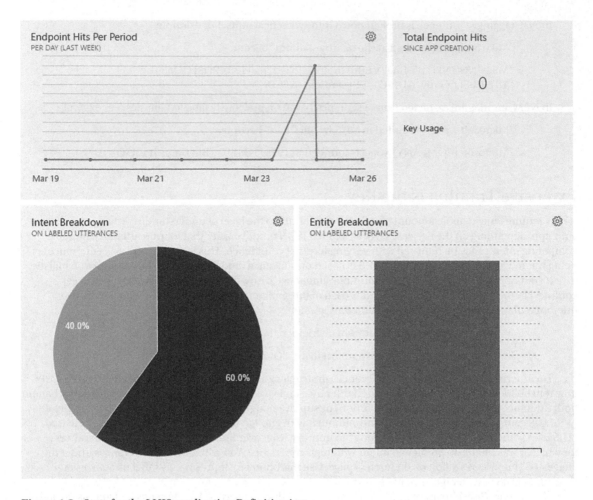

Figure 4-8. *Stats for the LUIS application DefinitionApp*

In Chapter 6, you will learn about the building blocks of a LUIS application, such as intents, entities, phrase lists, etc. You will learn to develop intelligent conversational interfaces by using a LUIS in a Bot Framework application. But before you can start using LUIS in your application, you need an Azure subscription key.

Getting an Azure Subscription for LUIS

Let's create a new Cognitive Services account for LUIS in Azure Portal, get the subscription keys, and apply them to your LUIS account on luis.ai.

Getting Subscription Keys on Azure Portal

1. Open Azure Portal. It's `https://portal.azure.com` in case you forgot.

2. From the left side menu, select New ➤ Intelligence + Analytics ➤ Cognitive Services APIs.

3. Fill in the form as shown in Figure 4-9. The API type should be "Language Understanding Intelligent Service (LUIS)." Choose the Subscription and Pricing tier as per your requirements. You may want to select the Free pricing tier (F0) at this initial stage. You can always upgrade to a paid tier later.

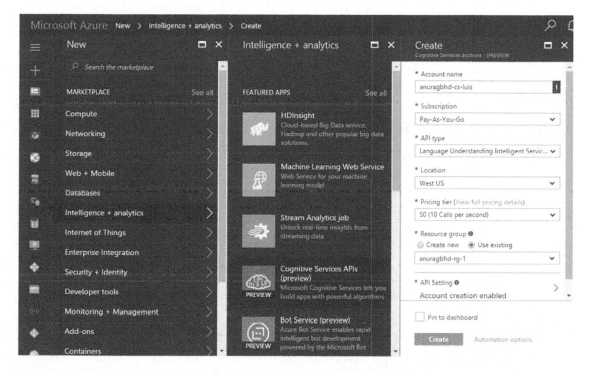

Figure 4-9. *Creating a new LUIS Cognitive Services account on Azure Portal*

4. Submit the form by clicking the Create button. It may take a couple of minutes to create your CS account. You can track the progress in the Notifications menu on the top-right.

5. Once your account is created, from the left side menu, go to All resources ➤ <your-LUIS-account> ➤ Keys. You should see a screen similar to the screenshot in Figure 4-10. Take a note of Key 1 and Key 2 values.

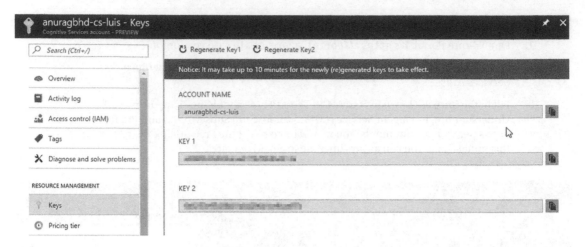

Figure 4-10. *LUIS subscription keys*

Applying Subscription Keys in LUIS

1. Open the LUIS website. That's `https://luis.ai`.

2. Log in using the same Microsoft account (email-password) that you use on Azure Portal. If this is your first login, you may be asked to accept license terms and grant LUIS permissions to access your Microsoft account.

3. Once you are in, and are through the optional getting started tutorial, visit the My Keys page.

4. You will see your programmatic API key under the My Keys heading. This is NOT your subscription key. This key is used along with LUIS' programmatic API we talked about earlier, something that allows you to manage your LUIS applications programmatically.

5. Under the section Endpoint Keys, click the "Add a new key" button. In the resulting dialog form, enter Key 1's value as in your Azure Portal. Name this key "Key 1." Refer Figure 4-11.

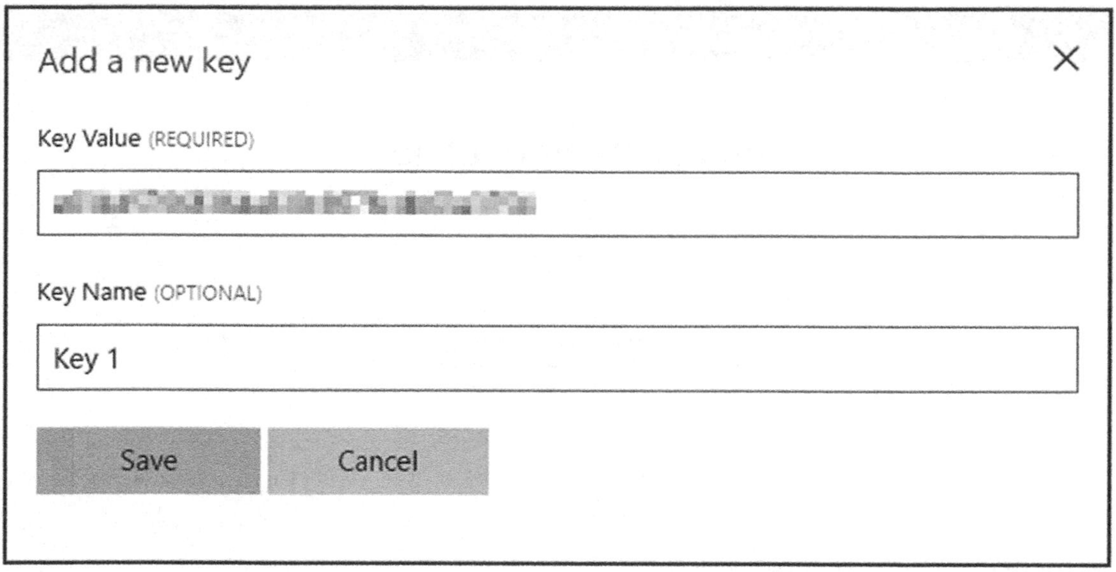

Figure 4-11. Adding a subscription key to your LUIS account at luis.ai

6. Repeat step 5 to add Key 2.

7. At this point, you are all set to create new LUIS applications. As many as you want. If your LUIS Azure account uses the Free (F0) pricing tier, your software application may access LUIS up to 5 times in a second and up to a total of 10,000 times in a month.

There is an External Keys section just along the Endpoint Keys one. In this section, you can add a subscription key for the Bing Spell Check API, which is also part of the Cognitive Services suite, to let LUIS perform auto spelling checks.

Demo: Definition App

We end this chapter with a screenshot (Figure 4-12) and code (Listing 4-1) for your extremely simple Definition App. You will learn to build more advanced conversational smart apps using LUIS and the Bot Framework in Chapter 6.

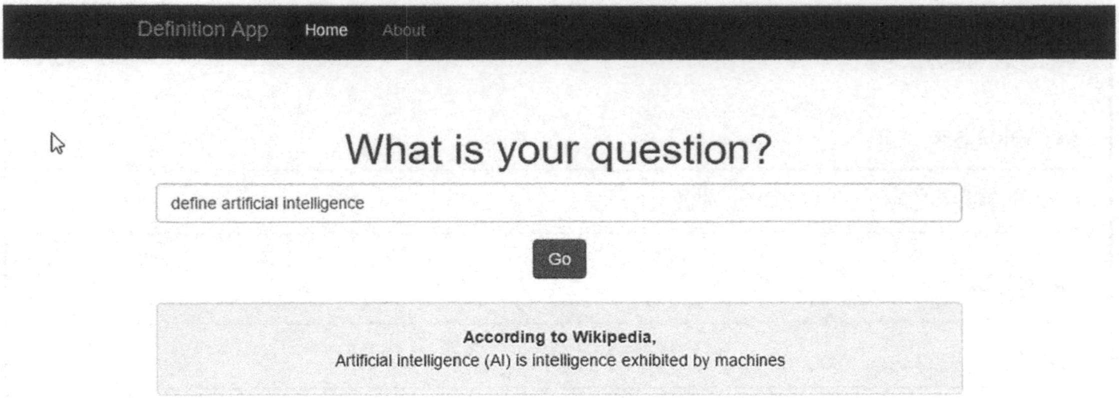

Figure 4-12. *Screenshot of the Definition App*

The Definition App is a one-page web app that was created using the following:

- Bootstrap (UI, CSS)

- jQuery (AJAX calls to your LUIS app)

- Wikipedia (the definitions data store)

- The code in Listing 4-1.

Listing 4-1. The Definition App

```
HTML
----
<div class="definition-app">
        <h1>What is your question?</h1>
        <form>
          <div class="form-group">
                <input type="text" class="form-control" id="utterance" placeholder='Eg.,
                "define artificial intelligence"'>
          </div>
          <button type="submit" class="btn btn-primary">Go</button>
        </form>
        <br>
        <div id="definition" class="well">Definition will appear here.</div>
</div>
JAVASCRIPT
----------
$(document).ready(function() {
        // Do this when the form is submitted;
```

```
// that is, the "Go" button is clicked
$('form').submit(function(e) {
        e.preventDefault(); // stop the default form submission behavior
        var utterance = $('#utterance').val(); // text entered by user in the textbox
        // Send the utterance to LUIS
        $.get("https://westus.api.cognitive.microsoft.com/luis/v2.0/apps/<app-
        id>?subscription-key=<key>&timezoneOffset=0.0&verbose=true&q=" + utterance,
        function(responseLuis) {
                if (responseLuis.intents.length > 0) { // at least 1 intent was
                detected
                        if (responseLuis.topScoringIntent.intent === "GetDefinition")
                        { // the top scoring intent is "GetDefinition"
                                if (responseLuis.entities.length > 0) { // at least
                                1 entity was detected
                                        var phrase = responseLuis.entities[0].entity;
                                        // ideally, we should check if entity type
                                        is "Phrase"
                                        // Get the definition from Wikipedia
                                        var wikipediaData = {
                                                "format": "json",
                                                "action":"query",
                                                "prop": "extracts",
                                                "exintro": "",
                                                "explaintext": "",
                                                "titles": phrase
                                        };
                                        $.get("https://en.wikipedia.org/w/api.php",
                                        wikipediaData, function(responseWikipedia) {
                                                var pages - responseWikipedia.query.
                                                pages;
                                                var summaryFirstLine = pages[Object.
                                                keys(pages)[0]].extract.split(". ")
                                                [0];
                                                $('#definition').html("<b>According
                                                to Wikipedia,</b><br>" +
                                                summaryFirstLine);
                                        });
                                }
                                else { // no entity was detected
                                        $('#definition').text("Sorry, I could not
                                        detect the phrase.");
                                }
                        }
                        else if (responseLuis.topScoringIntent.intent === "None") {
                        // the top scoring intent is "None"
                                $('#definition').text("Did you ask the right
                                question?");
                        }
                }
```

```
                          else { // no intent was detected
                                  $('#definition').text("Sorry, I did not understand.");
                          }
                  });
          });
});
```

Notes

- You will need to create your own LUIS application before you can use the above code.

- A web browser is bound by the same-origin policy for security reasons. What that means is your browser will block calls to the two external APIs: LUIS and Wikipedia. To get around this problem, we recommend that you use Google Chrome browser with the extension "Allow-Control-Allow-Origin" installed. Search online for more details on same-origin policy.

- The extent of the definition is limited to what's on Wikipedia. If Wikipedia does not have a page with a title that is your Phrase entity's value, the app will be unable to show a definition. As a result, the app does not support definitions for all dictionary words.

- As an exercise, add dictionary support to this app.
  Hint: Search for "dictionary api" online and you will see many free-to-use APIs.

Recap

In this chapter, you learned in detail about natural language understanding (NLU), its background, applications, and status quo. You saw why natural language is hard for machines to understand. Finally, you gained an in-depth understanding of Microsoft's NLP framework, LUIS.

To recap, you learned about

- Natural language understanding

- The history of NLU

- Complexities in natural languages that prevent machines from properly understanding them

- Microsoft LUIS

- A bird's eye view of a LUIS-enabled software application

- How the various components in such applications communicate

- Getting a subscription key for LUIS from Azure Portal

- A working LUIS-enabled web app

CHAPTER 5

■ ■ ■

Exploring a Cognitive Language Model

At this point, you should have a fair understanding of natural language processing. Until now, you have concentrated your efforts on learning language understanding and its associated concepts. NLP is much larger than that, as you have seen with our brief mentions of NLP tasks along the way. So, what else can we expect machines to do with natural languages? Let's have a look.

After completing this chapter, you will have learned

- Concepts behind and usage of four Language APIs other than LUIS

    - Bing Spell Check API

    - Text Analytics API

    - Web Language Model API

    - Linguistic Analytics API

- How Microsoft and others use language-based cognitive models in the real world

- Subtasks that each API offers

- A detailed explanation of request and response formats for each task's API

- Existing and new usage ideas to inspire your next smart app

The Bing Spell Check API

"bok a ticket"

"whats meaning of athiest"

"whois martin luther king"

"raiders of the lost arc"

Making spelling mistakes is one of the most common user behaviors. Spelling mistakes come in different forms and flavors, from benign and unintentional errors to careless and downright outrageous ones.

You don't have to be creating a text editor or a word processor to be using spell checking for correcting errors in documents. The market is already saturated with such editors. There are many other areas where spell checking helps. In fact, checking errors in text is sometimes a basic requirement for software to work correctly.

© Nishith Pathak 2017
N. Pathak, *Artificial Intelligence for .NET: Speech, Language, and Search*, DOI 10.1007/978-1-4842-2949-1_5

Take, for instance, search. A hearty percentage of websites and mobile apps offer a search textbox, in which users are free to type whatever they want, however they like. Here, users are not bound by any rules for searching; they are so used to using search engines like Google and Bing that they expect the search feature on other websites to just work. Giving users such unrestricted freedom comes with its own set of challenges. For example, it is not uncommon for users to make spelling errors while not even consciously aware of them. Consider a website that allows you to search for movies.

> *User*: "momento"

> *Website*: "No results found for 'momento.'"

Of course, the website could not find a movie with that name. "Momento" is a common misspelling of "Memento," and that's the actual name of the popular Christopher Nolan movie. Is it wise to blame the user for not knowing their spelling? No! A resounding, big no! In turn, it's shameful for the website to fail to detect such a basic spelling mistake. This situation could be totally avoided by using a simple dictionary-based spell-checker. How about this:

> *User*: "pursuit of happiness"

> *Website*: "No results found for 'pursuit of happiness.'"

The user would swear that they wrote each word of Will Smith's 2006 film correctly. Where's the problem? The actual name of the movie that the user is looking for is "The Pursuit of Happyness." The problem is not with the user's search keywords but with the movie title itself. *Happyness* is a deliberate misspelling of *happiness*. In any case, the website failed yet again. But it failed this time not because it could not catch a simple dictionary error. It failed because it didn't know the correct movie name. This is not a trivial problem as we are talking about making the website smarter by having it somehow learn all movie titles.

At any rate, you don't want to miss out on your users just because your application could not search correctly. Now you see why the ability to handle spelling errors is a basic requirement in some cases. A website that cannot return search results most of the time is bound to lose its most valuable asset: its users. A user who cannot find what they are looking for on a website will, in a matter of seconds, move on to another website to seek answers. In many scenarios, **a lost user translates into lost revenue**.

Figure 5-1 shows spell check at work on bing.com. If the Bing search results did not take into account spelling mistakes, would its users think twice about going over to Google?

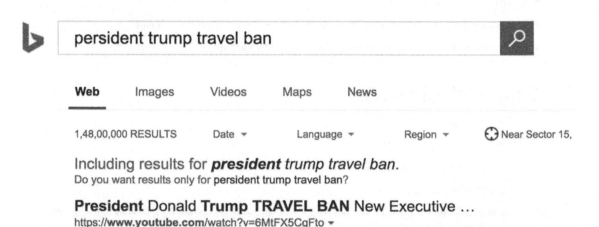

Figure 5-1. Spell check on Bing.com

How can we forget about conversational interfaces? The only way to interact with conversational UIs is to talk to them via text or speech. Where talking is involved, spelling mistakes are bound to happen. The following conversation with a bot could easily qualify for one of the most shameful user experiences.

User: I am feeling unwell. Please help.

Health Bot: What are your symptoms?

User: Head ache, back pain and fever

Health Bot: Have you taken any medicine?

User: Yes. Paracitamole.

Health Bot: Sorry, I couldn't understand.

User: Paracitamole.

Health Bot: Sorry, I couldn't understand.

User sighs, then thinks.

User: Parasitamole.

Health Bot: Sorry, I couldn't understand.

User closes bot app and calls a friend for help instead.

What Is It?

The Bing Spell Check API is an online spell-check service that can scan short to large pieces of text for spelling errors. For each detected error, it provides suggested corrections in decreasing order of confidence score. The API benefits from Bing's years of experience with user search queries and uses the exact same machine learning models as Bing. It is part of the Microsoft Cognitive Services suite, and is, as you might guess, smarter than the average spell-checker and does much more than just check spelling.

Traditional spell-checkers detect misspellings and provide suggestions for correct spelling using their underlying word dictionaries. Such spell-checkers are fast and small in size. But they usually are not accurate, can recognize only a limited set of proper nouns, and are updated only periodically to support new names and words. These spell-checkers are usually bundled with apps with a small footprint, such as web browsers and text editors.

Slightly more sophisticated spell-checkers can take into account rules of grammar and even additionally suggest grammatical mistakes. You have seen such spell-checkers in word processors such as MS Word, LibreOffice Writer, etc. These are larger in size than simple dictionary-based spell-checkers and are more accurate. Yet all the other restrictions of simple checkers apply.

The Bing Spell Check API works on the principles of machine learning. As you know, with sufficient training an ML model can be taught to understand patterns in data. That's what has happened with all of the Bing APIs. All of these APIs leverage Bing's extensively trained models that have learned not just from the engineers who created them but also from millions of users since Bing launched in 2009. Bing APIs provide a way to tap into the wealth of information it has learned and is still learning. You will learn about the Bing Speech API in Chapter 7. All other Bing APIs (Autosuggest, Image Search, News Search, Video Search, and Web Search) are covered in Chapter 8.

The Bing Spell Check API performs contextual spelling checks on text, meaning it detects errors not based on dictionary rules but how and where a word is used in a sentence. Consider the following sentence:

"Don't worry. I'll go home by Uber tonight."

By the rules of a dictionary, this sentence makes the wrong use of the word "uber." Uber comes from the German language and means above or beyond. In English, uber must be used either as a prefix (uber-cool, uberstylish) or as an adjective (uber intellectuals). But ask another person and they will tell you that the word as used in the sentence "I'll go home by…" refers to Uber, a cab-hailing service. You may recap our discussion on pragmatics in Chapter 5: contextual references are so common in natural languages that it would sound artificial and be tiresome to use full sentences all the time.

So, while other spell-checkers will complain about the usage of the word uber, the Bing Spell Check API will not detect any error because it will be aware of the context in which the word is used. In fact, it will warn against the wrong usage of the proper noun Uber as is seen in the following example.

User: "I'll take an uber tonight."

Bing Spell Check: "I'll take an uber Uber tonight."

Not only can the Bing Spell Check API recognize brands, persons, places, and other proper nouns, it also supports slang and broken words.

"Both knda kinda look the same."

"Are you going to ch eck check the kitchen?"

"Clerk Clark Kent is Superman."

"The policemen had guns in there their hands."

■ **Note**   As of writing this book, the Bing Spell Check API supports only English (US) text. Support for more English locales as well as other languages is in the cards for a near future release. Locales in the pipeline are British English (en-GB), Canadian English (en-CA), Australian English (en-AU), New Zealand English (en-NZ), and Indian English (en-IN), plus Chinese and Spanish.

How To Use It

As is the case with other Cognitive Services APIs, Bing Spell Check is also an online REST API that you access via its URL. But first you need an Azure subscription key. Refer the steps in Chapter 2 or Chapter 4 to get a free tier subscription key for the Bing Spell Check API.

■ **Note**   In this chapter, we have not written C# code for each service. Instead, we have used the valuable book space to explain in detail the request and response structure for each service. If you wish, you can reuse the C# code in Chapter 2 to call the services covered in this chapter. You are, however, encouraged to first use a REST API client, such as Postman, to try various combinations of request parameters and explore the response received for each Cognitive Services API.

Request

The Bing Spell Check API endpoint is enabled for both GET and POST requests, with only minor differences between the two methods. GET supports more options and should be the method of choice, unless it is not possible to control the request data format, in which case you should use POST (such as when handling data received through an HTML form).

Here is what a sample GET request looks like:

```
GET /bing/v5.0/spellcheck/?mode=spell&amp;mkt=en-us&amp;text=whois persident trumpp HTTP/1.1
Host: api.cognitive.microsoft.com
Ocp-Apim-Subscription-Key: abc123abc123abc123abc123abc123
Cache-Control: no-cache
```

Endpoint URL:

```
https://api.cognitive.microsoft.com/bing/v5.0/spellcheck/
```

All headers and params except those marked with an asterisk (*) are optional.

Request Headers:

- `Ocp-Apim-Subscription-Key`*: Should be set to your Azure subscription key for the Bing Spell Check API. Please note that the key used in the sample request above is for demonstration purpose only and is invalid.

Request Params:

- `mode`: Can be either Spell or Proof. Bing Spell Check works in two modes:

  - The Spell mode is optimized for search queries and small sentences. It provides fast and relevant results.

  - The Proof mode is optimized for long text strings. It is similar to the spell-checker in MS Word.

- `text`*: The text string to be checked for spelling errors. There is virtually no limit on the number characters in Proof mode. In Spell mode, up to nine words are supported.

- `preContextText`: Although the spell-checker automatically understands context, it is possible to manually provide context when the target word or phrase is known in advance. `preContextText` represents text that comes before the target word/phrase. So "Stephen Spielberg" may be a valid name of a person but "Director Stephen Spielberg" signifies the popular director Steven Spielberg. So "Stephen" becomes a misspelling when used with `preContextText` "Director."

- `postContextText`: This parameter is like `preContextText`, except it provides context after the target word/phrase, such as "inglorious bastards" vs. "inglourious basterds movie."

- `mkt`: The market your application targets. Optimizes spelling and grammar check based on the target market. This is automatically detected but can be manually overridden by supplying a valid value, such as en-us, pt-br, etc.

A sample POST request looks the following:

```
POST /bing/v5.0/spellcheck/?mode=spell&amp;mkt=en-us HTTP/1.1
Host: api.cognitive.microsoft.com
Ocp-Apim-Subscription-Key: abc123abc123abc123abc123abc123
Content-Type: application/x-www-form-urlencoded
Cache-Control: no-cache

Text=Bill+Gatas
```

Response

Let's analyze the JSON response received from the GET request:

```json
{
    "_type": "SpellCheck",
    "flaggedTokens": [
        {
            "offset": 0,
            "token": "whois",
            "type": "UnknownToken",
            "suggestions": [
                {
                    "suggestion": "who is",
                    "score": 1
                }
            ]
        },
        {
            "offset": 6,
            "token": "persident",
            "type": "UnknownToken",
            "suggestions": [
                {
                    "suggestion": "president",
                    "score": 1
                }
            ]
        },
        {
            "offset": 16,
            "token": "trumpp",
            "type": "UnknownToken",
            "suggestions": [
                {
                    "suggestion": "trump",
                    "score": 1
                }
            ]
        }
    ]
}
```

Response Properties:

- _type: An internal property that represents the type of Cognitive Services API. Okay to ignore.

- flaggedTokens: An array of all detected spelling errors, where each error is a token represented by an object with further properties.

- offset: Starting character position of token in the original text.

- token: The word that has an error. The value of this property combined with offset can be used to determine the misspelled word to replace in the original text.

- type: The type of spelling error.

- suggestions: An array of suggested corrections for the misspelled words. Each suggestion is accompanied by a confidence score between 0 and 1. It's a good idea to filter out suggestions with low scores.

Integration with LUIS

As we mentioned in Chapter 4, Bing Spell Check can be enabled in a LUIS application. Figure 5-2 shows what effect this has on the output received from LUIS.

```
{
  "query": "defnie rocket",
  "topScoringIntent": {
    "intent": "Hello",
    "score": 0.134179562
  },
  "intents": [
    {
      "intent": "Hello",
      "score": 0.134179562
    },
    {
      "intent": "GetDefinition",
      "score": 0.103685826
    },
    {
      "intent": "None",
      "score": 0.08644706
    }
  ],
  "entities": []
}
```

BEFORE

```
{
  "query": "defnie rocket",
  "alteredQuery": "define rocket",
  "topScoringIntent": {
    "intent": "GetDefinition",
    "score": 0.9508681
  },
  "intents": [
    {
      "intent": "GetDefinition",
      "score": 0.9508681
    },
    {
      "intent": "Hello",
      "score": 0.0463244952
    },
    {
      "intent": "None",
      "score": 0.0159818735
    }
  ],
  "entities": [
    {
      "entity": "rocket",
      "type": "Phrase",
      "startIndex": 7,
      "endIndex": 12,
      "score": 0.803182
    }
  ]
}
```

AFTER

Figure 5-2. *JSON results from a LUIS application before and after enabling Bing Spell Check*

Follow these steps to enable spell check in a LUIS application:

1. On the luis.ai homepage, go to the My Keys page.

2. In the External Keys section, click the "Add a new key" button. Fill the form as per Figure 5-3.

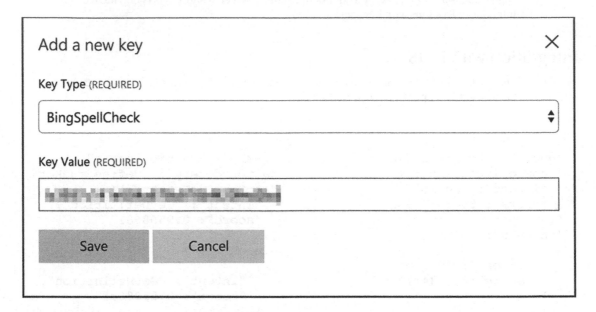

Figure 5-3. Adding a new external key in LUIS

3. Now open the LUIS application where you need to enable spell check. Go to the Publish App page.

4. Scroll down to the bottom. Click the "Add key association" button under the External Key Associations section and select the key you entered in step 2.

5. Finally, check the "Enable Bing spell checker" option and click Publish. Refer to Figure 5-4 for your app's settings.

Endpoint url

https://westus.api.cognitive.microsoft.com/luis/v2.0/apps/59e41f6d-7fa0-48d5-a76f-8781394c069c?subscription-key=a2980332d
9234caa9170cf6fdfad213a&timezoneOffset=0.0&verbose=true&spellCheck=true&q=

☑ Add verbose flag   ☑ Enable bing spell checker   Timezone

                                                                 (GMT) Western Europe Time, Lond ⬍

     Train   Publish

External Key Associations

  Add Key Association

Key Type	Key	Actions
BingSpellCheck	▨▨▨▨▨▨▨▨▨▨▨	🗑

Figure 5-4. *Enabling Bing Spell Check in a LUIS application*

The Text Analytics API

Data or text is broadly of two types: structured and unstructured. To understand the difference, let's consider a simple text file with the following content:

> I do not believe in a fate that falls on men however they act; but I do believe in a fate that falls on them unless they act.

Such a text file stored on file system would have metadata similar to the following:

Name: Quote.txt

User: Anurag Bhandari

Date created: April 01, 2017

Date modified: April 01, 2017

Size: 125 bytes

Can you guess which one is structured text, out of metadata and file contents? If you said metadata, you were right. Metadata has a structure: fields like name, user, size, etc. are the same in all text files; only the values of these fields change. Can you think of other structured data or text? Hint: spreadsheet, database, log file.

On the other hand, contents of the file are unstructured; they could be any text under the sun. File contents do not have a strict form or structure. This makes unstructured text harder to analyze. Suppose you had 10,000 such text files and were asked to programmatically find the file size using (a) metadata and (b) file contents. Even a child can guess that metadata would be more helpful and quicker in solving such a problem.

Analyzing unstructured text is what text analytics is about. There may be hundreds of problems to be solved that involve analyzing unstructured text. The really hard ones cannot be efficiently solved through traditional programming algorithms. And that's where machine learning comes handy. Microsoft Cognitive Services' Text Analytics API provides solutions for four such NLP problems: language detection, key phrase extraction, sentiment analysis, and topic detection. Text analytics is especially useful in accurately determining user or customer responses to your products.

Language Detection

Consider the following conversation with a chatbot.

> *Bot*: Hello. Tell me your problem and I will connect you with the concerned department.
>
> *User*: J'ai besoin d'aide pour la facturation.
>
> (I need help with billing.)
>
> *Bot*: Vous connecter avec notre expert en facturation francophone.
>
> (Connecting you with our French speaking billing expert.)

The bot detected the user's language as French and connected them to a French-speaking support operator from the Billing department. This bot would surely be mind-blowing (and handy) to many users due to its ability to deal with multiple languages. Such a bot would have a big edge over humans, with whom the ability to understand multiple languages is not a given trait.

Given a word, a phrase, or a larger piece of text, the Text Analytics API can detect its natural language through an HTTP call. The longer the piece of text, the more accurate the language detection.

Language detection can be useful in dozens of conversational UI scenarios. It can also be useful in, say, determining the first, second, and third most popular languages used to post replies to a tweet. Such information may be invaluable for a company trying to understand its product's audience.

Another place where language detection comes in handy is a search engine. Figure 5-5 shows how Microsoft Bing intelligently uses it to filter search results.

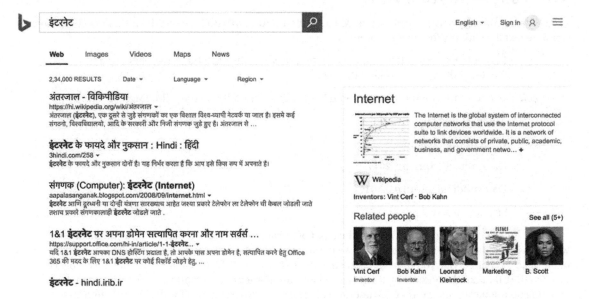

Figure 5-5. *Bing uses language detection to smartly filter search results based on the detected language. If the interface language (English in this case) is different from detected language (Hindi in this case), Bing also displays a summary of search keywords in the interface language.*

Request

The language detection, key phrase extraction, and sentiment analysis APIs all expect a POST request and share a common JSON body format. An XML body is not supported. The body format allows you to send multiple pieces of text to be analyzed in one go, each piece being a "document."

■ **Note** This API charges 1 transaction per document submitted. As an example, if you request sentiment for 1,000 documents in a single call, 1,000 transactions will be deducted. This is true for the language detection, key phrase extraction, and sentiment analysis APIs.

```
POST /text/analytics/v2.0/languages?numberOfLanguagesToDetect=5 HTTP/1.1
Host: westus.api.cognitive.microsoft.com
Ocp-Apim-Subscription-Key: abc123abc123abc123abc123abc123
Content-Type: application/json
Cache-Control: no-cache

{
  "documents": [
    {
      "id": "1",
      "text": "Hello. Tell me your problem and I will connect you with the concerned department."
    },
    {
      "id": "2",
      "text": "J'ai besoin d'aide pour la facturation."
    }
  ]
}
```

Endpoint URL:

```
https://westus.api.cognitive.microsoft.com/text/analytics/v2.0/languages
```

All params except those marked with an asterisk (*) are optional.

Request Params:

- numberOfLanguagesToDetect: An optional query string parameter to specify the maximum number of languages to detect per document. This is helpful for documents that contain text in several languages. The value must be an integer greater than or equal to 1. The default value is 1.

Request Body:

- documents*: An array of all documents to be analyzed in one API call. The maximum size of a single document that can be submitted is 10KB, and the total maximum size of submitted input is 1MB. No more than 1,000 documents may be submitted in one call. Rate limiting exists at a rate of 100 calls per minute. It is therefore recommended that you submit large quantities of documents in a single call.

- id*: A string that uniquely identifies a document in the list. The same is returned in the API response along with the detected language. It's up to the developer to specify an id however they like, given that each document's id is unique. Perhaps the simplest id scheme is 1, 2, 3, 4, etc. GUIDs can be used for more sophisticated id values.

- text*: The string to be analyzed.

Response

```
{
  "documents": [
    {
      "id": "1",
      "detectedLanguages": [
        {
          "name": "English",
          "iso6391Name": "en",
          "score": 1
        }
      ]
    },
    {
      "id": "2",
      "detectedLanguages": [
        {
          "name": "French",
          "iso6391Name": "fr",
          "score": 1
        }
      ]
    }
  ],
  "errors": []
}
```

Response Properties:

- documents: An array of results for each document supplied in the request.

- id: Document id specified in the request.

- detectedLanguages: An array of language(s) detected in the document text. The number of objects in this array may depend on the numberOfLanguagesToDetect request parameter.

- name: Full name of the detected language.

- iso6391Name: The two-character language short code as defined by ISO standards body. "en" is for English, "fr" for French, "es" for Spanish, "hi" for Hindi, and so on.

- score: Confidence level of detection, 0 being the lowest and 1 highest.

- errors: If a supplied document has error(s), the corresponding error will be in this array.

- id: The document in which the error was detected.

- message: Detailed error message.

■ **Note** Take extra care in specifying request params and body. Wrong values used with either may result in a JSON error response, which usually follows the following format:

```
{ "statusCode": number, "message": string }
```

where statusCode is the HTTP status code and message is the detailed message string.

Key Phrase Extraction

Sometimes it is desirable to extract just the key words and phrases, the main "talking points," from a given piece of lengthy, messy text. This information can be used to understand more clearly the context of a news article or a blog entry or a social network post. Once the main talking points of a text are known, one can do a variety of things with that knowledge.

Using extracted key phrases from multiple documents, it's possible to generate word clouds to easily visualize the most popular key phrases across documents. Figure 5-6 shows a word cloud that illustrates the main talking points in user reviews for the Android version of the popular mobile game Angry Birds Friends.

Figure 5-6. *Rovio, creators of the Angry Birds franchise, can see that users are talking mostly about power ups, expensive, tournament, etc. The company can use this information as invaluable feedback to improve its next release.*

In a similar fashion, the ability to extract key phrases is crucial to digital advertisement networks, such as Google AdSense and DoubleClick. Such networks use extracted key phrases from web pages where their ads are hosted to display more relevant ads to visitors.

Request

```
POST /text/analytics/v2.0/keyPhrases HTTP/1.1
Host: westus.api.cognitive.microsoft.com
Ocp-Apim-Subscription-Key: abc123abc123abc123abc123abc123
Content-Type: application/json
Cache-Control: no-cache

{
  "documents": [
    {
      "id": "1",
      "text": "Tesla will unveil an electric articulated lorry in September, chief executive
      Elon Musk has said. Additionally, he said an electric pick-up truck would be shown off
      in around 18-24 months.",
      "language": "en"
    },
    {
      "id": "2",
      "text": "La carta a Cristiano Ronaldo de la víctima de su presunta violación:
      'Te dije no, te grité, rogué que parases'",
      "language": "es"
    }
  ]
}
```

Endpoint URL:

https://westus.api.cognitive.microsoft.com/text/analytics/v2.0/keyPhrases

Request Params:

There are no params for this API.

Request Body:

The JSON request body is like the one you saw in language detection. One additional property in the document object is language. language is an optional property that should be specified for non-English documents. Currently, only English (en), Spanish (es), German (de), and Japanese (ja) languages are supported by this API.

Response

```
{
  "documents": [
    {
      "keyPhrases": [
        "electric articulated lorry",
        "September",
        "chief executive Elon Musk",
        "electric pick",
        "Tesla",
        "truck",
        "months"
      ],
      "id": "1"
    },
    {
      "keyPhrases": [
        "víctima",
        "Cristiano Ronaldo",
        "carta",
        "presunta violación"
      ],
      "id": "2"
    }
  ],
  "errors": []
}
```

Response Properties:

- documents: List of documents supplied in request.

- id: The unique document id specified in request.

- keyPhrases: An array of all key phrases detected in the corresponding document.

Sentiment Analysis

Sentiment analysis is a process used to determine whether the tone in a piece of text is positive, neutral, or negative. The given text is analyzed to arrive at an overall sentiment score, where 0 means very negative and 1 means very positive.

Sentiment analysis as a product feedback tool has been in use for a considerable amount of time. The big data revolution has allow companies, big and small, to tap into the wealth of user feedback available online in the form of direct comments, Facebook posts/comments, Twitter posts, blogs, and so on. Big data analytics tools and machine learning have enabled exponentially faster analysis of large volumes of data to determine the critical responses of users or customers toward an app or product.

Figure 5-7 shows the kind of visualizations that can be created with the help of sentiment analysis.

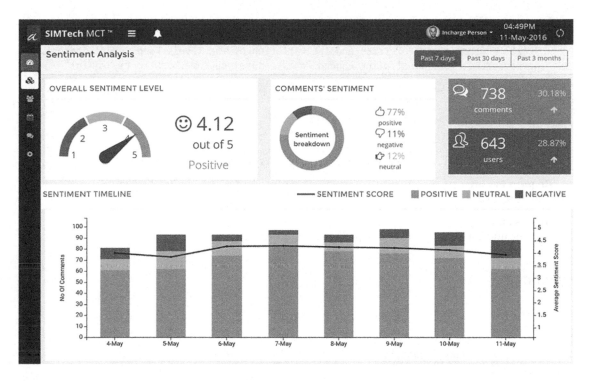

Figure 5-7. *Dashboard generated by online tool SIMTech MCT*

■ **Note** A sentiment score is generated using classification techniques. The input features to the classifier include n-grams, features generated from part-of-speech tags, and embedded words. The classifier was trained in part using Sentiment140 data. Supported languages are English (en), Spanish (es), French (fr), and Portuguese (pt).

Request

```
POST /text/analytics/v2.0/sentiment HTTP/1.1
Host: westus.api.cognitive.microsoft.com
Ocp-Apim-Subscription-Key: abc123abc123abc123abc123abc123
Content-Type: application/json
Cache-Control: no-cache

{
  "documents": [
    {
      "id": "1",
      "text": "You need to change it back! The new graphics are awful! Massive headache
      after a few minutes of play. Your graphic are what made candy crush different to other
      match 3 games now its a unplayable as the others. Im out till you fix it",
      "language": "en"
    },
```

```
   {
     "id": "2",
     "text": "Great mental exercise and the variation of the levels keeps your interest.
     Never boring, just frustrating enough to make sure you come back to try again!"
   }
  ]
}
```

Endpoint URL:

`https://westus.api.cognitive.microsoft.com/text/analytics/v2.0/sentiment`

Request Params:
There are no params for this API.

Request Body:
Nothing unusual here. The language property, as earlier, is optional.

Response

```
{
  "documents": [
    {
      "score": 0.0344527179662149,
      "id": "1"
    },
    {
      "score": 0.796423438202407,
      "id": "2"
    }
  ],
  "errors": []
}
```

Response Properties:
score signifies the overall sentiment of the document text. 0.03 is highly negative, while 0.79 is pretty positive.

Topic Detection

A topic is a brief one-line summary of a given text. It could be one word or multiple related words. Topic detection is not that different from key phrase extraction in that, just like the latter, it provides the main talking point or the highlight of a text. But instead of giving you multiple key phrases, it returns just one topic for the entire text.

■ **Note** This API is designed to work with short text documents, such as user reviews, comments, and other such feedback. It will not work well with long texts, such as book extracts, articles, etc.

Topic detection is especially helpful in making it easier to read long customer reviews about a book, movie, app or product. More than one review text may be assigned the exact same topic, based on their similarity. Normally, key phrase extraction and sentiment analysis are sufficient to get a good idea about the general customer sentiment for a product release. One should additionally go for topic detection to understand feedback in detail, which key phrases cannot provide.

Request

This API expects text documents in a format similar to the other three text analytics APIs. Calling the API, though, is not as straightforward. Topic detection is a time-intensive process. Microsoft mandates you to send at least 100 text documents in a single API call. There is no set limit for the maximum number of text documents, although the max size of 1 document cannot be more than 30KB and the max size of the entire request body must not exceed 30MB. As a reminder, each document in an API call counts as one transaction for billing purposes. You may make up to five API calls every 5 mins.

As topic detection is a time-consuming process, you do not get a response instantly. A request to the API submits the documents to a queue and returns, with an HTTP status code 202, a URL that should be periodically polled to retrieve the results.

```
POST /text/analytics/v2.0/topics HTTP/1.1
Host: westus.api.cognitive.microsoft.com
Ocp-Apim-Subscription-Key: abc123abc123abc123abc123abc123
Content-Type: application/json
Cache-Control: no-cache

{
    "documents": [
        {
            "id": "1",
            "text": "I love this product and have no complaints except that I cannot have 2 of them."
        },
        ...
        {
            "id": "100",
            "text": "The sound quality is not as good as my other speakers."
        }
    ],
    "stopWords": [
        "problem", "bug", "feedback"
    ],
    "topicsToExclude": [
        "create a ticket", "Amazon Echo"
    ]
}
```

Endpoint URL:

https://westus.api.cognitive.microsoft.com/text/analytics/v2.0/topics

All params except those marked with an asterisk (*) are optional.

Request Params:

- minDocumentsPerWord: An integer to specify the minimum number of documents for which a topic word is the same. For example, if you set it to 2, then all topic words that are assigned to only 1 document will be excluded. This param can help you exclude rare topic words.

- maxDocumentsPerWord: The opposite of minDocumentsPerWord. Use this to exclude very common topic words.

Request Body:

The document list format remains unchanged. There is no language property in the document object because English is the only supported language. A document whose text is in a language other than English will be ignored. Similarly, documents of a length less than three words will be ignored.

- stopWords: List of words that should not be part of detected topics. Helps to exclude words that are common and implicit in a given scenario. For example, if topic detection is being performed on feedback reviews, words such as problem, bug, feedback, etc. will not add any value to a topic. Apart from explicitly specified stop words, the API will also consider their plurals.

- topicsToExclude: Similar to the stopWords property. Allows you to specify full topic names to be excluded. Full and partial product names are good candidates for this property.

Response

The immediate response to the above POST request will have an empty body and 202 as its HTTP status code. It will have the following header:

```
'operation-location': 'https://westus.api.cognitive.microsoft.com/text/analytics/v2.0/
operations/<operationId>'
```

The value of the operation-location header is the URL endpoint that will eventually return the results when they are ready. How much time it takes for a request to be processed depends on the number and length of the documents supplied in the original POST request.

This URL must be polled periodically (the recommended duration is once per minute) to check for results.

```
GET https://westus.api.cognitive.microsoft.com/text/analytics/v2.0/operations/<operationId>
```

Each time the above call will return a JSON response with at least the property status, whose value can be one of notstarted, running, and succeeded. You want to poll until you get succeeded as a status value.

The final response will have the following form:

```
{
    "status": "succeeded",
    "operationProcessingResult": {
        "topics": [
            {
                "id": "d8f62239-4ab5-4f95-8067-b2fca96d0c40"
                "score": "7"
                "keyPhrase": "no complaint"
            },
```

```
        ...
        {
            "id": "8af50d44-92d0-464f-886a-9690542f259b"
            "score": "2"
            "keyPhrase": "sound quality not good"
        }
    ],
     "topicAssignments": [
        {
            "topicId": "d8f62239-4ab5-4f95-8067-b2fca96d0c40",
            "documentId": "1",
            "distance": "0.354"
        },
        ...
        {
            "topicId": "8af50d44-92d0-464f-886a-9690542f259b",
            "documentId": "100",
            "distance": "0.758"
        }
    ],
     "errors": []
    }
}
```

Response Properties:

- topics: An array of all distinct topics detected for the supplied documents.

    - id: A unique topic id generated by the API.

    - score: Number of documents that share this topic.

    - keyPhrase: The detected topic.

    - topicAssignments: An array of topic assignments for each document.

    - topicId: The unique id as seen in the topics array.

    - documentId: The unique document id that was supplied in the request.

    - distance: Document-to-topic affiliation score. Between 0 and 1. The lower the score, the higher the affiliation.

Usage Ideas

- **Election prediction**: Performing sentiment analysis on data collected from social media, news articles, public polls, and surveys is not new. But for a very long time, the methodologies used have largely been statistical. With the advent of machine learning, especially deep learning techniques, predicting the winner of an election will produce more accurate results.

- **Automatic MOM generation**. Collecting and articulating the minutes of a meeting (MOM) is a standard activity performed during formal meetings. Techniques such as topic detection and key phrase extraction can be a godsend in automating MOM generation in text-based meetings on platforms such as Slack and IRC.

- **Call record analysis**: As an auditing measure, a user's call to a call center support executive is usually recorded. Using speech-to-text, the textual transcripts can be generated from these recordings. The transcripts can then be used as documents to perform sentiment analysis and key phrase extraction to better analyze customers' satisfaction levels.

The Web Language Model (WebLM) API

Creating a language model for machine learning requires a suitably created corpus. As you learned in the previous chapters, the performance of an ML model is as good as its training data (corpus). The larger the corpus, the more the training data, the better the resulting model. Creating a large corpus by hand of the scale required for training is practically infeasible even for large corporations. Publicly available records of European Union court proceedings, translated into several languages, were used to create models for language translation systems. The EU docs are not the only free text that could be used to build language models. There is, of course, the WWW.

An awesome thing about the world-wide web is that it contains an infinite amount of text in its billions of web pages. It could form an incredibly large corpus for anybody to train their machine learning language models absolutely free of cost. That's exactly what Microsoft did with Bing's indexed web pages. They created vast corpora (plural of corpus) using text read from millions of web pages.

A corpus made using text collected from all over the Web is not suited for such applications as machine translation due to the presence of several anomalies: grammatical errors, slang, profanity, lack of punctuation, and so on. But a corpus made from the Web can give us a general idea about how the common populace uses language. Common patterns can be found in the incorrect usage of words and phrases. This is good enough to use the corpus for creating models to do stuff like predicting the next word in a sequence and breaking up a string of words that lacks spaces. Microsoft calls its language model created in this fashion the Web Language Model or WebLM.

Text may be present in different parts of a web page: body, title, anchor elements, and search queries. There are subtle to visible differences in text extracted from each of these four parts. While the phrase "tryout" may be common in anchor text and search queries, it's usually present in its more correct form of "try out" in the body part. Thus, Microsoft has created four different models using text from these four parts of a web page:

- Bing Anchor Model

- Bing Body Model

- Bing Query Model

- Bing Title Model

Currently, the only language supported by WebLM API is American English.

■ **Note**   The WebLM corpus is not as simple as a random collection of zillions of sentences. Instead of plain words and phrases, it contains what are called n-grams. Microsoft calls it Web N-gram Corpus.

An n-gram is a partial sequence of n items derived from a larger, more complete sequence. An item could be a character, a word, or a phrase. Consider the following example sentence:

"Bruno is a good dog."

n-gram sequences that can be derived from the above complete sequence are

1-gram (unigram) — Bruno, is, a, good, dog

2-gram (bigram) — Bruno is, is a, a good, good dog

3-gram (trigram) — Bruno is a, is a good, a good dog

MS Web N-gram Corpus has up to 5-gram sequences. It's using these n-grams so that tasks like word breaking and predicting the next word in sequence can be accomplished.

Figure 5-8 shows how Microsoft Bing probably uses WebLM to display search results.

Figure 5-8. *Word breaking and next word prediction in action on the Bing search page*

Not only was Bing Search able to break the word "happyeaster2017" into "happy easter 2017," it could also present similar search queries ("happy easter 2017 wallpaper") by checking its query language model for most common next words.

The WebLM API supports the following four tasks or operations:

- Breaking of strings with no spaces into words

- Joint probability of a word sequence

- Conditional probability of one word succeeding a given sequence of words

- Predicting the next word(s) that may follow a given sequence of words

Word Breaking

We know that breaking a contiguous string into individual words is a pretty useful thing. But where can we find instances of such weird strings? In other words, who in their right mind would write words joined together?

You may have seen such strings more than you may realize. Hash tags on social media are a very common example.

#iamfeelinggood #germanyvsargentinafootballllive #EpicFail

The ability to break hash tag strings into individual words can give data analytics systems plenty of otherwise hidden material to analyze. Contiguous strings may also be present in URLs and internal links.

```
www.example.com/topsellers, www.example.com/tutorial#creatinganewproject
```

Request

```
POST /text/weblm/v1.0/breakIntoWords?model=body&amp;text=germanyvsargentinafootballlive&amp;
order=5&amp;maxNumOfCandidatesReturned=3 HTTP/1.1
Host: westus.api.cognitive.microsoft.com
Ocp-Apim-Subscription-Key: abc123abc123abc123abc123abc123
Cache-Control: no-cache
```

Endpoint URL:

```
https://westus.api.cognitive.microsoft.com/text/weblm/v1.0/breakIntoWords
```

All params except those marked with an asterisk (*) are optional.

Request Params:

- `model`*: The Bing language model to use. One of anchor, body, query, and title.

- `text`*: The string to be split into individual words. If spaces are already present in the string, they will be maintained as such in the result.

- `order`: The order of n-gram. One of 1, 2, 3, 4, and 5. Default is 5.

- `maxNumOfCandidatesReturned`: Maximum matches to be returned. Default is 5.

This API does not require a request body.

Response

```
{
  "candidates": [
    {
      "words": "germany vs argentina football live",
```

```
      "probability": -12.873
    },
    {
      "words": "g ermany vs argentina football live",
      "probability": -19.08
    },
    {
      "words": "germany vs argentina football l i v e",
      "probability": -19.432
    }
  ]
}
```

Response Properties:

- candidates: An array of all possible matches, limited by themaxNumOfCandidatesReturned request param.

  - words: Broken-up individual words In a candidate match.

  - probability: Less negative values represent high confidence.

Joint Probability

Joint probability tells you how often a certain sequence of words occurs together. For example,

> here I come => quite probable

> hello dude => somewhat probable

> Microsoft washing machine => not probable at all

Request

```
POST /text/weblm/v1.0/calculateJointProbability?model=body&amp;order=5 HTTP/1.1
Host: westus.api.cognitive.microsoft.com
Ocp-Apim-Subscription-Key: abc123abc123abc123abc123abc123
Content-Type: application/json
Cache-Control: no-cache

{
    "queries":
    [
            "but",
            "wide world",
            "natural language processing",
            "natural language dinner"
    ]
}
```

Endpoint URL:

https://westus.api.cognitive.microsoft.com/text/weblm/v1.0/calculateJointProbability

All params except those marked with an asterisk (*) are optional.

Request Params:

- model*

- order

Request Body:

- queries: An array of strings. Each string is a sequence whose joint probability must be calculated. Single word queries are valid.

Response

```
{
  "results": [
    {
      "words": "but",
      "probability": -2.9
    },
    {
      "words": "wide world",
      "probability": -6.381
    },
    {
      "words": "natural language processing",
      "probability": -6.807
    },
    {
      "words": "natural language dinner",
      "probability": -12.939
    }
  ]
}
```

Response Properties:

- results: An array of results, one for each query specified in a request body.

  - words: The query sequence from the request.

  - probability: The lower the negative score, the more common the word or sequence.

Conditional Probability

Conditional probability tells you how common it is for a word to come after a certain sequence of words. For example,

> top selling artist => very probable
>
> top selling author => very probable
>
> top selling guy => mildly probable
>
> top selling rat => not probable at all

Possible use cases are

- Unscramble a jumbled sentence.
- Correctly guess a short search query in which words are incorrectly ordered.

Request

```
POST /text/weblm/v1.0/calculateConditionalProbability?model=body&amp;order=5 HTTP/1.1
Host: westus.api.cognitive.microsoft.com
Ocp-Apim-Subscription-Key: abc123abc123abc123abc123abc123
Content-Type: application/json
Cache-Control: no-cache

{
    "queries":
    [
        {
            "words": "top selling",
            "word": "artist"
        },
        {
            "words": "top selling",
            "word": "rat"
        },
        {
            "words": "game of",
            "word": "thrones"
        }
    ]
}
```

Endpoint URL:

https://westus.api.cognitive.microsoft.com/text/weblm/v1.0/calculateConditionalProbability

All params except those marked with an asterisk (*) are optional.

Request Params:

- model*
- order

Request Body:

- queries
  - words: The sequence of words that precede the target word.
  - word: The target word.

Response

```json
{
  "results": [
    {
      "words": "top selling",
      "word": "artist",
      "probability": -2.901
    },
    {
      "words": "top selling",
      "word": "rat",
      "probability": -5.848
    },
    {
      "words": "game of",
      "word": "thrones",
      "probability": -0.475
    }
  ]
}
```

Next Word Prediction

You saw earlier in Figure 5-8 how next word prediction works by suggesting the words that may come after the search query. Using this API, it is possible to generate next word suggestions for a certain sequence of words. For example,

> new york city
>
> new york times
>
> new york university

Request

```
POST /text/weblm/v1.0/generateNextWords?model=body&amp;words=Microsoft Windows&amp;order=5&amp;maxNumOfCandidatesReturned=5 HTTP/1.1
Host: westus.api.cognitive.microsoft.com
Ocp-Apim-Subscription-Key: abc123abc123abc123abc123abc123
Cache-Control: no-cache
```

Endpoint URL:

`https://westus.api.cognitive.microsoft.com/text/weblm/v1.0/generateNextWords`

All params except those marked with an asterisk (*) are optional.

Request Params:

- `model*`

- `order`

- `maxNumOfCandidatesReturned`

- `words*`: A string that is the sequence of words for which next word suggestions need to be generated. The sequence may contain only one word.

This API does not require a request body.

Response

```
{
  "candidates": [
    {
      "word": "7",
      "probability": -0.892
    },
    {
      "word": "xp",
      "probability": -0.998
    },
    {
      "word": "currentversion",
      "probability": -1.047
    },
    {
      "word": "server",
      "probability": -1.123
    },
    {
      "word": "8",
      "probability": -1.201
    }
  ]
}
```

The Linguistic Analysis API

The operations offered by this API deal with analyzing the language structure of a given text. The output of this analysis may be useful in better understanding the meaning and context of text.

The Linguistic Analysis API supports the following three operations:

- **Sentence separation and tokenization**: Breaking text into sentences and tokens.

- **Part-of-speech tagging**: Categorizing each word of a sentence as a grammatical component (noun, verb, adjective, etc.).

- **Constituency parsing**: Breaking text into all possible phrases.

This sort of linguistic analysis is usually done as a first step for other NLP tasks, such as natural language understanding, text-to-speech, machine translations, and so on. Apart from its usefulness as a preliminary step in the field of NLP itself, linguistic analysis has applications in consumer-facing cognitive apps.

To be able to perform the three analyses, a system must be trained using a treebank. A treebank is a corpus that contains a wide collection of POS-tagged words and parsed phrases. Microsoft, for this API, used Penn Treebank 3 to train its systems.

Sentence Separation and Tokenization

Breaking up large pieces of text into individual sentences and tokens is a pretty common requirement in software development. But do we not already know the solution? Consider the following text:

> It was nice to meet you. Goodbye and see you again.

The first thing that comes to mind when breaking text into sentences is to split it around the full-stop or dot (.) symbol. Sure, let's do that with the above text. We get two sentences.

> Sentence 1: It was nice to meet you.

> Sentence 2: Goodbye and see you again.

How about the following text:

> He said, "I am going to the concert." And, poof, he was gone!

Splitting it around full-stops gives us the following:

> Sentence 1: He said, "I am going to the concert.

> Sentence 2: " And, poof, he was gone!

You surely did not want this. At this point, you no doubt realize that not all sentences end with a full-stop. For example,

> How did I do? Was I good?

> Are you crazy! I don't have anything to do with this.

> What?! Are you out of your mind?

This is where cognitive sentence separation comes handy. You may use the API to extract all sentences from a very long article or book and store them for further analysis. Or you may be simply looking to limit a large piece of text somewhere on your app or website to a few sentences.

Tokenization, or breaking up sentences into individual words and other tokens, is another story. Just like sentence separation, tokenization cannot be simply achieved by always splitting a sentence around white spaces. Stuff like contractions and possessives must be taken care of, among other things. And languages such as Chinese do not always have spaces between words.

The sentence "I don't have anything to do with Ronnie's broken glasses, I swear." contains the following tokens:

I - do - n't - have - anything - to - do – with - Ronnie -'s - broken - glasses - , - I - swear - .

n't is a *contraction* for not. 's is a *possessive*. The dot and comma are *punctuation*. These are some tokens apart from the usual words that should be detected for a proper further analysis.

Request

```
POST /linguistics/v1.0/analyze HTTP/1.1
Host: westus.api.cognitive.microsoft.com
Ocp-Apim-Subscription-Key: abc123abc123abc123abc123abc123
Content-Type: application/json
Cache-Control: no-cache

{
        "language": "en",
        "analyzerIds": ["08ea174b-bfdb-4e64-987e-602f85da7f72"],
        "text": "How did I do? Was I good?"
}
```

Endpoint URL:

https://westus.api.cognitive.microsoft.com/linguistics/v1.0/analyze

All params except those marked with an asterisk (*) are optional.

Request Params:

This API doesn't have request params.

Request Body:

- language*: The ISO 639-1 two letter code for the language of the text to be analyzed.

- analyzerIds*: An array of GUIDs of analyzers to be used (Tokens, POS_Tags, or Constituency_Tree).

- text*: The piece of text to be analyzed.

■ **Note**   You can use all three analyzers at once on the same piece of text. To get the list of all supported analyzers (three at the time of writing) along with their GUIDs, make a GET call to https://westus.api. cognitive.microsoft.com/linguistics/v1.0/analyzers using the Language Analytics API subscription key.

Response

```
[
  {
    "analyzerId": "08ea174b-bfdb-4e64-987e-602f85da7f72",
    "result": [
      {
        "Len": 13,
```

123

```
    "Offset": 0,
    "Tokens": [
      {
        "Len": 3,
        "NormalizedToken": "How",
        "Offset": 0,
        "RawToken": "How"
      },
      {
        "Len": 3,
        "NormalizedToken": "did",
        "Offset": 4,
        "RawToken": "did"
      },
      {
        "Len": 1,
        "NormalizedToken": "I",
        "Offset": 8,
        "RawToken": "I"
      },
      {
        "Len": 2,
        "NormalizedToken": "do",
        "Offset": 10,
        "RawToken": "do"
      },
      {
        "Len": 1,
        "NormalizedToken": "?",
        "Offset": 12,
        "RawToken": "?"
      }
    ]
  },
  {
    "Len": 11,
    "Offset": 14,
    "Tokens": [
      {
        "Len": 3,
        "NormalizedToken": "Was",
        "Offset": 14,
        "RawToken": "Was"
      },
      {
        "Len": 1,
        "NormalizedToken": "I",
        "Offset": 18,
        "RawToken": "I"
      },
```

```
    {
      "Len": 4,
      "NormalizedToken": "good",
      "Offset": 20,
      "RawToken": "good"
    },
    {
      "Len": 1,
      "NormalizedToken": "?",
      "Offset": 24,
      "RawToken": "?"
    }
  ]
 }
]
 }
]
```

Note that the result is not an object but an array of objects. This is because this API gives you the option to perform multiple analyses at once on the same text. Each analyzer's result is returned as an object of the root array.

Response Properties:

- `analyzerId`: GUID of the analyzer used for the corresponding result set.

- `result`: The result of the analysis. An array of sentences.

  - Len: Total number of characters in the sentence.

  - Offset: Starting position of sentence in the text. Starts from 0.

  - Tokens: Array of tokens in the sentence.

    - Len: Number of characters in the token.

    - Offset: Starting position of token in the sentence.

    - RawToken: The detected token.

    - NormalizedToken: The token represented in a format that is safe to be used in a parse tree.

Part-of-Speech Tagging

Remember when you were in school and just starting to learn to identify the grammatical structure of a sentence.

"Subject-verb-object," your teacher would say and then proceed to define subject and object in terms of proper and common nouns. After this you gradually learned to spot adjectives, adverbs, prepositions, and conjunctions in a sentence. Think of that technique to spot grammatical structure taught by your teacher as a simplified version of POS tagging.

Things like nouns and verbs and adjectives are called parts of speech. POS tagging is a common disambiguation technique, something that makes confusing/ambiguous words clearer; it's used to identify parts of speech in a given sentence based on their respective position and context. That is, for each word in a sentence, POS tagging will tell you what part of speech that word is. Consider the following sentence:

He is going to contest the election.

An interesting thing about the sentence is the word "contest," which could be a noun or a verb. In this case, it is used as a verb. A POS tagger must smartly detect the context and surrounding words to tag a word correctly. Here is a POS-tagged version of the above sentence:

He (PRP) is (VBZ) going (VBG) to (TO) contest (VB) the (DT) election (NNS).

The following tags were detected:

PRP = pronoun, personal

VBZ = verb, present tense, third person singular

VBG = verb, present participle, or gerund

TO = "to" as preposition or infinitive marker

VB = verb, base form

DT = determiner

NNS = noun, common, plural

A comprehensive list of all possible tags may be found online as well as on Microsoft's documentation for POS tagging.

POS tagging is especially helpful in NLU and language translation.

Request

```
POST /linguistics/v1.0/analyze HTTP/1.1
Host: westus.api.cognitive.microsoft.com
Ocp-Apim-Subscription-Key: abc123abc123abc123abc123abc123
Content-Type: application/json
Cache-Control: no-cache

{
        "language": "en",
        "analyzerIds": ["4fa79af1-f22c-408d-98bb-b7d7aeef7f04"],
        "text": "He is going to contest the election"
}
```

Endpoint URL:

https://westus.api.cognitive.microsoft.com/linguistics/v1.0/analyze

All params except those marked with an asterisk (*) are optional.

Request Params:

This API doesn't have request params.

Request Body:

- language*
- analyzerIds*
- text*

Response

```
[
  {
    "analyzerId": "4fa79af1-f22c-408d-98bb-b7d7aeef7f04",
    "result": [
      [
        "DT",
        "VBZ",
        "JJ",
        "."
      ],
      [
        "PRP",
        "VBP",
        "PRP",
        "."
      ]
    ]
  }
]
```

Response Properties:

The result is an array of tags in each sentence. Tags are in the same sequence as words in a sentence.

Constituency Parsing

Constituency parsing is used to detect phrases in a given sentence. This is different from the key phrase extraction you saw in the Text Analytics API in that, unlike KPE, constituency parsing does not only return the key phrases but all possible phrases. Such information may be useful to KPE analysis itself.

> I want to buy a laptop with graphics card.

How many phrases can you identify in the above sentence?

Let's see. "I want to buy a laptop," "buy a laptop," "a laptop with graphics card," and "graphics card" are all valid phrases. Can you find more? See Figure 5-9 when you're done.

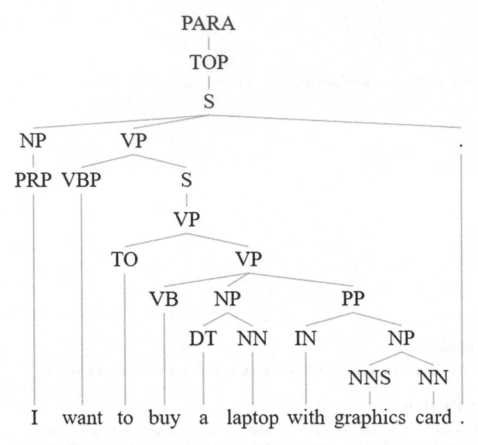

Figure 5-9. *A parsed tree for the above sentence. Words including and between each pair of nodes in the above binary tree are a valid phrase.*

It is important to note that a phrase is not simply any group of words. A phrase is something that may be replaced or moved as a whole in a sentence such that the sentence remains grammatically correct and easy to understand. For example, "I want to buy" and "a laptop with graphics card" are the two main phrases in the above sentence. If we interchange their positions, the sentence remains understandable:

a laptop with graphics card I want to buy

Since "to buy" is not a phrase, changing its position makes the sentence incomprehensible:

to buy I want a laptop with graphics card

Phrases are usually nested within one another and can be hard to find without an understanding of the grammatical structure of the sentence.

Request

```
POST /linguistics/v1.0/analyze HTTP/1.1
Host: westus.api.cognitive.microsoft.com
Ocp-Apim-Subscription-Key: abc123abc123abc123abc123abc123
Content-Type: application/json
Cache-Control: no-cache

{
        "language": "en",
        "analyzerIds": ["22a6b758-420f-4745-8a3c-46835a67c0d2"],
        "text": "I want to buy a laptop with graphics card."
}
```

Endpoint URL:

https://westus.api.cognitive.microsoft.com/linguistics/v1.0/analyze

All params except those marked with an asterisk (*) are optional.

Request Params:

This API doesn't have request params.

Request Body:

- language*

- analyzerIds*

- text*

Response

```
[
  {
    "analyzerId": "22a6b758-420f-4745-8a3c-46835a67c0d2",
    "result": [
      "(TOP (S (NP (PRP I)) (VP (VBP want) (S (VP (TO to) (VP (VB buy) (NP (DT a) (NN laptop))
      (PP (IN with) (NP (NNS graphics) (NN card))))))) (. .)))"
    ]
  }
]
```

Response Properties:

The result is an array of parsed sentences. Try to map the rounded brackets format of the parse with Figure 5-9 to see how to interpret it.

Recap

In this chapter, you learned about NLP tasks other than language understanding (NLU), which you learned about in the previous chapter.

To recap, you learned about

- The four APIs in the Language category of Cognitive Services: Bing Spell Check, Text Analytics, WebLM, and Linguistics Analysis

- Theory and application for each API and all of its operations

- A detailed overview of using the APIs

- Live implementation examples and new usage ideas

In the **next chapter**, you will apply your knowledge of LUIS and the Bot Framework to build an enterprise-grade chat bot.

CHAPTER 6

■ ■ ■

Consuming and Applying LUIS

Welcome to the conclusion! This chapter is where you put the knowledge you gained in the previous chapters to work.

In Chapter 2, you learned how to set up the development environment.

In Chapter 3, you learned about the conversational user interface (CUI), a new paradigm for creating natural language-based intelligent apps. In that chapter, you also learned to create a very basic, albeit unintelligent, chat bot using the Bot Framework. You did not, however, deploy your bot to one or more of the several supported channels.

In Chapter 4, you took a deep dive into natural language understanding (NLU), the thing that lets computer programs interpret humans the way they do each other. You got a glimpse of Microsoft LUIS and behind the scenes of how an app might use LUIS to understand its users more naturally.

In this chapter, we continue the story of the Health Checkup bot. You will use LUIS to make the otherwise dumb bot way smarter. You will create a LUIS app, one step at a time, to be used with the bot. Finally, you will integrate this LUIS app in the Bot Framework. By the end of this chapter, you will have learned

- The anatomy of a LUIS application

- Intents, entities, phrase lists, and other LUIS components

- How to methodically create a LUIS application from scratch

- How to test, train, and publish a LUIS application

- How to make the Bot Framework use LUIS

- How to publish a bot to a channel such as Skype and Facebook Messenger

Planning Your App

When creating conversational apps, it is of the utmost importance to make a formal plan. For GUI apps, developers use mockups and other design documents for visual reference. This makes it easy to develop the various components of a GUI app by visualizing their final designs. Conversational apps do not have a lot of visual components. The workflow must be understood in terms of text-based conversations between the app and its users.

Such a workflow may be represented in a variety of ways, such as a flow diagram. Whatever way you choose, it is essential you first have answers to the following questions:

- What should the bot be able to do? **Tasks**

- What information does the bot need from the user? **User context**

- What should be done in LUIS? **Intents and entities**

- What should be done in the Bot Framework? **Logic and answers**

Let's have a look at each for the Health Checkup bot.

© Nishith Pathak 2017

N. Pathak, *Artificial Intelligence for .NET: Speech, Language, and Search*, DOI 10.1007/978-1-4842-2949-1_6

What Should the Bot Be Able to Do?

The version of the bot that you created in Chapter 3 could do just one thing: schedule an appointment with the doctor. What other task(s) should it handle? Remember, it's a health checkup bot. How about a basic diagnosis? That is, given a list of symptoms, arrive at a list of potential diseases or conditions. This is the sort of self-help that your bot can provide to a user sitting at home. Let's add this to your bot's list of tasks.

> *User*: I am feeling pain in my lower abdomen, and there is some swelling as well.

> *Bot*: You may be suffering from Appendicitis, Constipation, or Food Poisoning.

Now coming back to the appointment scheduling aspect, the Chapter 3 bot was clearly based on the assumption that there was only one doctor. In the real world, that is not the case unless the bot is specifically built for a clinic. The bot could cater to a hospital, a chain of hospitals, or a network of doctors. In any case, a user is dealing with several types of doctors and multiple doctors of the same type. Your bot should be able to identify the type of doctor from a user's request: "schedule an appointment with the **dentist**," "I want to consult a **gynecologist**," or "how can I meet a **cardiologist**?"

A user may also optionally specify a convenient time range during which they wish to meet a doctor: "schedule an appointment with the dentist between 9 am and 12 pm." The bot should be able to detect requested time frames.

In sum, the bot should be able to deal with the following two tasks:

1. Perform a basic diagnosis by providing a list of diseases/conditions based on a given set of symptoms.

2. Schedule an appointment with a physician or a specialist for the requested date and close to the requested time frame.

What Information Does the Bot Need from the User?

Now that you have a clear idea about the capabilities of your bot, it's easy to list all the data that it needs from the user to carry out its tasks.

Two common pieces of data that your bot needs from the user are their **name and age**. The same set of symptoms may affect people of different age groups differently. And, at any rate, this information is essential in scheduling an appointment.

■ **Tip**   You can additionally ask for a contact number and email address.

For performing a basic diagnosis, **a list of all symptoms** is required. The user may provide this list in a simple sentence or individually.

For scheduling an appointment, the **type of doctor**, **date** and, optionally, a convenient **time range** are needed.

What Should Be Done in LUIS?

This is easy to answer. LUIS is quite simply the language understanding component in your app. It cannot do anything more than help your bot understand the meaning of a given sentence. It cannot store or provide answers. Nor can it perform calculations or process logic. But it can break down a sentence into intent and entities.

Now, it's a good idea to name your intents and entities beforehand. This will give you an idea about the exact number of intents and entities you will need to later create your LUIS app. Table 6-1 shows a helpful way of designing a LUIS app. You can follow it later while handling the LUIS part or pass it on to a colleague as a design document to let them create the LUIS app.

Table 6-1. *Data Dictionary for the Health Checkup Bot's LUIS App*

Utterance	Answer	Intent	Entities
Hi Hello Hey Help me	Hello, there. Tell me your symptoms and I will tell you possible conditions. Or ask me to schedule an appointment with a doctor. But first I need to know your name and age.	Greet	--
I am Anurag Bhandari. I am 29 years old.	Hi, Anurag. How can I help you today?	PatientDetails	PatientName::FirstName = Anurag, PatientName::LastName = Bhandari, PatientAge = 29 years
I am feeling confusion and anxiety. I vomited a few minutes ago.	You might be suffering from Hypoglycemia.	GetCondition	Symptom = confusion, Symptom = anxiety, Symptom = vomited
I am feeling pain in my lower abdomen, and there is some swelling as well.	You might be suffering from Appendicitis, Constipation, or Food Poisoning.	GetCondition	Symptom = pain, Symptom = swelling BodyPart = lower abdomen
Schedule an appointment with the dentist tomorrow between 9 am and 12 pm	I have scheduled an appointment with Dr. John Doe for Sunday, May 07 at 11 am.	ScheduleAppointment	DoctorType = dentist, datetime = tomorrow, AppointmentTime::StartTime = 9 am, AppointmentTime::EndTime = 12 pm
I want to see a doctor	I have scheduled an appointment with Dr. John Doe for Sunday, May 07 at 11 am.	ScheduleAppointment	-- (Since no entity is specified in utterance, assuming default values. DoctorType = physician, datetime & AppointmentTime = first available slot)

The above table does not comprehensively cover all possible use cases. It is intended only to give you a format for your design document. As a practice assignment, expand the above data dictionary to cover as many use cases as you can think of. You may not always be able to cover all cases in the first draft itself, and you may have to revisit the dictionary several times during the development of the bot. LUIS is very flexible in terms of adding and modifying intents and entities, as well as retraining already labelled utterances.

What Should Be Done in the Bot Framework?

Pretty much everything else. You learned to build a bot in Chapter 3, and so you know that the Bot Framework will provide you with the tools (its developers' API) to create a bot. How you use its API is entirely up to you. This is the place where you write the entire logic for the bot, including interacting with LUIS. This is also where you give the users answers to their questions after performing your calculations and talking to LUIS. Answers can come from a database or can simply be stored statically in the code itself.

Two very important questions arise at this point:

- How to deduce diseases from symptoms?

- How to check a doctor's availability during certain time of day?

You aren't thinking of creating a database of all possible symptoms and conditions, are you? Not only you are not an expert in the medical profession, maintaining such a database would be a cephalgia (headache). The basic rule of thumb when creating apps is to never reinvent the wheel. A quick Google search led us to www.apimedic.com, which provides a symptom checker API that would be a good fit in this scenario. Although their API is paid, they do have a free tier that allows 100 API calls per month.

Similarly, you can use something like the Google Calendar API to create appointments and get available slots. Alternatively, the drchrono API provides a full-fledged doctor-patient management system.

To summarize, the tasks to be done using the Bot Framework include

- Receiving user input

- Sending user input to LUIS for analysis

- Taking action(s) based on intent and entities received from LUIS

- Sending a response back to the user

Creating a LUIS App

You now have a plan. You know what inputs to expect from users and what responses to provide, as well as what actions to perform on the way. You also have a clearly defined data dictionary for use with LUIS.

Creating a LUIS app is not difficult. You may have already done that during practice in Chapter 4. Let's create a new LUIS app for the Health Checkup Bot.

While logged into the luis.ai website, go to My Apps and click the New App button. Take hints from Figure 6-1 to fill in the new app form.

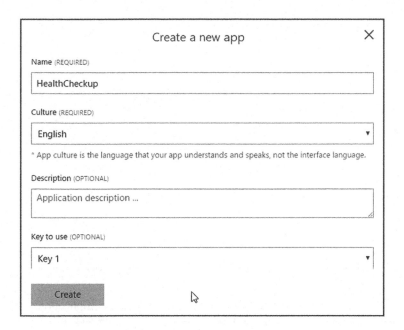

Figure 6-1. *Creating a new LUIS app*

■ **Note**   Without a key, you will not be able to publish the app. Refer to Chapter 2 for the steps to get a LUIS subscription key at Azure Portal, and Chapter 4 for steps to attach subscription keys to your LUIS account.

Congratulations. You have just created a new LUIS app. Time to add intents.

Adding Intents

After creating a new LUIS app, you should have been auto-redirected to the app's overview page. If that did not happen, click the newly created app from the list on the My Apps page.

To add a new intent, from left sidebar, go to the Intents page. Referring to Table 6-1, the very first intent should be Greet. Click the Add Intent button, specify "Greet" as the intent name, and click Create. You should be redirected to the Greet intent's page.

Adding/Labeling Utterances

On this page, start adding sample utterances. Think of all possibilities of how a user may start a conversation with your bot. You may start with "hi," "hello," and "hey", which are common conversation starters. After adding the initial utterances, click the Save button to commit your changes. Figure 6-2 shows the changes done so far. At this point, your LUIS app cannot yet make predictions for user input because it is not trained yet. Adding utterances to an intent is NOT the same as training LUIS.

Utterances (3)   Entities in use   Suggested utterances

| | Type a new utterance & press Enter ... | ✕ |

| 💾 Save   ✕ Discard   🗑 Delete   Reassign Intent ⌄ | | Labels view (Ctrl+E): | Entities ▼ |
| | | Search in utterances ... 🔍 | ▽ |

☐	Utterance text	Predicted Intent
☐	hey	Not trained
☐	hello	Not trained
☐	hi	Not trained

Figure 6-2. Adding utterances to an intent

Let's train the app. From the left sidebar, go to the Train and Test page and click the Train Application button. Once training completes in a few seconds, test the app you've created so far. In the Interactive Testing section, try "hi" and "hello." In the results pane on the right, you should get Greet as the top scoring intent, along with a confidence score. Figure 6-3 shows the results.

Interactive Testing   Batch Testing

| ☐ Enable published model | | Labels view (Ctrl+E) | Entities ▼ | Reset console |

Type a test utterance & press Enter	→	**Current version results**
hello		Top scoring intent **Greet (0.99)**
hi		Other intents **None (0.13)**

Figure 6-3. Testing utterances on the Train and Test page

At this point, the confidence score will be high (ideally 1, otherwise always greater than 0.9). As a matter of fact, you will notice that LUIS will return Greet with high confidence even for all other utterances. Try with "how far is paris from london." This is because you have only one intent at this point.

To be more precise, your app has a total of two intents right now: Greet and None. The None intent is something that LUIS creates by default. It is a built-in intent that cannot be deleted. The purpose of None is to reduce the kind of confusion we just talked about. All utterances that your app is not supposed to handle should be added to the None intent.

Let's go back to the Intents page and open the None intent page from the list. Add "how far is paris from london." Save and retrain the app. If you test this utterance now, None will be returned as the top scoring intent. Try other similar utterances, like "how far is delhi from Mumbai." You should still see None winning.

Test some more utterances: "who are you," "hello bot," and "how are you?" If LUIS returns None, go back to the Greet intent page and add these utterances to the list. Newly added utterances will appear in a different color, as seen in Figure 6-4.

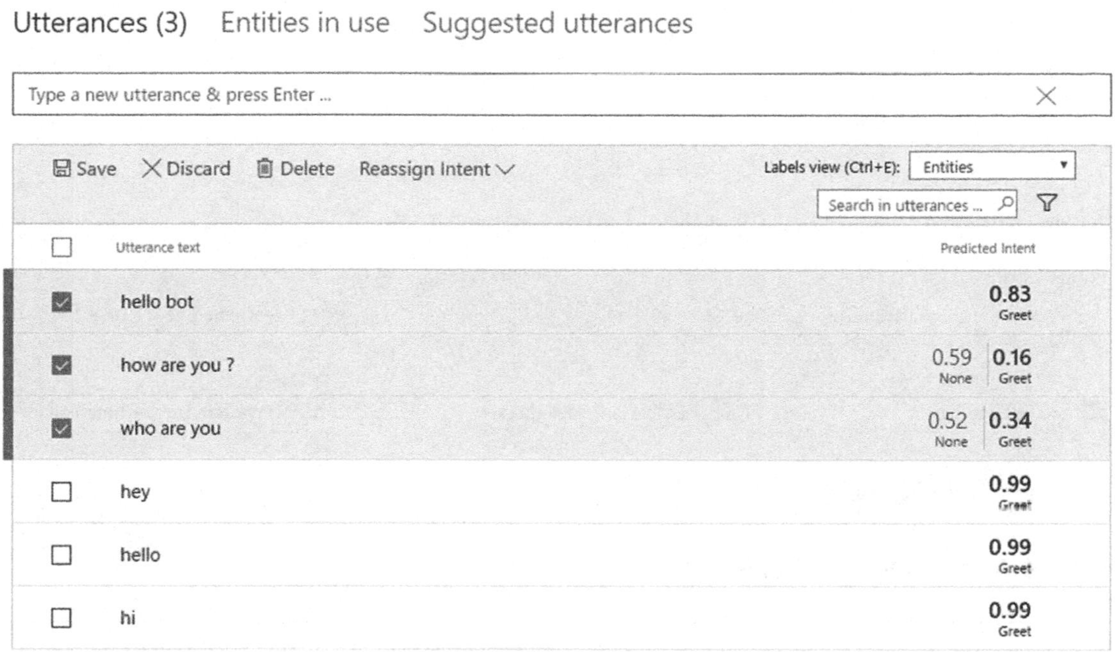

Utterances (3)   Entities in use   Suggested utterances

	Utterance text	Predicted Intent	
☑	hello bot		**0.83** Greet
☑	how are you ?	0.59 None	**0.16** Greet
☑	who are you	0.52 None	**0.34** Greet
☐	hey		**0.99** Greet
☐	hello		**0.99** Greet
☐	hi		**0.99** Greet

Figure 6-4. *Adding more utterances to an existing intent*

Train your app again and verify that the new utterances are returning the correct intent.

Publishing Your App

Publishing you app would be the logical final step in the development of a LUIS application. But since you want to ensure that your training is going in the right direction, it's essential for you at this point to publish your app. Publishing simply means deploying your application's most recently trained model to an HTTP endpoint URL.

The endpoint is nothing but a web service to access a LUIS app. The endpoint receives an utterance via a query string parameter and returns a JSON output with a corresponding intent-entities breakdown. When you are publishing for the first time, an endpoint URL is generated for you based on your application's ID and subscription key. This URL remains constant throughout the lifetime of your LUIS app.

The reason you want to publish your app at this point is not to see how the JSON output looks, but to verify your training until now. It's not unusual for results received from the HTTP endpoint to be different from the results received on the Interactive Testing page for the exact same utterance. Ultimately, it's the endpoint results that matter because that is what your bot will get.

From the left sidebar, go to the Publish App page. Scroll down and click the Publish button, while making sure Production is selected as the Endpoint Slot. Like training, publishing takes a few seconds to complete. Figure 6-5 shows the result.

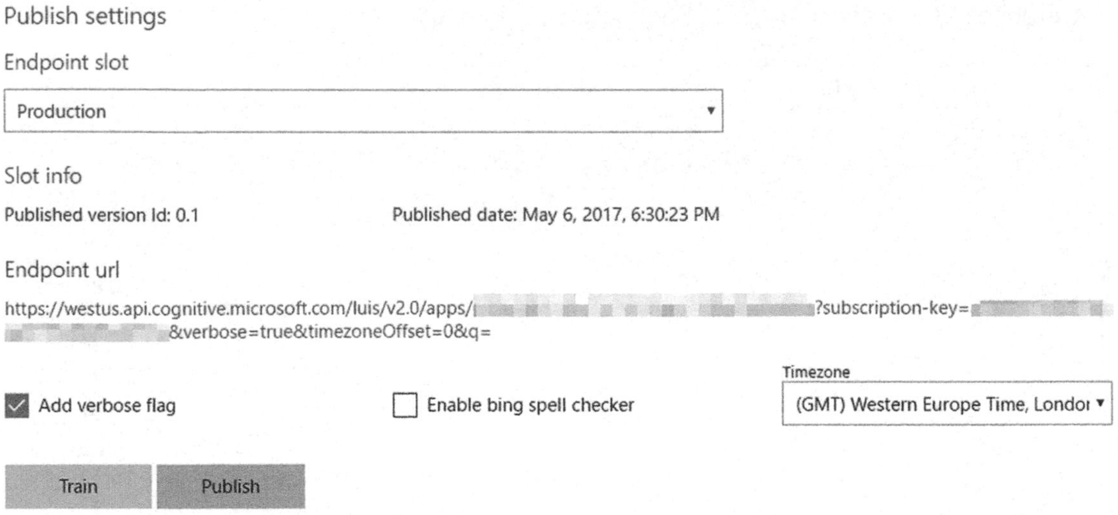

Publish settings

Endpoint slot

Production ▼

Slot info

Published version Id: 0.1   Published date: May 6, 2017, 6:30:23 PM

Endpoint url

https://westus.api.cognitive.microsoft.com/luis/v2.0/apps/▮▮▮▮ ▮▮ ▮▮▮ ▮▮▮▮▮?subscription-key=▮▮▮▮▮▮
▮▮▮▮▮▮▮▮▮▮&verbose=true&timezoneOffset=0&q=

Timezone

☑ Add verbose flag   ☐ Enable bing spell checker   (GMT) Western Europe Time, Londoi ▼

Train	Publish

Figure 6-5. *Publishing a LUIS application*

■ **Note**   You may wonder why there is a Train button right next to the Publish button when there is a dedicated page for training. This is to save time. When dealing with production LUIS applications, one usually relies on published endpoint results more than interactive testing results. Thus, it's common to skip the training and testing after labeling utterances and come directly to the Publish App page.

Copy the endpoint URL and paste it in your browser's address bar. The q parameter of the query string is where an utterance must be specified. Here is the JSON result for "hello bot" we received when we tested it:

```
https://westus.api.cognitive.microsoft.com/luis/v2.0/apps/<id>?subscription-key=<key>
&verbose=true&timezoneOffset=0&q=hello bot
```

```
{
  "query": "hello bot",
  "topScoringIntent": {
    "intent": "Greet",
    "score": 0.9999995
  },
  "intents": [
    {
      "intent": "Greet",
      "score": 0.9999995
    },
    {
      "intent": "None",
      "score": 0.0768341646
    }

  ],
  "entities": []
}
```

We find that in the result received from the endpoint, Greet is still the top scoring intent with 99% confidence. This matches with the interactive testing results we saw earlier. So far, so good.

Adding Entities

You did not need entities for simple greeting utterances. As per the dictionary in Table 6-1, you'll need entities for all other intents. Let's start by creating a new intent. Go to the Intents page and create the ScheduleAppointment intent.

Add the entity-less utterance "schedule an appointment." And then one with an entity "schedule an appointment with the dentist." Hover on the word "dentist" in the just-added utterance to see it surrounded with square brackets. Clicking the word will give you the option to either label it as an existing entity or a new entity. Figure 6-6 shows how to create a new entity called DoctorType like this.

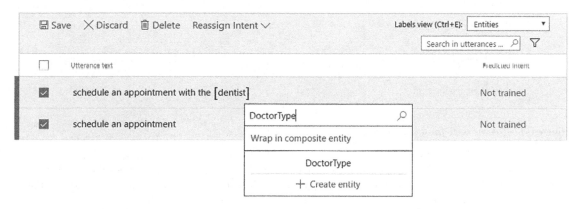

Figure 6-6. *Creating a new entity directly from an intent's page*

An entity created like this is called a *simple* entity. There are two other types of entities: *hierarchical* and *composite*. And then there are *prebuilt* entities. You'll see them in a bit.

Add more variations of "schedule an appointment," such as "set an appointment," "I want to see a dentist," etc. Also, add utterances to cover more types of doctors: "I want to see a dermatologist," "schedule an appointment with the cardiologist," etc. Figure 6-7 shows the result of adding new utterances.

Utterance text	Predicted Intent
schedule an appointment with the [$DoctorType]	Not trained
i want to see a [$DoctorType]	Not trained
set an appointment	Not trained
schedule an appointment with the [$DoctorType]	Not trained
schedule an appointment	Not trained

Figure 6-7. *Adding more variations of the same utterance*

Notice in the above list that it's not possible to distinguish "dentist" from "dermatologist." Both are labeled as $DoctorType. Click the Labels view drop-down and select Tokens. Figure 6-8 shows the updated view, where it's possible to discern entity values.

Figure 6-8. *Tokens view for the utterance list*

Now visit the Train and Test page and do a fresh training. Once that is complete, check the "Enable published model" option in the Interactive Testing section. This will let you compare interactive testing and published model results side-by-side, as in Figure 6-9.

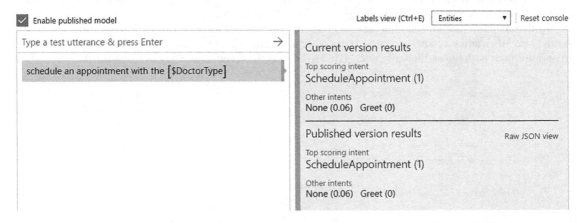

Figure 6-9. *Testing results with published model results enabled*

It's important to note that using the enable published model option will make hits to the published endpoint and thus add to the LUIS subscription key usage limit. The JSON result from the above testing is as follows:

```
{
  "query": "schedule an appointment with the dentist",
  "topScoringIntent": {
    "intent": "ScheduleAppointment",
    "score": 0.9981268
  },
  "intents": [
    {
      "intent": "ScheduleAppointment",
      "score": 0.9981268
    },
    {
      "intent": "None",
      "score": 0.0598709881
    },
    {
      "intent": "Greet",
      "score": 7.16493842E-09
    }
  ],
  "entities": [
    {
      "entity": "dentist",
      "type": "DoctorType",
      "startIndex": 33,
      "endIndex": 39,
      "score": 0.95532
    }
  ]
}
```

Simple Entities

The entity DoctorType that you created earlier is an example of simple entity. A simple entity is a type of custom entity in LUIS that can be used to label your app's domain-specific keywords. It's the simplest of all custom entity types.

Other custom entities include hierarchical and composite. They are custom because, unlike prebuilt entities, they need to be properly trained through utterances or features (details later), whereas prebuilt entities are ready-to-use, pretrained things.

Let's create a simple entity named Symptom. From the left sidebar, go to the Entities page and click the Add custom entity button. In the Add Entity dialog, type in "Symptom" as the entity name, select Simple as the entity type, and click Save. The symptom entity will appear alongside the DoctorType.

That's it. There's nothing more to do here. Unlike for an intent, you cannot add utterances specifically for an entity. Another important point is regarding the reusability of entities. An entity is not tied to an intent. It can be, and should be, use across intents.

Referring to Table 6-1, we know that the only intent where the Symptom entity is used is *GetCondition*. This intent does not exist yet. Create the intent and add a few utterances to it, as shown in Figure 6-10.

☐ i am feeling [pain] in my [lower abdomen] , and there is some [swelling] as well .	**Tokens View**
☐ i am feeling [confusion] and [anxiety] . i [vomited] a few minutes ago	
☐ i have [pain] , [swelling] and [stiffness] in my [ankle]	
☐ i am feeling [$Symptom] in my [$BodyPart] , and there is some [$Symptom] as well .	**Entities View**
☐ i am feeling [$Symptom] and [$Symptom] . i [$Symptom] a few minutes ago	
☐ i have [$Symptom] , [$Symptom] and [$Symptom] in my [$BodyPart]	

Figure 6-10. *A few example utterances for the GetCondition intent*

Add many more similar and different-but-related utterances. Cover as many symptoms and body parts as you can. Do a Google search for common diseases and their symptoms for some assistance. Figure 6-11 shows interactive testing results after training the intent with about 10 utterances.

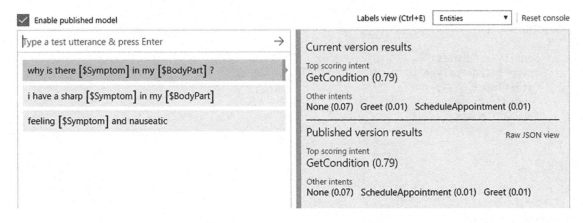

Figure 6-11. *The more you train, the better the results. "why is there <symptom> in my <body part>" has a low confidence score. Also, "nauseatic" was not recognized as a symptom. Misses like these can be easily corrected with more training.*

Composite Entities

Consider the following JSON:

```
{
  "query": "there is pain in my ankles, swelling and stiffness in my knees",
  "topScoringIntent": {
    "intent": "GetCondition",
    "score": 0.9803361
  },
```

```json
  "intents": [... ],
  "entities": [
    {
      "entity": "ankles",
      "type": "BodyPart",
      "startIndex": 20,
      "endIndex": 25,
      "score": 0.920250833
    },
    {
      "entity": "knees",
      "type": "BodyPart",
      "startIndex": 57,
      "endIndex": 61,
      "score": 0.9399164
    },
    {
      "entity": "pain",
      "type": "Symptom",
      "startIndex": 9,
      "endIndex": 12,
      "score": 0.9281677
    },
    {
      "entity": "swelling",
      "type": "Symptom",
      "startIndex": 28,
      "endIndex": 35,
      "score": 0.9131367
    },
    {
      "entity": "stiffness",
      "type": "Symptom",
      "startIndex": 41,
      "endIndex": 49,
      "score": 0.9450974
    }
  ]
}
```

For the given utterance, LUIS could successfully determine the intent and all entities correctly. But that's not enough to correctly predict the underlying condition. Why? Because there are two sets of symptoms involved, one that relates to ankles and the other that relates to knees. Unless you can infer which symptoms are related to which body part, how can you come up with a diagnosis? After all, "swelling in ankles" and "pain in knees" may pertain to totally different conditions.

A clever thought may cross your mind. For each entity, a startIndex and an endIndex is returned in the JSON. Perhaps you can leverage the index bit to put a condition in your code to relate all symptoms that occur **before** a body part in an utterance to the part. Not a bad thought at first. But what if the utterance is "my ankles have pain, my knees have swelling and stiffness?" Or, worse, "there is pain in my ankles, also my knees have swelling and stiffness." A logic solely based on an index fails miserably here.

A composite entity helps define relationships among entities. In other words, it helps create a **group** of entities. A composite entity is nothing but a logical container/wrapper for existing entities in your application. It defines a has-a relationship. For example, you could have a composite entity called SymptomGroup consisting of Symptom and BodyPart entities. Go back to Entities page and create a composite entity, as shown in Figure 6-12.

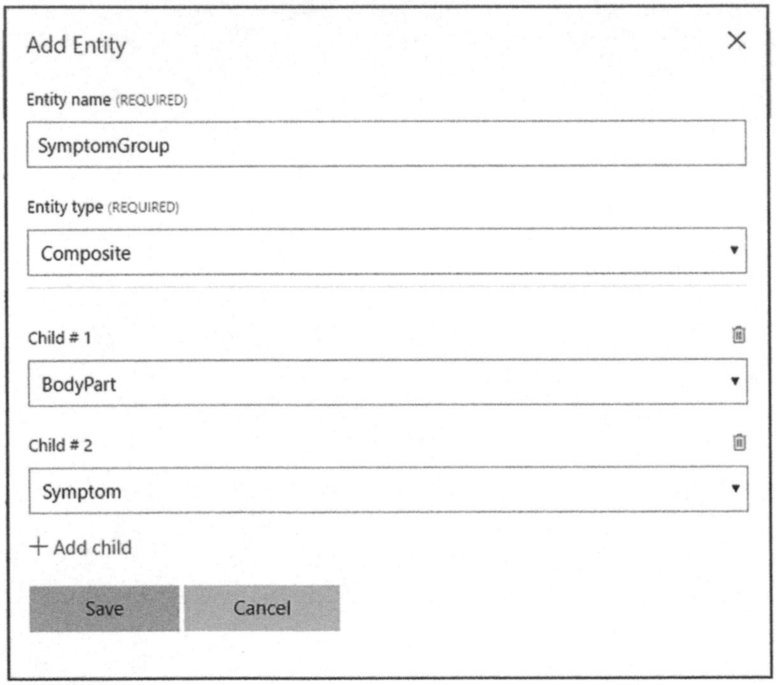

Figure 6-12. *Creating a composite entity in LUIS*

This is a job half done. The main work is to now label utterances with your new composite entity. Go to the GetCondition intent's page, and add the utterance "there is pain in my ankles, swelling and stiffness in my knees." Label the symptoms and body parts as you would normally do. Now click the first symptom, "pain," then click "Wrap in composite entity, and finally select SymptomGroup. This begins the process of wrapping. You will see a curly starting bracket just before "pain." Click "ankles" to finish wrapping. You have successfully added a composite entity into the utterance. Do the same for the other part, "swelling and stiffness in my knees."

Train and publish the application. LUIS will now return an array of composite entities, each with its child entities. Writing logic to calculate the right condition(s) is way more easy now:

```
{
  "query": "there is pain in my ankles, also my knees have swelling and stiffness",
  "topScoringIntent": {
    "intent": "GetCondition",
    "score": 0.9933607
  },
  "intents": [... ],
  "entities": [... ],
  "compositeEntities": [
```

```
{
    "parentType": "SymptomGroup",
    "value": "pain in my ankles",
    "children": [
      {
        "type": "BodyPart",
        "value": "ankles"
      },
      {
        "type": "Symptom",
        "value": "pain"
      }
    ]
  },
  {
    "parentType": "SymptomGroup",
    "value": "knees have swelling and stiffness",
    "children": [
      {
        "type": "BodyPart",
        "value": "knees"
      },
      {
        "type": "Symptom",
        "value": "swelling"
      },
      {
        "type": "Symptom",
        "value": "stiffness"
      }
    ]
  }
 ]
}
```

Hierachical Entities

A hierachical entity is like a composite one in that it also has child entities. But the similarity ends there. Rather than defining a has-a relationship, a hierarchical entity defines an is-a relationship. Also, it does not rely on existing simple entities. You create children while creating the entity itself. Deleting the entity deletes all its children as well. This is, however, not the case with composite entities, which, when deleted, leave behind the child entities intact; only the relationship gets deleted.

For example, a hierarchical entity Location may have two children: Source and Destination. Similarly, PatientName can have FirstName and LastName as its children. Use hierarchical entities when you want a group of similar entities that have an is-a relationship with its parent.

■ **Note**   Each LUIS application comes with a maximum limit for total number of entities it can have. At the time of writing, this limit is 30. One hierarchical entity with 5 children does not result in adding 2, only 1 to its application's total entities. Each hierarchical entity can have up to 10 children. When planning your application, you may want to use hierarchical entities to reduce the entity footprint if your application is expected to have a large number of total entities.

Another reason to use a hierarchical entity is to force LUIS into recognizing logical groups of entities, such as full name. Try this experiment in a separate application: create two simple entities called FirstName and LastName. Now label utterances such as the following appropriately:

- "my name is anurag Bhandari"
- "i am nishith Pathak"
- "hi, I am rohit"

Now, when LUIS encounters "i am anurag Bhandari," it will correctly identify FirstName and LastName. LUIS will, however, fail to recognize the entities for names it has not been trained for, such as "i am priyanka chopra." LUIS may still be able to recognize common English first and last names, but not Indian, Chinese, European, etc. names.

To fix this, use a hierarchical entity with first and last names as its children. This will force LUIS into recognizing patterns such as one where a pair of words that follow "i am" or "my name is" as entities.

Go to Entities page, and create a new hierarchical entity named PatientName, as shown in Figure 6-13.

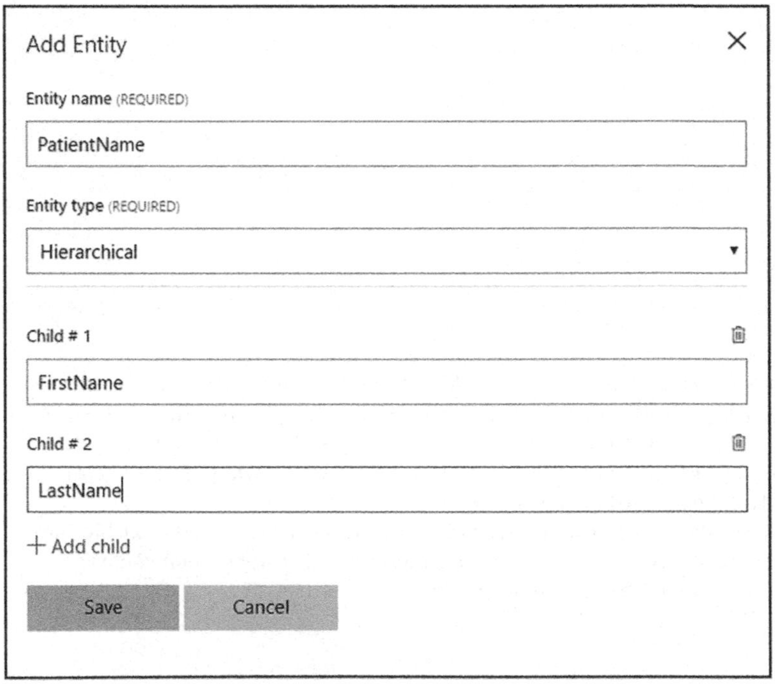

Figure 6-13. *Creating a hierarchical entity in LUIS*

You will need the `PatientName` entity for the `PatientDetails` intent. Let's create and train the `PatientDetails` intent, as shown in Figure 6-14.

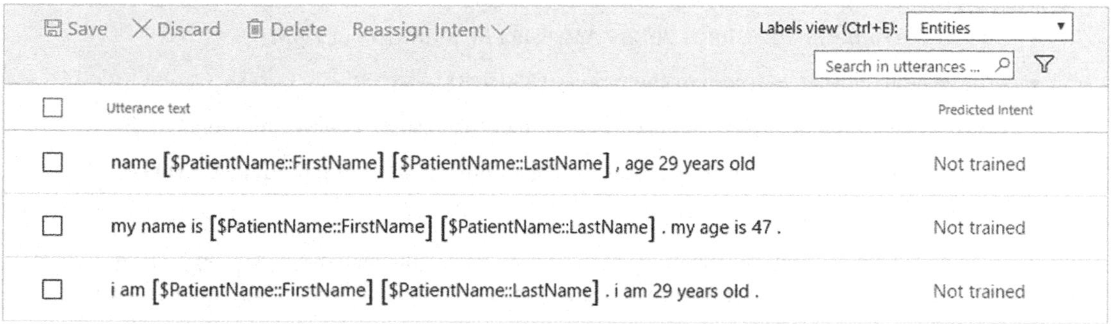

	Utterance text	Predicted Intent
☐	🖫 Save ✕ Discard 🗑 Delete Reassign Intent ∨	Labels view (Ctrl+E): Entities ▼ / Search in utterances ... 🔍 ▽
☐	name [$PatientName::FirstName] [$PatientName::LastName] , age 29 years old	Not trained
☐	my name is [$PatientName::FirstName] [$PatientName::LastName] . my age is 47 .	Not trained
☐	i am [$PatientName::FirstName] [$PatientName::LastName] . i am 29 years old .	Not trained

Figure 6-14. Labeling utterances with a hierarchical entity

The detected entities are returned in Parent::Child format in the JSON output:

```
"entities": [
    {
      "entity": "anurag",
      "type": "PatientName::FirstName",
      "startIndex": 11,
      "endIndex": 16,
      "score": 0.9718365
    },
    {
      "entity": "bhandari",
      "type": "PatientName::LastName",
      "startIndex": 18,
      "endIndex": 25,
      "score": 0.791057765
    }
  ]
```

■ **Note**   Now that you know how to create hierarchical entities, create another one named `AppointmentTime` for use with the `ScheduleAppointment` intent. Refer to Table 6-1 for a sample utterance.

Prebuilt Entities

While training the `PatientDetails` intent, you did not handle the patient's age. You need an entity to recognize the age. You can create a simple entity named `PatientAge` and then train it through labels, such as "29 years old," "52-year-old," etc. Or, instead, you can use the age prebuilt entity.

A *prebuilt entity* is a ready-to-use entity that has already been trained extensively by Microsoft through its Bing platform. LUIS comes with a lot of prebuilt entities, such as

- age (10-month-old, 19 years old, 58 year-old)

- datetime (June 23, 1976, Jul 11 2012, 7 AM, 6:49 PM, tomorrow at 7 AM)

- dimension (2 miles, 650 square kilometres, 9,350 feet)

- email (user@site.net, user_name@mysite.com.eg, user.Name12@website.nets)

- geography (Antarctica, Portugal, Dubai, Sanjiang County, Lake Pontchartrain, CB3 0DS)

- number (ten, forty two, 3.141, 10K)

And more, such as encyclopedia, money, ordinal, percentage, phonenumber, temperature, and url. It is highly recommended to use a prebuilt entity, whenever possible, instead of creating a custom entity.

■ **Tip**   You cannot add the same prebuilt entity more than once in the same app.

From the Entities page, add the age prebuilt entity to your LUIS application. That's it. No further labeling is required in the PatientDetails intent. The next time you train and test utterances, age will automatically be recognized for you, as shown in Figure 6-15.

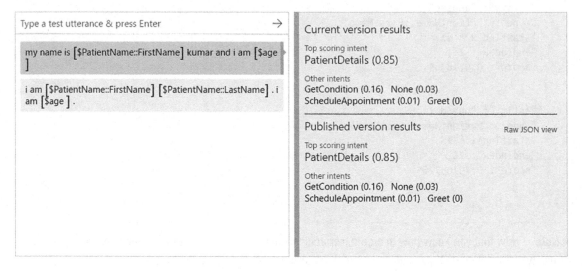

Figure 6-15. *Once a prebuilt entity is added to a LUIS application, all utterances that have words or phrases that match the prebuilt entity's patterns are detected automatically*

Here is the JSON of the age entity:

```
{
  "entity": "29 years old",
  "type": "builtin.age",
  "startIndex": 27,
  "endIndex": 38,
  "resolution": {
```

```
      "unit": "Year",
      "value": "29"
   }
}
```

Adding a Phrase List

Remember when we asked you to add more utterances to cover as many types of doctors as possible? We said the same thing for symptoms. With the help of a phrase list, you won't have to do so.

Depending on the domain and requirements, there may be hundreds of variations of an utterance and dozens of values of entities involved in those utterances. That equates to thousands of permutations and combinations to train LUIS. A *phrase list* is a comma-separated list of possible values of an entity or a phrase in an utterance.

For example, a phrase list named SeeDoctor may have the values "see a doctor," "consult a doctor," "schedule appointment with doctor," "meet with doctor," and so on. All these phrases mean the same thing. We can say that the phrases are interchangeable.

Similarly, a Cities phrase list may have values such as "London," "New Delhi," "Paris," "Chicago," etc. These possible values, however, are not interchangeable. London is not the same as New Delhi.

LUIS allows you to create both exchangeable and non-exchangeable phrase lists. Figure 6-16 shows the TypesOfDoctor phrase list, something that will hugely improve the quality of results in your application. From the left sidebar, go to the Features page and click the "Add phrase list" button in the Phrase list features section.

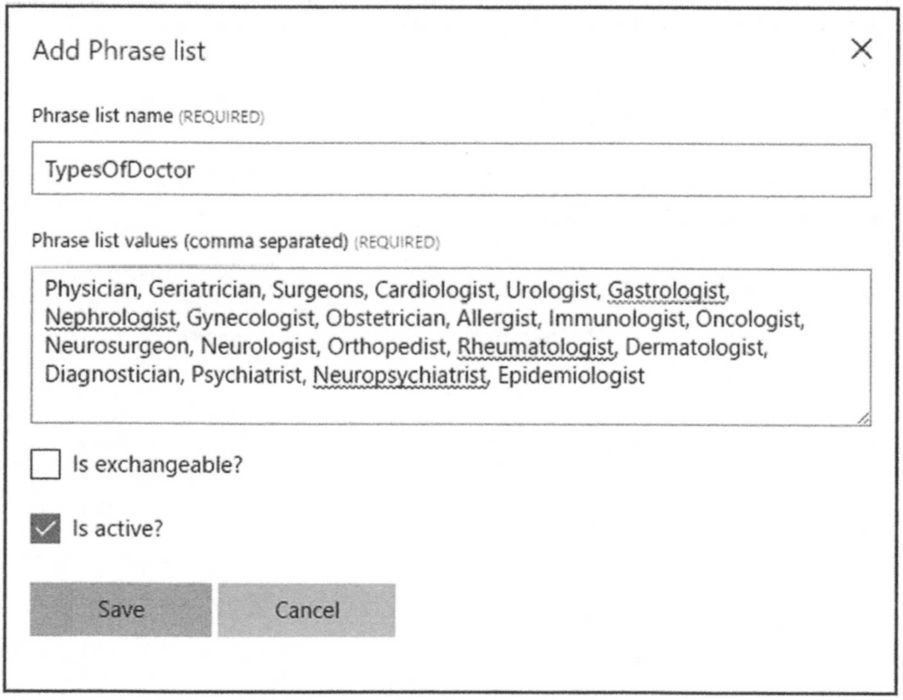

Figure 6-16. Adding a phrase list in LUIS

Train and publish the model. Now if you test an utterance, such as "schedule an appointment with a neurologist," you will see that "neurologist" is correctly detected as the entity DoctorType. If that does not happen, add a few more utterances with two or three values from the phrase list.

Suggested Next Steps

The following sections cover some ideas for next steps.

Active Learning Through Suggested Utterances

When you start building a LUIS application, you rely on a bunch of utterances for the training that you and/or a few others thought of during the planning stage. Once your application goes live into production and users start interacting with it, it generally happens that the application receives a lot of user queries that are very different from the initial bunch.

For some or most of user queries, LUIS may be able to answer correctly and confidently. For the others, it may fail miserably. Over time, LUIS keeps on accumulating the users' utterances that it thinks are different from the ones it was trained with. This wealth of data is what it then suggests to its developers for further training itself, a process known as *active learning*. It is one thing to train a model with initial utterances and another thing to do so with data collected from live, real-world users.

Figure 6-17 shows a few suggested utterances for the GetCondition intent. By just selecting these utterances and clicking Save, you can give your nod of approval to LUIS that its result was all right. Alternatively, you can label missed entities, change wrongly detected ones, or reassign the intent altogether. This is an activity you and your fellow developers should follow regularly to improve your application's responses and make it more natural.

Dashboard   Suggested utterances

	Utterance text	Suggested Intent
☐	my name is [akshay] kumar and i am [49 - years - old]	**0.74** PatientDetails
☐	i am [akshay] [kumar] . i am [49 years old] .	**0.7** PatientDetails
☐	schedule an appoint with a [psychiatrist]	**0.73** ScheduleAppointment
☐	i have a [headache] and am feeling [nauseatic]	**0.97** GetCondition

Suggest utterances for : GetCondition

💾 Save   ✕ Discard   🗑 Delete   Reassign Intent ∨   Labels view (Ctrl+E): Tokens   Search in utterances ...

Figure 6-17. *Suggested utterances on the Overview page*

Suggested utterances can be accessed from the Overview page, an intent's details page, or the Entities page.

Using LUIS Programmatic API for Automation

LUIS comes with a set of rich RESTful API to let developers manage an application entirely programmatically. Tasks such as creating intents, entities, and phrase lists, as well as adding and labelling utterances and training and publishing the model can all be automated via the API.

You may want to use the programmatic APIs for a bunch of reasons:

- To create a custom website for non-developers for the purpose of training and active learning

- To retrieve detailed statistics about your application to create dashboards and graphs

- To simply to create an entirely new version of the LUIS website if, for some reason, you aren't satisfied with the one that Microsoft offers at luis.ai

To see all the options or to explore all functionalities exposed by the API, visit www.luis.ai/home/help#api-docs or do a web search for "luis programmatic api."

Integrating LUIS with the Bot Framework

Before going ahead, you are highly encouraged to go back to Chapter 3 for a quick refresher of the Bot Framework. In that chapter, you created a *static* sort of bot, something that responded to user queries based on simple if-else conditions. But you got the gist of how to use the Bot Framework SDK for creating a quick and dirty chat bot.

As promised, it's now time to delve a bit further and create an intelligent bot that uses LUIS' natural language understanding capabilities to respond to its users. You have your LUIS application ready, something that you built one step at a time earlier in this chapter. It's time now to integrate it with the Bot Framework.

Adding LUIS support in the Bot Framework will require you to use its dialogs. As a result, the approach you will follow now will be a bit different from what you did in Chapter 3. So rather than reusing HealthCheckupBot's code, you'll create another project from scratch. This gives you an excuse to give a better name to your bot.

So, let's first get the matter of naming the bot out of the way. In real life, a name such as HealthCheckupBot is not only unnatural but it also outright gives the impression that you are dealing with an automated software. What should you call it? **Dr. Checkup** sounds just right!

Creating a Project in Visual Studio

Fire up Visual Studio and create a new Bot Framework type project, as you did in Chapter 3. Name it DrCheckup. A fully functional bot will be created for you that you can run and test using the Bot Framework Emulator. But all the bot does by default is echo back the text user sends it. The entire logic can be found in Controllers ➤ MessagesController.cs. Let's leave things as is here. You need to create a LuisDialog class to integrate your LUIS application.

Right-click the DrCheckup project in Solution Explorer and selected Add ➤ New Folder. Call it Dialogs. Now create a new class in the Dialogs folder called HealthCheckupDialog.cs. This class will derive from LuisDialog. Listing 6-1 shows the boilerplate code.

Listing 6-1. Boilerplate Code for HealthCheckupDialog.cs

```
using System;
using System.Collections.Generic;
using System.Linq;
```

```
using Microsoft.Bot.Builder.Dialogs;
using Microsoft.Bot.Builder.Luis;
using Microsoft.Bot.Builder.Luis.Models;
using System.Threading.Tasks;

namespace DrCheckup.Dialogs
{
    [LuisModel("luis-app-id", "luis-subscription-key")]
    [Serializable]
    public class HealthCheckupDialog : LuisDialog<object>
    {

    }
}
```

In the LuisModel class attribute, pass in your HealthCheckup LUIS application's id and your subscription key. Get the app id from the Overiew page of the application and the subscription key from the My keys page in LUIS. You are now all set up to start handling intents in this class.

Handling an Entity-less Intent

Let's start simple. What's the most basic intent in your app? Why, Greet, of course. The utterances that are mapped to Greet are simple. Also, this intent has zero associated entities. To handle it in the bot, create the following method in the HealthCheckupDialog class:

```
[LuisIntent("Greet")]
public async Task Greet(IDialogContext context, LuisResult result)
{

}
```

Here is how it works:

1. Bot receives a message from the user.

2. Bot sends the message to the configured LUIS application.

3. LUIS returns the top-scoring intent.

4. Bot checks for the method corresponding to the detected intent in the LuisDialog class. If it finds it, the code inside that method is executed.

In other words, a method with the exact same name as its corresponding intent or with an intent name passed to the LuisIntent attribute will act as that intent's handler. Either of the conditions should be true; we are doing both for convenience. There is no code inside the Greet method. Let's add the following code to send an appropriate message back to the user as bot's response:

```
[LuisIntent("Greet")]
public async Task Greet(IDialogContext context, LuisResult result)
{
        string message = "Hello, there. Tell me your symptoms and I will tell you possible
        conditions. " +
                "Or ask me to schedule an appointment with a doctor. " +
```

```
            "But first I need to know your name and age.";
        await context.PostAsync(message);
        context.Wait(MessageReceived);
}
```

context.PostAsync(message) sends your message to the user. context.Wait(MessageReceived) suspends the dialog until the user's next message is received. We haven't explored the result argument yet. We'll do that in a bit, but know that it's usually used to extract entities.

Setting Up Your Bot to Use HealthCheckupDialog

You'll handle other intents later. One step at a time, remember? First, let's test what you have done so far. For the bot to call LUIS, you need to set up code in MessagesController.cs to redirect received messages to HealthCheckupDialog.

In MessageController's Post method, replace all code in the if (activity.Type == ActivityTypes. Message) condition with the following:

```
if (activity.Type == ActivityTypes.Message)
{
        await Conversation.SendAsync(activity, () => new HealthCheckupDialog());
}
```

Now, all activities of type Message will be redirected to HealthCheckupDialog.

Testing the Bot in an Emulator

Run your code in Visual Studio by pressing F5. It will open your default browser and point it to http://localhost:3979/.

Open the Bot Framework Emulator from the Start menu. Enter http://localhost:3979/api/messages in the address bar. Leave the App Id and App Password fields empty, and click the Connect button. Once a connection with your bot is established, ping a greeting message. You should get the response shown in Figure 6-18.

Figure 6-18. *Testing a LUIS-enabled bot in the Bot Framework Emulator*

It works!

153

Handling an Entity-Full Intent

Let's write a method to handle `PatientDetails`, an intent that involves entities. But first, let's add a few class variables that will act as the dialog's state. Add the following code at the top of the `HealthCheckupDialog` class:

```
string patientFirstName, patientLastName, patientAge;
```

These three variables, which pertain to a patient's (user) details, will become the dialog's state. What that means is that once set, their values will remain persistent throughout the user's session with the bot. So, when your bot receives an utterance that matches the `PatientDetails`' intent, your state variables can be set to values extracted from the corresponding entities, PatientName and age. Patient details are things you'd like to retain for subsequent user utterances, so that you can use them to schedule an appointment with a doctor (name would be essential) or to determine condition(s) based on symptoms (age would be helpful).

Now, add the following method to the `HealthCheckupDialog` class:

```
[LuisIntent("PatientDetails")]
public async Task PatientDetails(IDialogContext context, LuisResult result)
{
        EntityRecommendation patientFirstNameEntity, patientLastNameEntity, patientAgeEntity;

        if (!result.TryFindEntity("PatientName::FirstName", out patientFirstNameEntity))
        {
                patientFirstNameEntity = new EntityRecommendation() { Entity = "Unknown" };
        }
        if (!result.TryFindEntity("PatientName::LastName", out patientLastNameEntity))
        {
                patientLastNameEntity = new EntityRecommendation() { Entity = "Unknown" };
        }
        if (!result.TryFindEntity("builtin.age", out patientAgeEntity))
        {
                patientAgeEntity = new EntityRecommendation() { Resolution = new
                Dictionary<string, object>() { { "value", "29" } } };
        }

        patientFirstName = patientFirstNameEntity.Entity;
        patientLastName = patientLastNameEntity.Entity;
        patientAge = patientAgeEntity.Resolution["value"].ToString();

        string message = $"Hi, {patientFirstName}. How can I help you today?";

        await context.PostAsync(message);
        context.Wait(MessageReceived);
}
```

Let's break it down:

```
EntityRecommendation patientFirstNameEntity, patientLastNameEntity, patientAgeEntity;
```

154

The EntityRecommendation class represents an object in the entities array in the JSON output. It has properties, such as Entity, Type, Score, StartIndex, etc. You have created three EntityRecommendation instances to represent the three possible entities you may receive with a PatientDetails utterance:

```
if (!result.TryFindEntity("PatientName::FirstName", out patientFirstNameEntity))
{
        patientFirstNameEntity = new EntityRecommendation() { Entity = "Unknown" };
}
```

The TryFindEntity method of the LuisResult class looks for the entity of the specified type in the result. On success, it sets the out parameter of the EntityRecommendation type to the found entity and returns true. On failure, it returns false without affecting the out param. The above if condition is a good way to set a default value for an entity in case it is not present in LUIS result.

Remember, PatientName is a hierarchical entity. The entity type PatientName::FirstName refers to its child, FirstName. To find simple entities, simply pass in the entity name without the colons (like Symptom).

```
if (!result.TryFindEntity("builtin.age", out patientAgeEntity))
{
        patientAgeEntity = new EntityRecommendation() { Resolution = new Dictionary<string,
        object>() { { "value", "29" } } };
}
```

A prebuilt entity's resolved value is returned in its resolution property in JSON. The resolved value is more usable than the value returned in the entity property. resolution.value stores the numeric part whereas resolution.type stores the unit part. In C#, Resolution is a <string, object> dictionary.

```
patientFirstName = patientFirstNameEntity.Entity;
patientLastName = patientLastNameEntity.Entity;
patientAge = patientAgeEntity.Resolution["value"].ToString();
```

You set the state variables to the values of their corresponding entities. And, finally, you send back to the user a message that contains an extracted entity: the patient's first name.

Run the bot and test it in the emulator. You should get a response that looks something like Figure 6-19.

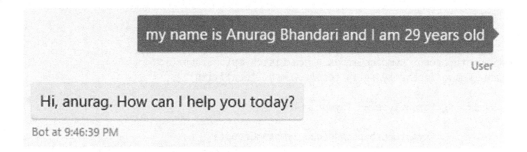

Figure 6-19. *A response that contains an entity (first name) extracted from user's message*

Handling an Intent with Composite Entities

You saw earlier that composite entities are returned in the compositeEntities array in JSON. A composite entity object looks like this:

```
{
  "parentType": "SymptomGroup",
  "value": "pain in my ankles",
  "children": [
        {
          "type": "BodyPart",
          "value": "ankles"
        },
        {
          "type": "Symptom",
          "value": "pain"
        }
  ]
}
```

C# obeys this structure. The LuisResult instance result has a property named CompositeEntities that is an array of composite entities that follow the above structure. As such, this structure requires a bit of work to get access to a composite entity's children. It's a good idea to create custom models to represent your composite entities and then make the above structure to the models.

Add a new folder in the DrCheckup project named Models. In this folder, create the following class:

```
public class SymptomGroup
{
        public string BodyPart { get; set; }
        public string[] Symptoms { get; set; }
}
```

Now, let's create the handler for the GetCondition intent. As this intent involves composite entities, the very first thing that you'll do is map the result.CompositeEntities array to your model.

```
[LuisIntent("GetCondition")]
public async Task GetCondition(IDialogContext context, LuisResult result)
{
        IList<SymptomGroup> symptomGroups = new List<SymptomGroup>();
        foreach (CompositeEntity sg in result.CompositeEntities)
        {
                if (sg.ParentType == "SymptomGroup")
                {
                        symptomGroups.Add(new SymptomGroup() {
                                BodyPart = sg.Children.Where(x => x.Type == "BodyPart").
                                FirstOrDefault().Value,
                                Symptoms = sg.Children.Where(x => x.Type == "Symptom").
                                Select(x => x.Value).ToArray()
                        });
                }
        }
}
```

You leverage a little LINQ to selectively pick out values from the `CompositeEntity` objects. If you are unfamiliar with LINQ, think of it as having an SQL-like syntax. It greatly simplifies querying IEnumerable objects in C# that are either formed purely in code or as a result of an SQL query execution.

Now that you have groups of symptoms by body parts, you can call a third-party API to fetch possible conditions/diseases:

```
string[] conditions = { };

// TODO: Call ApiMedic API using extracted symptom group(s)

string message;
if (conditions.Length < 1)
{
        message = "I'm sorry, I could not determine your condition.";
}
else
{
        message = $"You might be suffering from {string.Join(" or ", conditions)}.";
}
```

■ **Tip**   Also, write code to handle situations where instead of composite entities, simple entities (`Symptom` and `BodyPart`) are returned directly. If you recall, you had initially added utterances to the `GetConditions` intent that did not have composite entities. It's fairly possible to sometimes have symptoms that either do not affect one specific body part or are implicitly associated with one, like nausea, headache, diarrhea, anxiety, etc.

Figure 6-20 shows the entities detected in the utterance "there is pain in my ankles, also my knees have swelling and stiffness" while the code was running in debug mode.

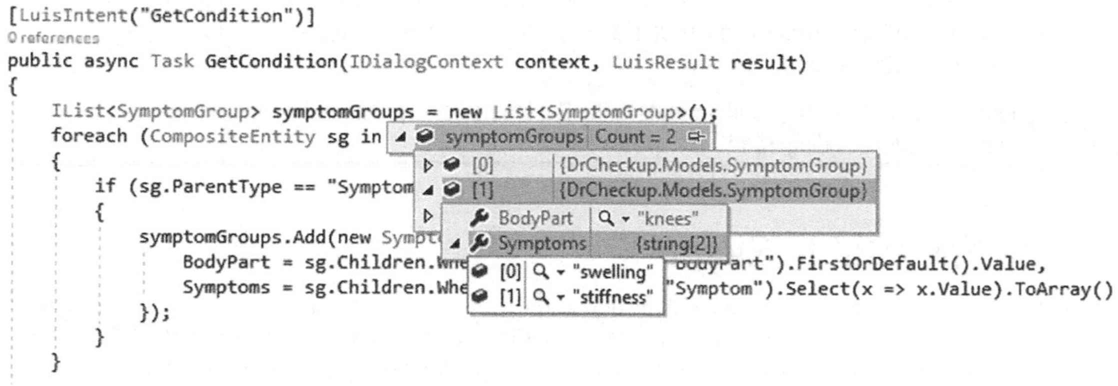

```
[LuisIntent("GetCondition")]
0 references
public async Task GetCondition(IDialogContext context, LuisResult result)
{
    IList<SymptomGroup> symptomGroups = new List<SymptomGroup>();
    foreach (CompositeEntity sg in  ◢ ● symptomGroups Count = 2 ⊡
    {                                ▷ ● [0]        {DrCheckup.Models.SymptomGroup}
        if (sg.ParentType == "Symptom ◢ ● [1]        {DrCheckup.Models.SymptomGroup}
        {                            ▷  ♪ BodyPart   Q ▾ "knees"
            symptomGroups.Add(new Sympt ◢ ♪ Symptoms   {string[2]}
                BodyPart = sg.Children.Whe ● [0] Q ▾ "swelling" bouyPart").FirstOrDefault().Value,
                Symptoms = sg.Children.Whe ● [1] Q ▾ "stiffness" "Symptom").Select(x => x.Value).ToArray()
            });
        }
    }
}
```

Figure 6-20. *Composite entities in a LUIS result were successfully mapped to your custom models*

Handling the None Intent

To wrap things up, let's handle the None intent as well.

```
[LuisIntent("")]
public async Task None(IDialogContext context, LuisResult result)
{
        string message = "Sorry, I did not understand.";
        await context.PostAsync(message);
        context.Wait(MessageReceived);
}
```

EXERCISE

Complete the LUIS Integration

After going through the section "Integrating LUIS with the Bot Framework," you should have the know-how to handle intents and all types of entities in the Bot Framework. Use this knowledge to complete the integration of your HealthCheckup LUIS app in the DrCheckup Bot Framework project.

- Handle the `ScheduleAppointment` intent, along with default values for involved entities. Make use of Google Calendar or drchrono API for creating appointments.

- Returning users may jump straight to asking their question before introducing themselves. In that case, you may want to ask them to mention their name and age first.

- Try adding a few UI elements here and there in your flow. Rather than making your bot a purely text-based experience, make it a hybrid CUI app. Check the Connector Service ➤ Attachments, Cards and Actions page in the Bot Framework's official documentation. The section on buttons and card actions may especially interest you. For example, you can use buttons to display a few common symptoms to make it easy for the user to interact with your bot.

Lastly, learn more about dialogs and prompts in the Bot Framework. These greatly improve user experience and reduce coding effort.

Adding Your Bot to Skype

The time has come to move your bot beyond the boundaries of your own computer. Let's see it live in your favorite channels. As a first step, you need to publish (deploy) your bot at a web-accessible URL. With a valid Azure subscription, it's a matter of a few clicks to publish a Bot Framework application as an app service using Visual Studio.

Publishing Your Bot

Right-click the DrCheckup project in Solution Explorer and select Publish. On the "Pick a publish target" prompt, ensure that the Create New option in Microsoft Azure App Service is selected. Click OK/Next and follow the instructions to create a new app service and deploy your application to it.

Once publishing is complete, take a note of the site URL of your newly created app service. It should be of the form `http://<appname>.azurewebsites.net`.

■ **Tip** You can test the published bot in the emulator. Just put the generated site URL in the address bar, leave the app id and password fields empty, and click Connect. You may require ngrok to be installed to be able to test remote URLs in the emulator.

Registering Your Bot

Follow the steps below to register your bot at the Bot Framework website. This will give you the option to later add the bot to one or all supported channels, including Skype.

1. Head to `dev.botframework.com` and log in with your Microsoft account.

2. Go to the "Register a bot" page. Fill the Bot profile section as desired.

3. In the Configuration section, copy-paste your deployed app service's site URL in the Messaging endpoint field, like this: `https://<appname>.azurewebsites.net/api/messages`.

4. Click "Create Microsoft App ID and password" button. This will open a new tab/window with a newly generated App ID for your bot. On this page, click the Create password button to generate a new password for the above App ID. Securely save your App ID and password in a local text file. Microsoft will not show you the password ever again.

5. Come back to the "Register a bot" page, and fill in the app ID field.

6. Scroll down to the bottom and read the terms of use. Once you are satisfied, check "I agree..." and click the Register button.

At this point, your bot is registered at the Bot Framework's developer portal. But it is not yet published on any channel. Before doing that, go back to Visual Studio. In DrCheckup's `Web.config`, update the `MicrosoftAppId` and `MicrosoftAppPassword` keys in <appSettings> to the values you saved earlier. Use any value for the BotId key, say DrCheckup. These configuration settings are necessary to securely authenticate a bot at the Bot Framework developer portal. Republish the project.

Go back to the Bot Framework website. Open the My bots page and select Dr Checkup. If you scroll down a bit, you will see a list of enabled and other available channels. By default, Skype will be added in the enabled channels list. Leave the settings as is.

Scroll to the top of this page. Click the Test button in the "Test connection to your bot" section. After a few seconds, you should get the message "Endpoint authorization succeeded." If that is not the case, verify that the app ID and password values that you used while registering the bot exactly match the values in bot's `Web.config`.

Now, click the Publish button on the top-right to start the publishing process. Fill out the form very carefully. Think of this step as adding an Android app on Google Play Store. All submitted apps have to go through a formal review by Google. Only apps that pass the review are finally published on Play Store. Similarly, Microsoft reviews all bot submissions to verify that they comply with its terms of use and code of conduct. After filling out all the fields carefully, click the "Submit for review" button. You shall be notified when the review is complete.

Recap

In this chapter, you created a production-quality LUIS application from start to finish using your prior understanding of NLU. You also saw how to integrate LUIS in a bot and publish the bot in a Skype directory.

To recap, you learned about

- Creating a LUIS application

- The building blocks of a LUIS application, such as intents, entities, and phrase lists

- Various entity types in LUIS

- Training and publishing a LUIS application

- Adding LUIS support in a Bot Framework app

- Publishing a bot to one of the supported channels

In the **next chapter**, you will learn about integrating speech capabilities into a .NET application.

CHAPTER 7

■ ■ ■

Interacting with the Speech API

The way we interact with devices these days has changed dramatically. There are lots of new methods coming each day and they are disruptive enough to affect our daily lives. Most of these interactions would have been a wonder a decade ago or earlier. Among these innovations, speech is becoming very popular. One of the interesting things that gives the edge to a voice as a communication medium over anything else is that it's faster and of course more natural. Today, more and more devices have built-in speech recognition and speech synthesis capabilities. In fact, there are a lot of systems already available and in use that utilize these smart systems and interactions. Consider personal digital assistants like Cortana and Siri, which have entirely changed the way we interact with mobile applications. Take another example of smart cars. We have had voice controlled cars for a long time now but what's innovative is the natural interaction. All of this integrated stuff is making systems intelligent and more interactive.

If you have ever thought about creating an accessibility-based application using speech; if you have ever thought about creating speech recognition-based software; if you have ever thought about how hard it is to recognize people's voices; if you have ever thought about talking to a machine and having it talk back to you; or if you have ever thought about how complex it would be to create a hands-free application, then this chapter is going to resolve most of your unanswered queries. Thanks to the ever-evolving world of Cognitive Services, these interactions are quite easy to implement in any application. In fact, you are going to see a couple of interactions of using Microsoft Speech in this chapter. The Microsoft Speech API comes with 20+ years of research on speech.

■ **Note**   Back in 1995, Microsoft's first version of a speech API (also called SAPI) was part of Windows 95. Since then, there has been a tremendous focus on Speech, and various version of Speech have been released with various OS offering flavors of both speech-to-text and text-to-speech capabilities. With the advent of the Speech API in Cognitive Services, Microsoft provides the best speech capabilities available on the cloud and they can be consumed in easy-to-use REST APIs.

Let's understand the various flavors of the Speech API. At the end of the chapter, you will understand how to

- Use the Speech API to recognize speech

- Use the Speech API to have a machine speak

- Use the Speech API to recognize voices

Ways to Interact with Speech

Depending on where you want to host an application and its usage, you have a couple of options of Speech flavors in Visual Studio 2017.

1. If you are using Windows 10 and want to develop an application that is primarily going to be deployed on the Universal Windows Platform, and works in disconnected scenarios, you should primarily use the Speech Recognizer class.

2. If your application requires some other platforms to be used or you would like to deploy it in cloud environment, Microsoft has two options:

    a. Download the Cognitive Speech SDK

    b. Consume the functionality by calling the Cognitive REST API

In order to consume the speech functionality in the client application, you must install the Bing Speech NuGet package. Right-click your project and select the Manage NuGet Packages option, as shown in Figure 7-1.

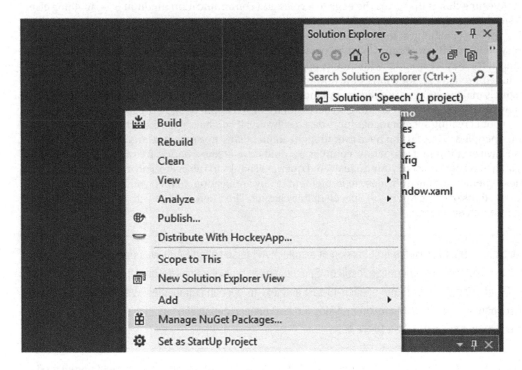

Figure 7-1. *Managing a NuGet package in Visual studio*

In the next window, set the package source to Nuget.org. Search for "Bing speech." You must install the Microsoft.Bing.speech package as shown in Figure 7-2.

Figure 7-2. *The Bing NuGet package found in NuGet Package Manager*

■ **Note** Cognitive Services come from Project Oxford. If you do a search on Oxford speech, you may get a x86 version and a X64 version of the NuGet package. Some developers who play with cognitive speech may be familiar with the Oxford Speech NuGet package. We strongly recommend using `Microsoft.Bing.speech`.

Installing the NuGet package of Speech provides an opportunity to create a speech application using a strongly typed object. Once you choose the project, the entire speech library resides in namespace `Microsoft.Bing.speech`. Accessing the client library is not covered in detail but most of the functionality works similar to the REST API, which we are covering in detail in this chapter.

The Cognitive Search API

The Speech API provides the easiest way to enhance your application with speech-driven scenarios. The Speech API provides ease of use by abstracting all of the complexity of speech algorithms and presents an easy-to-use REST API. Broadly, the functionality of the Speech API can be categorized into three main areas:

- Bing Speech API
  - Speech Recognition: Recognizing speech and converting it to text
  - Speech Synthesis: Converting text into audio
  - Understanding the intent of spoken audio
- Custom Speech Service (previously named CRIS)
  - Custom Language Model
  - Custom Audio Model
  - Deploying the model to an endpoint
- Speaker Recognition

Speech Recognition

Speech recognition, also referred to as speech-to-text, allows you to handle spoken words from your users in your application via a recognition engine and converting it into textual form. This text transcription can eventually be used for a variety of purposes. For example, a great use case for the Speech to Text API is to create an accessibility mobile solution for the deaf so they can read text of what others are saying. In fact, areas of speech recognition can be anywhere you want the user to speak rather than type. Any hands-free application requires speech recognition capabilities. These spoken words can come directly from a microphone, speaker, or even from an audio file. All of this is possible without even typing a single character.

Here's the bitter truth about speech recognition: most of the speech recognition engines across the globe are not 100% correct. However, speech recognition has certainly improved a lot in the recent past. There is still a ways to go to make these recognition engines understand conversational speech. In fact, while we were writing this book, Mark Zuckerberg (CEO of Facebook) was working on creating Jarvis.

> *"Speech recognition systems have improved recently, but no AI system is good enough to understand conversational speech just yet. Speech recognition relies on both listening to what you say and predicting what you will say next, so structured speech is still much easier to understand than unstructured conversation."*
>
> —Mark Zuckerberg

This interesting quote has a lot of meaningful testimony to address, certainly not to make you worry but to bring up a point about speech. Every day new research and inventions are happening in this area, so maybe by the time you read this book, this comment will be incorrect. Fingers crossed!

Getting Started

Cognitive Services does the amazing work of abstracting all internal usage of the algorithm. All calls go through the API, which is hosted on an Azure cloud server, which is supported by a combination of very powerful deep learning and a neural network working behind the scene. In order to consume the Bing Speech REST API, you need to follow these steps:

1. Get the JSON Web Token (JWT) by calling the token service.

2. Put the JWT token in the header and call the Bing Speech API.

3. Parse the text.

Getting the JSON Web Token First

Every call to the API needs to be authenticated before responding back to the user. All requests to the Speech endpoint require access_token to pass as an Authorization header. The first step in order to consume the Speech endpoint is to get your access token. access_token is a JWT token passed as a base 64 string in a speech request header. To obtain the JWT token, a user needs to send a POST message to the token service along with a subscription key, as shown:

```
POST https://api.cognitive.microsoft.com/sts/v1.0/issueToken HTTP/1.1
Host: api.cognitive.microsoft.com
Ocp-Apim-Subscription-Key:••••••••••••••••••••••••••••••••
```

Listing 7-1 shows a way to get a new token in C#. You can reuse the same solution developed in Chapter 2. In the code, you first create an instance of an HTTP client and then add your subscription key as a header before giving a POST call to the token site.

Listing 7-1. Getting a New Token

```
private static string GetFreshToken ()
    {
        using (var client = new HttpClient())
        {
            client.DefaultRequestHeaders.Add("Ocp-Apim-Subscription-Key", ApiKey);

            var response = client.PostAsync("https://api.cognitive.microsoft.com/sts/
            v1.0/issueToken", null).Result;

            return response.Content.ReadAsStringAsync().Result;
        }
    }
```

The token has an expiry period of 10 minutes so your solution needs to ensure that this token gets retrieved and activated every 10 minutes. There are multiple ways to handle this. Listing 7-2 refreshes the current token before it terminates. This strategy will also refresh the present token. It will likewise plan itself to run again before the recently gained token's expires by one minute.

Listing 7-2. Refreshing the Current Token

```
private const int TokenExpiryInSeconds = 600;
private string Token;

private void getValidToken()
    {
        this.token = GetFreshToken();
        this.timer?.Dispose();
        this.timer = new Timer(
            x => this. getValidToken(),
            null,
//Specify that token should run after 9 mins
TimeSpan.FromSeconds(TokenExpiryInSeconds).Subtract(TimeSpan.FromMinutes(1)),
TimeSpan.FromMilliseconds(-1));
// Indicates that this function will only run once
    }
```

You have not added code to get exclusive access to the current token. If you have a multi-threaded application, you may want to lock the token before calling the getValidToken method.

Calls to a token service with the right subscription key will return a JWT token as text/Plain with content type as application/jwt. The JWT token returns can then be used to call a speech endpoint for subsequent calls.

Free tier usage keeps on varying while writing this book; up to 5K transaction calls per month are available free with the caveat of 20 calls per minute. Go to www.microsoft.com/cognitive-services/en-us/subscriptions for more details.

The Consume Speech API

All audio is passed through HTTP POST to a speech endpoint. Once you receive your access token, the second step is to make another POST request to https://speech.platform.bing.com/recognize with additional HTTP query parameters. All of these parameters are described in detail in Table 7-1.

Table 7-1. *Parameters Used to Call the Bing Speech API*

Name	Description
Version	API version used by the client. We have been using API Version 3.0 for most of the requirements, which is the latest.
RequestId	A globally-unique id for an API call. It's a good idea to use a GUID.
appID	Must be D4D52672-91D7-4C74-8AD8-42B1D98141A5.
Format	The format in which you would like to get your data returned. We suggest format=json for most scenarios. You can also opt for other options like XML.
Locale	Language code of the audio being passed. It is case agnostic. There are 28 locales supported, which will increase over a period of time. For most of our demos, we use locale=en-us.
Device.os	Specifies the OS from where the call was made. Options are Window OS, Window Phone OS, Android, iPhone OS, and Xbox.
Instanceid	GUID that uniquely identifies the device making the request

Listing 7-3 shows how to call a speech endpoint with appropriate parameters that take audio, converts it into text, and returns it back to the user.

Listing 7-3. Calling a Speech Endpoint

```
private GUID instanceID;
public async Task<string> GetTextFromAudioAsync(Stream audiostream)
        {
            var requestUri = @"https://speech.platform.bing.com/recognize?scenarios
            =smd&appid=D4D52672-91D7-4C74-8AD8-42B1D98141A5&locale=en-US&device.os=
            WindowsOS&version=3.0&format=json&instanceid=instanceID3&requestid=" + Guid.
            NewGuid();

            using (var client = new HttpClient())
            {
                var token = this.getValidToken();
                client.DefaultRequestHeaders.Add("Authorization", "Bearer " + token);

                using (var binaryContent = new ByteArrayContent(StreamToBytes(audiostream)))
                {
                    binaryContent.Headers.TryAddWithoutValidation("content-type", "audio/
                    wav; codec=\"audio/pcm\"; samplerate=18000");
```

```
var response = await client.PostAsync(requestUri, binaryContent);
var responseString = await response.Content.ReadAsStringAsync();
dynamic data = JsonConvert.DeserializeObject(responseString);
return data.header.name;
        }
    }
```

If you look at this code, the first thing that has been done was to create a URL pointing to a speech endpoint with the necessary parameters. It is important to ensure that each parameter is used only once or you will get an error response of HTTP 400. It is also important to ensure that your subscription key is valid before calling a speech endpoint; if not, you will get an error response of HTTP 403. As mentioned earlier, JWT tokens expire every 10 mins, so it's important to call the getValidToken method created earlier before calling the above method to ensure that your token is valid. Once you've validated a JWT token, it needs to be passed as an authorization header prefixed with the string Bearer. All the audio needs to be converted from analog to a digital version. In an order to convert audio from analog to a digital version for passing to the Speech Recognition API, codecs are used. The Speech Recognition API supports three types of codecs:

- PCM

- Siren

- SirenSR

You should use PCM most of the time unless you need near real-time transcription for scenarios like conferencing, for which you would require the Siren codec. You then call the Speech API, which returns a JSON response. You can use any JSON converter to deserialize it an in .NET object.

Speech Synthesis

Speech synthesis, also known as text-to-speech (TTS) is not a new concept. Machines have been using speech synthesis features in one form or another since the 18th century. TTS allow you to speak words or phrases back to users through a speech synthesis engine. Virtually every Windows machine nowadays has a built-in speech synthesizer that converts text into speech. This built-in synthesizer is especially beneficial for anyone who can't read text printed on the screen. However, since these systems are not constantly upgraded and are dependent on the system's memory, they are better for handling simple to mildly complex scenarios. In order to build enterprise systems, a speech-based model should comply with the following prerequisites:

- Should be easy to use

- Should improve speed over a period of time

- Should be upgraded continuously to be more performant and accurate

- Should be able to compute complex computations

- Should be cost-effective

- Should be uniformly available to all platforms, even low-end mobile devices

The Bing Text to Speech API provides all of these features in an easy-to-consume REST API. By now, you are familiar with consuming the Text to Speech API.

Similar to TTS, Bing Speech to Text has all interactions done through HTTP Post. All requests to text every request to the Text to Speech API require a JWT token. We already covered how to obtain JWT in the previous section. One key thing to understand is that the Bing Text to Speech API supports Speech Synthesis Markup Language (SSML).

■ **Note** In today's world, speech synthesis can be applied in various places through a variety of ways. Looking back at history, most of the big software companies were working on developing speech using proprietary protocols that were tightly coupled with a specific platform. This software succumbs to the problem of speech-related aspects like pronunciation and pitch not being uniformly available. The ability to enable speech-related systems is a crucial need for a large number of organizations. In addition, newly developed applications need to make speech uniformly available to existing platforms, and businesses need to enable uniformity of speech. Back in early 2000s, this was a major issue for all the major software vendors, and they all wanted to use a widely accepted and adopted suite of protocols. To solve this issue, industry leaders such as Microsoft, IBM, BEA, and Sun came up with the W3C specification called Speech Synthesis Markup Language. SSML provide a uniform way of creating speech-based markup text. Check the official spec for the complete SSML syntax at `www.w3.org/TR/speech-synthesis`.

Calling the Text to Speech API is similar to using the Speech to Text API. You first need to get a valid token. For that, you can reuse your `getValidToken()` method. Next, make a POST request to `https://speech.platform.bing.com/synthesize`. You have seen several times in this book how POST and GET requests work in C# using `HttpClient`. For your Text to Speech code example, you will make use of a popular third-party HTTP library called RestSharp. Easy installation of RestSharp in Visual Studio is supported via NuGet. Consider Listing 7-4.

Listing 7-4. Code

```
public byte[] convertTextToSpeech(string ssml)
{
    var token = this.getValidToken();
    var client = new RestClient("https://speech.platform.bing.com/synthesize");
    var request = new RestRequest(Method.POST);
    request.AddHeader("authorization", "Bearer " + token);
    request.AddHeader("x-search-clientid", "8ae9b9546ebb49c98c1b8816b85779a1");
    request.AddHeader("x-search-appid", "1d51d9fa3c1d4aa7bd4421a5d974aff9");
    request.AddHeader("x-microsoft-outputformat", "riff-16khz-16bit-mono-pcm");
    request.AddHeader("user-agent", "MyCoolApp");
    request.AddHeader("content-type", "application/ssml+xml");
    request.AddParameter("application/ssml+xml", ssml, ParameterType.RequestBody);
    IRestResponse response = client.Execute(request);
    return response.RawBytes;
}
```

RestSharp has a neat-looking API to set up HTTP request objects, as you can see above. The request body is a string in SSML format. There are no request params to set. Instead, you set a few headers. A breakdown of possible headers is as follows:

- `Authorization`: *Required*. A valid token generated by the IssueToken API.

- `x-search-appid`: *Optional*. A hyphen-less GUID that uniquely identifies your application.

- `x-search-clientid`: *Optional*. A hyphen-less GUID that uniquely identifies your application per installation.

- x-microsoft-outputformat: *Required.* Format of the output audio file. Can be one of

  - ssml-16khz-16bit-mono-tts

  - raw-16khz-16bit-mono-pcm

  - audio-16khz-16kbps-mono-siren

  - riff-16khz-16kbps-mono-siren

  - riff-16khz-16bit-mono-pcm

  - audio-16khz-128kbitrate-mono-mp3

  - audio-16khz-64kbitrate-mono-mp3

  - audio-16khz-32kbitrate-mono-mp3

- **user-agent**: *Required.* Name of your application.

- **content-type**: *Optional.* The only recommended value is "application/ssml+xml".

The convertTextToSpeech() method returns a byte array of the audio sent back as response by the Text to Speech API. What do you do with the byte array? Let's first see how to call the above method, and what a valid SSML string looks like:

```
string ssml = "<speak version='1.0' xml:lang='en-US'><voice xml:lang='en-US'
xml:gender='Female' name='Microsoft Server Speech Text to Speech Voice (en-US,
ZiraRUS)'>Hello, how may I help you?</voice></speak>";
byte[] TTSAudio = this.convertTextToSpeech(ssml);
SoundPlayer player = new SoundPlayer(new MemoryStream(TTSAudio));
player.PlaySync();
```

The most common use case is to play the audio as soon as it is received in response. The above code will convert the text "Hello, how may I help you?" into speech. SoundPlayer is a built-in .NET class to play audio files and streams. The format of this audio file is determined by the value of the x-microsoft-outputformat header. As SoundPlayer only supports WAV audio files, you use "riff-16khz-16bit-mono-pcm" as the value for the outputformat header.

You can write a separate method to generate valid SSML strings. Listing 7-5 shows one way to generate SSML.

Listing 7-5. Generating SSML

```
private string GenerateSsml(string locale, string gender, string name, string text)
{
    var ssmlDoc = new XDocument(
                        new XElement("speak",
                            new XAttribute("version", "1.0"),
                            new XAttribute(XNamespace.Xml + "lang", "en-US"),
                            new XElement("voice",
                                new XAttribute(XNamespace.Xml + "lang", locale),
                                new XAttribute(XNamespace.Xml + "gender", gender),
                                new XAttribute("name", name),
                                text)));
    return ssmlDoc.ToString();
}
```

text is the text to be converted to speech. gender could be either Female or Male. For a complete list of possible values for locale and name, check the official Text to Speech API reference documentation at https://docs.microsoft.com/en-us/azure/cognitive-services/speech/api-reference-rest/bingvoiceoutput.

Speech Recognition Internals

At a high level, the recognition engine takes audio input or speech from a user's microphone and processes it by trying to match audio signals to patterns in the different databases. These signal patterns are then associated with known words, and if the engine finds a matching pattern in the database, it returns the associated word as text (see Figure 7-3). The speech jargon is covered concisely below:

- Individual sounds in speech are called *phonemes*. Phonemes can also be termed as a unit for a language. For example, the word "Nishith" is made of three phonemes: "Ni," "shi," and "th."

- The process of converting sound waves into phonemes is called *acoustic modeling*. This works like mapping sound waves into one or more phonetic units. As you can see in Figure 7-3, this is the first step in any speech recognition process.

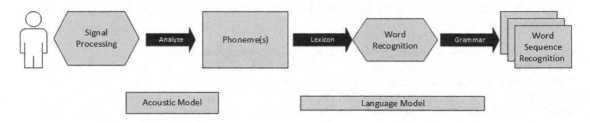

Figure 7-3. *The entire flow of speech recognition*

- A catalog of a language's words is called a *lexicon*.

- A system of rules combining those words into meaningful sentences is called *grammar*.

- The *language model* is a combination of lexicon and grammar. A language model also helps in identifying the right context between words and phrases. This is important as sometimes different words and phrases sound the same. For example, "the stuffy nose" and "the stuff he knows" sound similar but have different meanings.

As you can see, it is important to know the domain and context of that environment. In order for any speech recognition systems to perform well, it needs to be trained well. The Microsoft Speech to Text engine has been trained well with a massive amount of speech training. It is best in class. It works exceedingly well in generic scenarios. However, sometimes you need speech recognition systems in a closed domain or for a specific environment. For example, there is a need for speech recognition in environments with background noise, specific jargon, and diverse accents. Such scenarios mandate customization on both acoustics and the language model in order to get decent performance. This is where the Custom Speech Service comes into the picture.

Custom Speech Service

The Custom Speech Service (CSS), previously known as the Custom Recognition Intelligent Service (CRIS), enables you to customize speech recognition systems by creating custom language models and acoustic models that are specific to your domain, environment, and accents. While writing the book, it was available in public preview. Most of the concepts are unlikely to change, apart from the URLs.

Custom Acoustic Model

Creating a custom acoustic model requires four steps:

- Create a set of audio file(s) of speech data.

- Create a text file containing a transcript of each audio file.

- Upload the audio file(s) and transcripts in the CSS web portal to make acoustic dataset "ready."

- Create a custom acoustic model using an acoustic dataset.

The audio file should be recorded in the same environment and by the same set of people who are going to actually use this custom speech recognition system. This is important because some people have diverse accents. People may be using it in a noisy environment. Background noise is one of the most difficult challenges for modern custom speech recognition systems. Recording the audio in the same environment helps the underlying recognition platform to get familiar with the production environment and be performant as well.

Audio file(s) being uploaded need to follow some underlying rules:

- All audio file must be of the WAV format. This is a limitation of CSS for now. We hope that Microsoft will soon be able to accept audio of other types in future.

- Audio must be encoded with a sampling rate of 8KHz or 16KHz. Most VOIP communication, telephones, and wireless transmission use one of these rates, so it is definitely adequate for human speech.

- Only single channel (mono) is supported.

- Each audio file should not be more than 1 minute. During the very initial days of CRIS, it was 10 seconds. We hope this amount will increase later and can be based on size as well.

- Each file should start and end with at least 1 millisecond of silence.

- All audio file(s) for a specific dataset should have a unique name.

- All audio file(s) should be zipped in single archive file, which should have only audio file(s), no folders/subfolders.

- The file size after zipping shouldn't be more than 2GB.

■ **Tip**   Microsoft Custom Speech Service doesn't provide any recording tools to record the audio. You will need to use some of the existing Windows tools. Personally, we use Audacity (www.audacityteam.org/download/) for recording audio. It can also export the .WAV format. Don't forget to set the channel to mono and the sampling rate as 8KHz for recording as CSS won't provide a detailed description other than mentioning it as "Invalid audio." You are free to use any audio tool given you adhere to the audio prerequisites mentioned above.

Once you have recorded all the audio files with the above rules, the next step is to create a simple text file containing a transcription of all audio files. This transcription file needs to follow some basic rules of writing and normalization:

- There should be just one transcription file for all the .WAV files created.

- Each line in the transcription file should have the name of the audio file with the transcription separated by the tab (/t). For example,

  Audio01.wav This is my first audio file

  Audio02.wav I am excited to use CRIS API

- The text of the transcription should only use the ASCII printable character set.

- Avoid Unicode and replace with its ASCII substitution wherever applied. For example, rather than saying **Nishith's work** (right single quotation mark), it should be **Nishith's work** (apostrophe).

- Abbreviations should be written out in words. For example, Dr. Sanjay should be Doctor Sanjay.

- Words with no alphabet characters should be pronounced. For example, 363, SW should be written as three sixty-three, south west.

Once the audio files and transcription file have been prepared, they can be imported into the Custom Speech Portal. In order to use Custom Speech, you need to go to the CRIS site (`https://cris.ai`). (Since the name of CRIS has been changed to Custom Speech Service, the portal site URL may likely get changed. We advise you to go on the Cognitive Services home page to get the actual URL.) The current home page is shown in Figure 7-4.

Figure 7-4. *The portal page of Custom Speech Service*

If you are accessing it on public preview, you need to click the "Create an account" option that redirects you to the sign-in page. If you have access to the speech portal, you need to sign into the system by clicking the "Sign In" button on the top right side. Once you are logged into the system, you will see the page shown in Figure 7-5.

Figure 7-5. *The Custom Speech Service portal after signing in*

Click the Custom Speech drop-down menu and select Adaptation Data. Since this is your first time on this page, you'll see the empty table named Acoustic Datasets, shown in Figure 7-6.

Datasets

Acoustic Datasets	Import
Language Datasets	Import
Pronunciation Datasets	Import

Figure 7-6. *The Adaptation Datasets page when clicked for the first time*

By default, the locale is set to en-us. While writing this book, Custom Speech Service supports two locales (en-US and Zh-CN). If you choose to change the locale, use the drop-down on the top right. Note that the en-US locale support all three datasets (Acoustic, Language, and Pronunciation) while Zh-CN only supports the Acoustic and Language datasets. This may change over time. To import audio and transcript data, click the Import button next to the Acoustic Datasets. It then validates your subscription key and prompts you to associate it either with a free subscription or connect with any existing subscription, as shown in Figure 7-7.

Subscriptions

No active subscription found.

This is the list of subscription keys you can select for billing. You can have subscriptions to several pricing tiers. The names are your free choice. You can select from them when starting an adaptation or deployment. The associated key will then be used.

Connect existing subscription

You don't have any subscription registered. To start using Custom Speech Service, we can create a free subscription for you. Would you like us to create a free subscription for you now?

Get free subscription

Figure 7-7. *Subscription options to select before importing data*

After validating your subscription key, you are taken to the import page for importing the data, as shown in Figure 7-8.

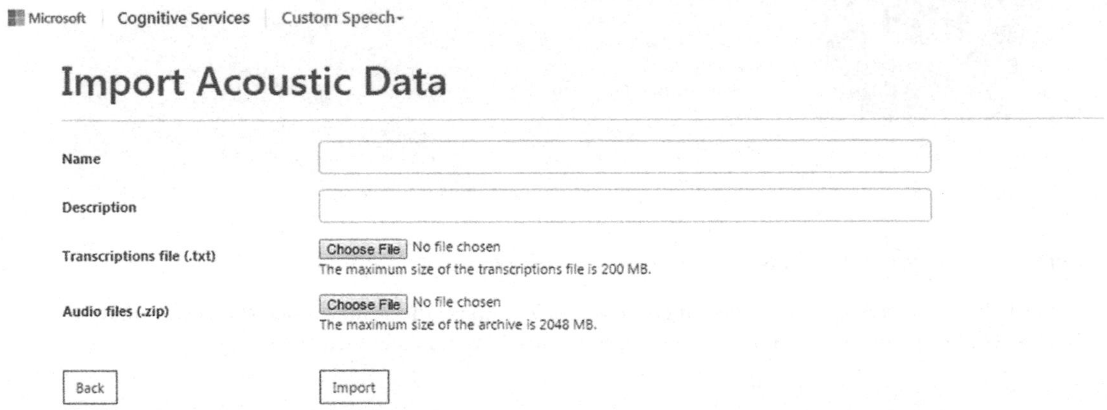

Figure 7-8. *The Import Acoustic Data page*

Enter a name and description. Choose the appropriate transcription file and a zip file containing all the audio by clicking on the Choose file button. Click the Import button to upload your data to the Custom Speech data center. If you have uploaded valid files, you will be redirected back to the Acoustic Dataset table, which now has one entry, as shown in Figure 7-9.

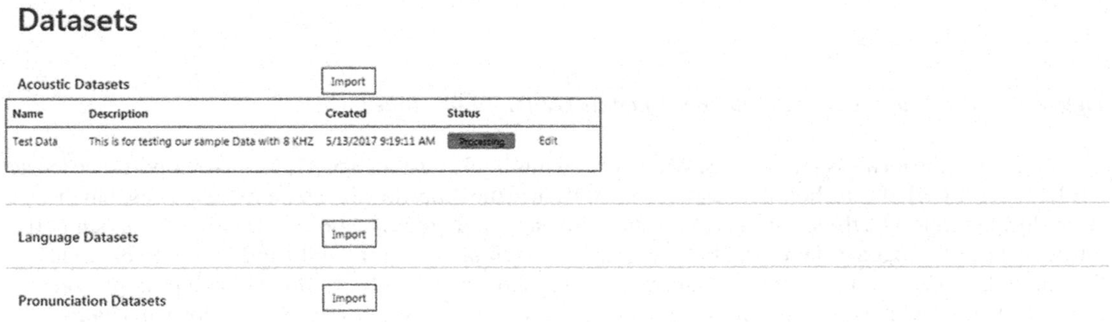

Figure 7-9. *The Datasets page with one entry after importing data*

You can change the name and description of the audio by clicking the Edit link. If you've uploaded a lot of audio, you may get a status of "Waiting" or "Processing". Waiting means you have uploaded the video but it is in the queue for processing. Processing means the Speech Service engine is doing internal validation of the audio and transcription that includes checking the file length, sampling rate, normalization of transcript data, etc. Once the file is uploaded with the proper rules, it will set the status as Complete. Figure 7-10 shows one of the datasets having a status marked as Failed and the other marked as Complete.

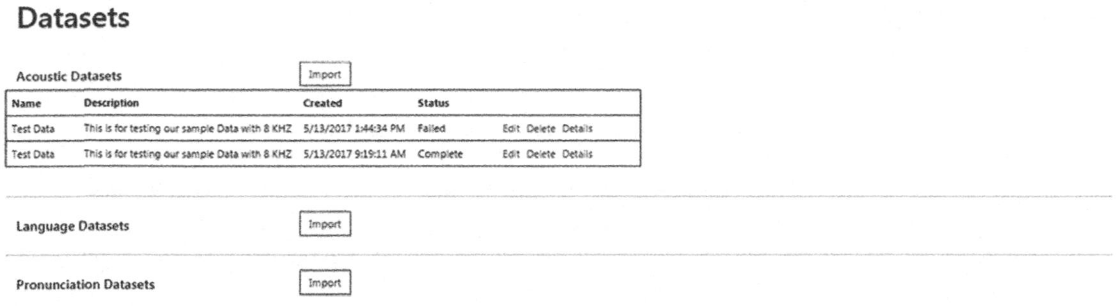

Figure 7-10. *Two records in the Acoustic dataset, one marked as Failed and the other as Complete*

Clicking now on the Details link for the dataset marked as the complete record will show that the utterance of the recording was successful. This means the audio has passed the CSS validation successfully, as shown in Figure 7-11.

Figure 7-11. *The successful utterances of the dataset marked as complete*

You may forget to follow the rules for the audio and transcription files. If both transcription file and the zip file are incorrect and don't follow the rules, you will get the error message "An error occurred while processing your request." This will be accompanied by the exact reason mentioned in the URL of the page and you will end up seeing something like `https://cris.ai/AcousticDatasets/Create?errorMessage=The%20name%20and%20the%20two%20files%20are%20required`. Your dataset status will be marked as Failed, as shown in Figure 7-8. Clicking the Details link will provide you additional context on the number of failed and successful utterances. If the status is marked as Failed, this means that none of the utterances for recording were successful. There can be multiple reasons for failure. The primary reason is that you didn't create the file at 8KHZ. Another potential reason can be that the transcript file didn't follow the rules and as such, you can get an error line by line stating "*The format of this line is incorrect, should be <wavefile><tab><transcription>.*"

In order to create a custom acoustic data model, your acoustic dataset should have the status of Complete. In order to create a custom acoustic model, click Custom Speech and then choose Acoustic model as an option. In order to create any custom acoustic model, you need to use some acoustic model as a base model for customization. Since this is the first time you are accessing this link, you will see two base acoustic models that come with CSS, shown in Figure 7-12.

Acoustic Models

Create New

Base models

Name	Description
Microsoft Conversational Model	Microsoft Conversational Model for recognizing speech spoken in a conversational style (i.e. speech directed at another person).
Microsoft Search and Dictation Model	Microsoft Search and Dictation Model for speech directed to an application, such as commands, search queries or dictation.

Figure 7-12. *Two base predefined acoustic models that come with CSS*

Microsoft Search and Dictation AM-1.1 is the base acoustic model that acts as a starting point for customization most of the time. This model has a REST endpoint of a speech recognition service. This model is more or less the same as the one used in Cortana. The Microsoft Conversational Model is the base model used to recognize conversational speech. You use this model when building any CUI-based application that requires custom speech scenarios. You can't delete these models. You always have an option to create an additional custom acoustic model and use it as the base model for other custom acoustic models. In order to create a new model, click the Create New option shown in Figure 7-12 and you will be redirected to a new screen, shown in Figure 7-13.

Create Acoustic Model

Name	
Description	
Base Acoustic Model	Microsoft Conversational Model ▼
Acoustic Data	Test Data ▼
Subscription	Nishith Pathak ▼
Accuracy Testing	☐

Back		Create

Figure 7-13. *The form to create the new acoustic model*

Enter the name and description. Since this is the first time you are creating an acoustic model, your base acoustic model drop-down should have two options: Microsoft Conversational Model and Microsoft Search and Dictation Model. Once you have created an additional custom model, you can see it listed in this drop-down as well. Select Test Data as the acoustic data set to evaluate the custom model. This was the only dataset with a status of Complete. All your subscriptions are also shown in the Subscription drop-down menu. If you are just part of the free subscription, you will also get an option for Custom Speech Service-Free Subscription.

Click the Create button to create the model. Creating an acoustic model will take about the same time or more as creating your dataset. As soon as you click Create, you will be redirected to the Acoustic Model home page, shown in Figure 7-14. Now you will see three records.

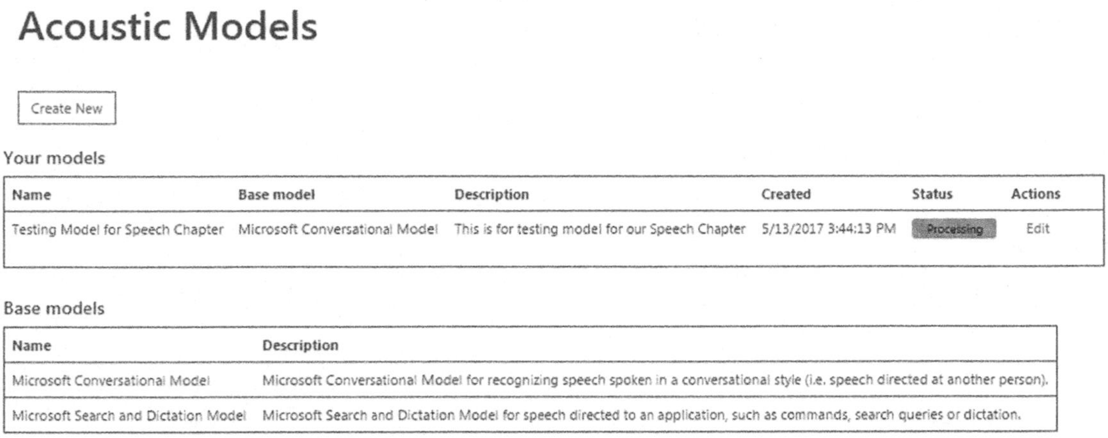

Acoustic Models

Create New

Your models

Name	Base model	Description	Created	Status	Actions
Testing Model for Speech Chapter	Microsoft Conversational Model	This is for testing model for our Speech Chapter	5/13/2017 3:44:13 PM	Processing	Edit

Base models

Name	Description
Microsoft Conversational Model	Microsoft Conversational Model for recognizing speech spoken in a conversational style (i.e. speech directed at another person).
Microsoft Search and Dictation Model	Microsoft Search and Dictation Model for speech directed to an application, such as commands, search queries or dictation.

Figure 7-14. *The creation of new acoustic model*

As you can see, the status is marked as Processing. In fact, if it's in the queue, it should be Waiting. Once the processing is complete, the status is marked as Complete, as shown in Figure 7-15. Click Edit to change the name and description. The View Result option is valid only when you want to view the results of offline testing.

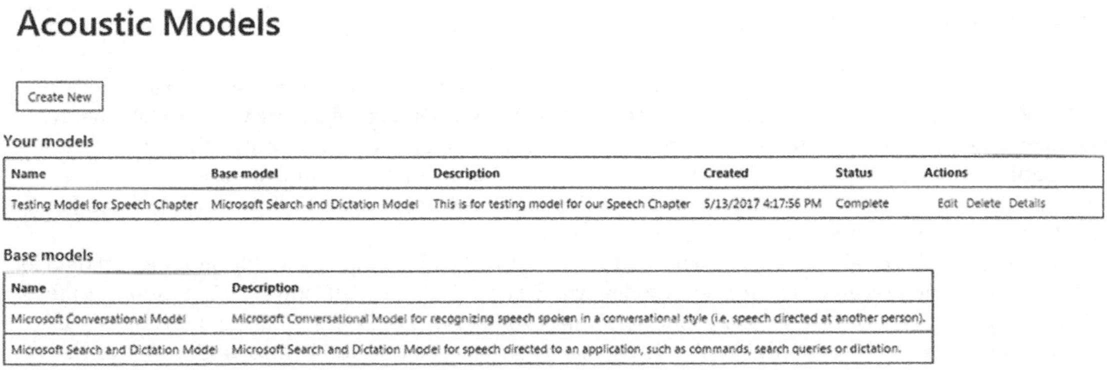

Acoustic Models

Create New

Your models

Name	Base model	Description	Created	Status	Actions
Testing Model for Speech Chapter	Microsoft Search and Dictation Model	This is for testing model for our Speech Chapter	5/13/2017 4:17:56 PM	Complete	Edit Delete Details

Base models

Name	Description
Microsoft Conversational Model	Microsoft Conversational Model for recognizing speech spoken in a conversational style (i.e. speech directed at another person).
Microsoft Search and Dictation Model	Microsoft Search and Dictation Model for speech directed to an application, such as commands, search queries or dictation.

Figure 7-15. *The acoustic model marked as Complete*

Clicking Details will show you the custom acoustic model creation details shown in Figure 7-16.

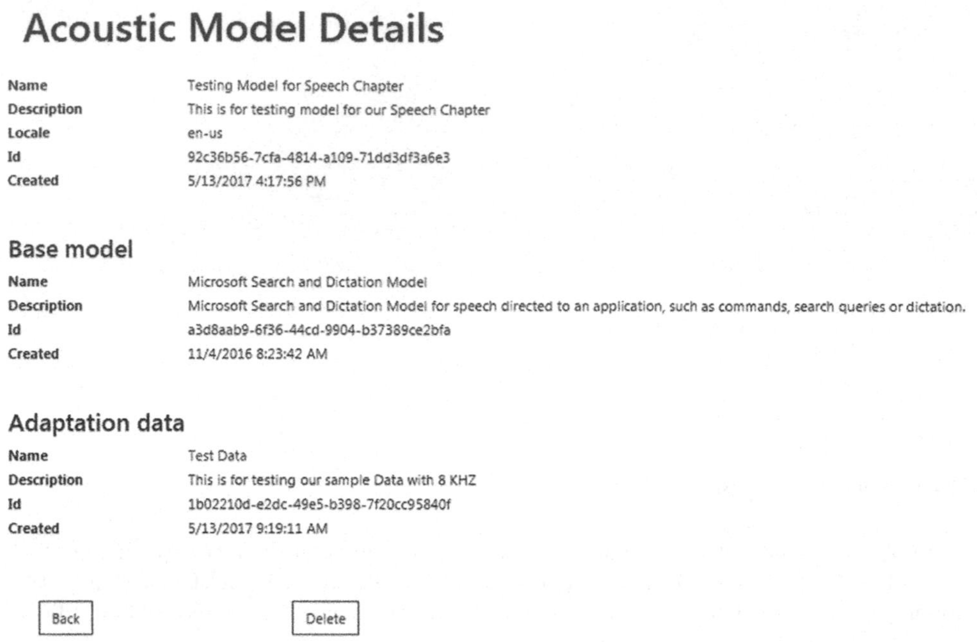

Acoustic Model Details

Name	Testing Model for Speech Chapter
Description	This is for testing model for our Speech Chapter
Locale	en-us
Id	92c36b56-7cfa-4814-a109-71dd3df3a6e3
Created	5/13/2017 4:17:56 PM

Base model

Name	Microsoft Search and Dictation Model
Description	Microsoft Search and Dictation Model for speech directed to an application, such as commands, search queries or dictation.
Id	a3d8aab9-6f36-44cd-9904-b37389ce2bfa
Created	11/4/2016 8:23:42 AM

Adaptation data

Name	Test Data
Description	This is for testing our sample Data with 8 KHZ
Id	1b02210d-e2dc-49e5-b398-7f20cc95840f
Created	5/13/2017 9:19:11 AM

Back   Delete

Figure 7-16. *New acoustic model details*

CSS also lets you test your "new" adaptation model against some test data. If you want to test your model, check the Accuracy Testing checkbox. This gives you the advantage of testing your model directly. You do not need to send data to your new endpoint hosting your adapted model. During the private preview (now public), the Accuracy Testing checkbox was named Offline Testing. I was one of the early feedback providers who suggested a title change from Offline Testing as end user might think of *offline* as *local*. In fact, you always need an internet connection to use Custom Speech.

Checking the Accuracy Testing checkbox requires you to select the language model and the test data for testing. If you haven't created any language models, you will get the Microsoft Universal LM model as the only language model in the drop-down. Microsoft Universal LM is a baseline language model and is used in various other cognitive services as well. You also need to select test data for testing your model, as shown in Figure 7-17. It is important to select different data than that used for creation. This will help in the true testing of your model performance as well. If you have selected the option for offline testing, you might see the status as Testing when the evaluation is being performed.

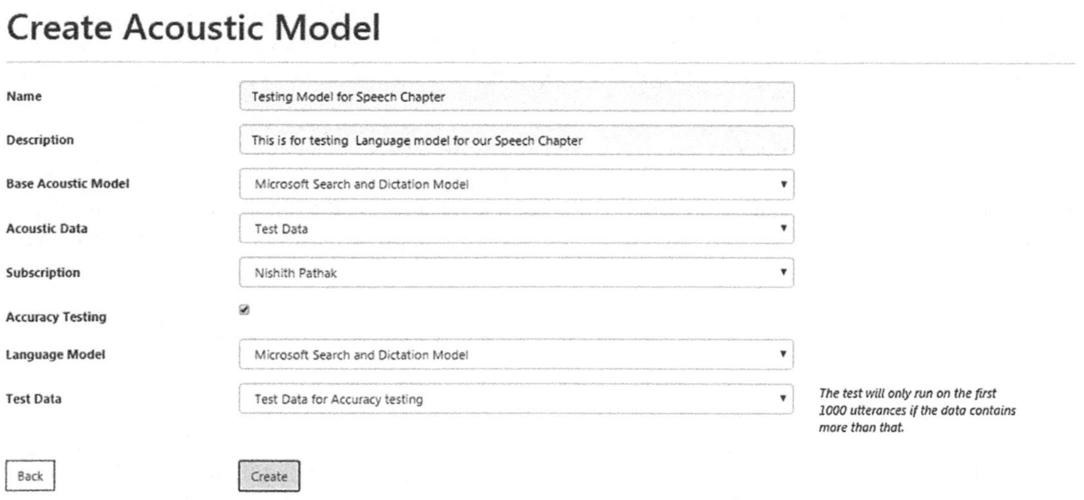

Create Acoustic Model

Name	Testing Model for Speech Chapter
Description	This is for testing Language model for our Speech Chapter
Base Acoustic Model	Microsoft Search and Dictation Model ▾
Acoustic Data	Test Data ▾
Subscription	Nishith Pathak ▾
Accuracy Testing	☑
Language Model	Microsoft Search and Dictation Model ▾
Test Data	Test Data for Accuracy testing ▾

The test will only run on the first 1000 utterances if the data contains more than that.

Back   Create

Figure 7-17. *The acoustic model creation with accuracy testing on*

Once created, you will get additional accuracy test results in the acoustic model details, as shown in Figure 7-18.

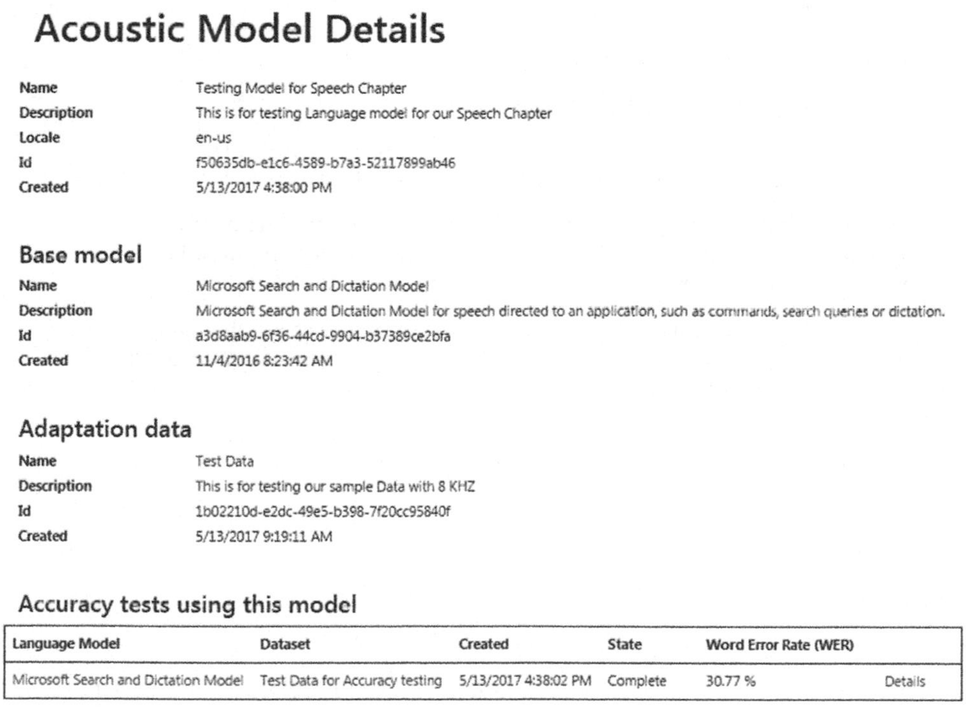

Acoustic Model Details

Name	Testing Model for Speech Chapter
Description	This is for testing Language model for our Speech Chapter
Locale	en-us
Id	f50635db-e1c6-4589-b7a3-52117899ab46
Created	5/13/2017 4:38:00 PM

Base model

Name	Microsoft Search and Dictation Model
Description	Microsoft Search and Dictation Model for speech directed to an application, such as commands, search queries or dictation.
Id	a3d8aab9-6f36-44cd-9904-b37389ce2bfa
Created	11/4/2016 8:23:42 AM

Adaptation data

Name	Test Data
Description	This is for testing our sample Data with 8 KHZ
Id	1b02210d-e2dc-49e5-b398-7f20cc95840f
Created	5/13/2017 9:19:11 AM

Accuracy tests using this model

Language Model	Dataset	Created	State	Word Error Rate (WER)	
Microsoft Search and Dictation Model	Test Data for Accuracy testing	5/13/2017 4:38:02 PM	Complete	30.77 %	Details

Figure 7-18. *Additonal details*

As shown above, the word error rate was 30.77%. Clicking the Details link will show more details about the accuracy tests. You can also see all of the accuracy tests or create new accuracy test by directly choosing Accuracy Tests from the Custom Speech menu at the top-left of the Custom Speech page.

Custom Language Model

As discussed earlier, creating a language model is important to understand the right context of words. For example, think about a phrase like "slow children;" this can be spoken in a variety of ways and have different meanings:

```
Slow, Children.
Slow, Children?
Slow Children!
Slow Children?
```

Depending on the right environment and context, the above words can have different meanings. The Custom Language Model follows a simpler process than creating the custom acoustic model. You no longer need to create audio files; rather you work with only one transcript file. Here are the steps:

- Prepare the language data.

- Upload the language data into the CSS portal to make the language dataset complete.

- Create a custom language model using the language dataset.

Creating a language data file requires you to follow a set of rules:

- Your language model data should be in a plain text file.

- Your language model supports US-ASCII or UTF-8 if you are using the en-US locale. If you are using zn-CN, you need to have the text file in the UTF-8 format.

- Each line in a file should have just one utterance. The reason I call it an utterance and not a sentence is that it should exactly represent actually spoken input rather than being grammatically correct.

- Every line has a default weight of 1. You have an option to give more weight to any line. Weight is an integer number greater than 1. The weight number is equivalent to repeating that line those number of times.

- In order to add any weight, just append the number separated by tab(\t), as shown below. The following example would result in successful acceptance of the language data file:

  This is my first audio file\t5
  I am excited to use CRIS API
  This text is been used a lot here

- The maximum size of the file should not be more than 200MB.

Once your language data is ready, it's time to get it uploaded. Similar to adding an acoustic dataset, click Custom Speech and then select Adaptation Data. Provide an appropriate name and description to identify the language data. Choose the right language data file, as shown in Figure 7-19, and click Import to import your data set.

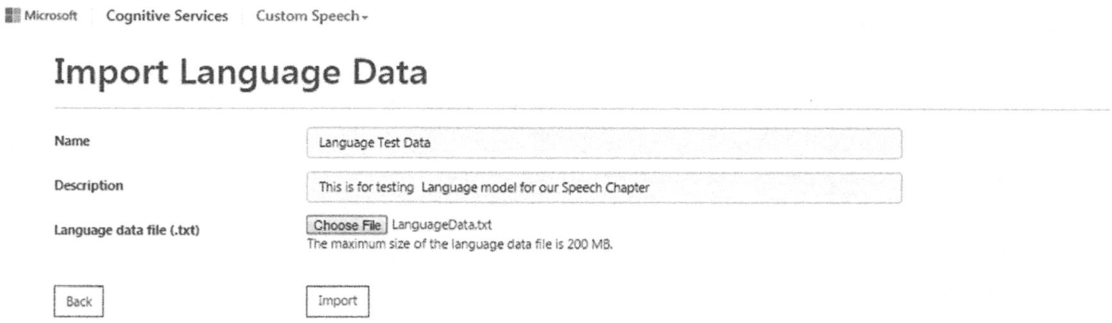

■■ Microsoft　　Cognitive Services　　Custom Speech ▾

Import Language Data

Name	Language Test Data
Description	This is for testing Language model for our Speech Chapter
Language data file (.txt)	[Choose File] LanguageData.txt The maximum size of the language data file is 200 MB.

[Back]　　　　　　　　　[Import]

Figure 7-19. *Importing language data*

You will be redirected back to the language data page and now you will see one record, as shown in
Figure 7-20. Your language data has been assigned a unique ID and has the status of Waiting, Processing,
or Complete. Figure 7-20 shows a status of Complete, which means your language data file has successfully
passed the data validation checks and is now ready to create a custom language model. You can click the
Details link to see a list of successful utterances.

Language Datasets　　　　　　[Import]

Name	Description	Created	Status			
Language Test Data	This is for testing Language model for our Speech Chapter	5/13/2017 5:54:43 PM	Complete	Edit	Delete	Details

Figure 7-20. *A subset of the Dataset page showing a language dataset*

Like your custom acoustic model, in an order to create a custom language data model, your language
dataset should have the status of Complete. Click Custom Speech and then choose Language model to
create a custom language model. Similar to the acoustic model, since this is the first time you are accessing
this link, you will see two records: Microsoft Conversational Model and Microsoft Search and Dictation
Model. These models serve as base models for creating new custom models. You can't delete these models.
You always have an option to create additional custom language model and use it as the base model for
other custom language models. Click Create New to create a new language model.

Like your custom acoustic model, you will now get the screen shown in Figure 7-21 to create a language
model. Enter the name and description to uniquely identify your language model. Choose one of the two
base language models as the base model. Select the language data as the language dataset previously
created. Click Create to create the language model. You also have the option to accuracy test the language
model without accessing the custom endpoint.

Create Language Model

Name	Language Test Data
Description	This is for testing Language model for our Speech Chapter
Base Language Model	Microsoft Search and Dictation Model ▼
Language Data	Language Test Data ▼
Pronunciation Data (optional)	You may want to add pronunciation data to be able to use it in adaptations.
Subscription	Custom Speech Service - Free subscription ▼
Accuracy Testing	☐

Back   Create

Figure 7-21. *The language test model creation page*

You will be redirected to the Language Model home page and will get the additional record. Remember to ensure that you have sufficient data when creating a language model or your language model status will be set as Failure with the reason of "Language dataset doesn't contain enough words to form a language model." If all goes well, you will get the status of Complete, as shown Figure 7-22.

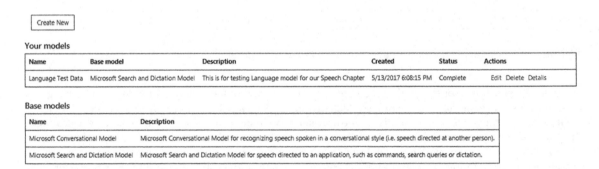

Create New

Your models

Name	Base model	Description	Created	Status	Actions
Language Test Data	Microsoft Search and Dictation Model	This is for testing Language model for our Speech Chapter	5/13/2017 6:08:15 PM	Complete	Edit Delete Details

Base models

Name	Description
Microsoft Conversational Model	Microsoft Conversational Model for recognizing speech spoken in a conversational style (i.e. speech directed at another person).
Microsoft Search and Dictation Model	Microsoft Search and Dictation Model for speech directed to an application, such as commands, search queries or dictation.

Figure 7-22. *The language model page after creating a custom language model*

Pronunciation Data

While creating a custom language model, you also have an option to add a custom pronunciation dataset that can eventually be used to understand new terms or acronyms. In order to create a pronunciation dataset, you need to create a simple text file that should have two columns (Display form and Spoken form), like so:

```
Display form    Spoken form
Cavity          kay vity
Cephalic        see pha lic
Cholesterol     kho les trol
Generic         Jeneric
Xerosis         Zerosis
```

Save the above or a similar file in a .txt file and go to Custom Speech ➤ Adaptation Data and choose the Import button next to the pronunciation dataset. You will get the form shown in Figure 7-23. Enter a name and description and choose the pronunciation data file previously created and click the Import button.

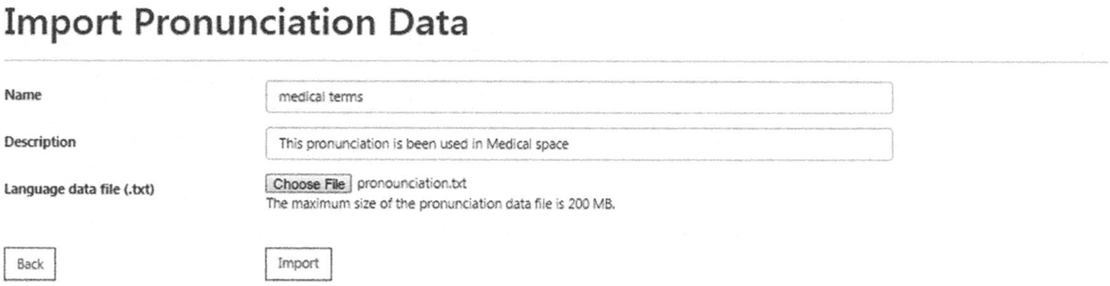

Import Pronunciation Data

Name	medical terms
Description	This pronunciation is been used in Medical space
Language data file (.txt)	Choose File pronounciation.txt The maximum size of the pronunciation data file is 200 MB.

Back   Import

Figure 7-23. *The Import Pronunciation Data page*

If the pronunciation data file is as per the above guidelines, you will be redirected to the acoustic data set home page, where you will see one entry in the pronunciation dataset marked as Complete, as shown in Figure 7-24.

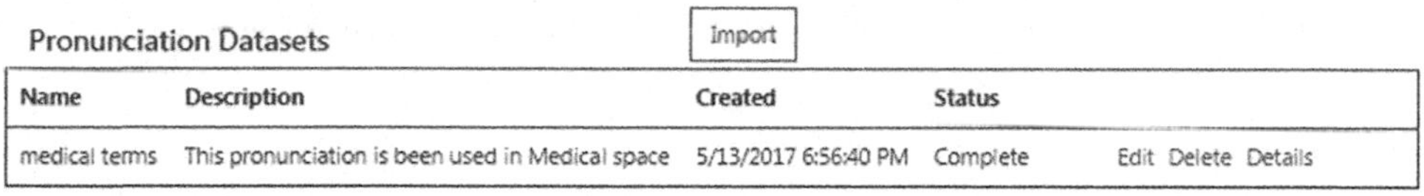

Pronunciation Datasets   Import

Name	Description	Created	Status	
medical terms	This pronunciation is been used in Medical space	5/13/2017 6:56:40 PM	Complete	Edit Delete Details

Figure 7-24. *The pronunciation dataset*

Once you have pronunciation dataset marked as complete, it can then be used in creating language models by specifying it.

Custom Speech-to-Text Endpoint

One of the unique features of the Microsoft Cognitive Speech API is that it allows you to create your own custom speech-to-text endpoint that suits your specific requirements. Once your custom acoustic models and custom language models are ready, you can create custom speech-to-text endpoints using a combination of these newly created custom models with each other or with the base model. In order to create a new custom speech-to-text endpoint, click Deployments under the Custom Speech menu. Click the Create New option to create the new custom endpoint. Enter a name and description to uniquely identify your custom endpoint. Select the base model as Microsoft Search and Dictation Model or Microsoft Conversational Model. Depending on the option chosen, you will get a list of custom acoustic models and language models previously created. You also have an option to use any of the base models, as shown in Figure 7-25. Click Create to create a new endpoint.

Create Deployment

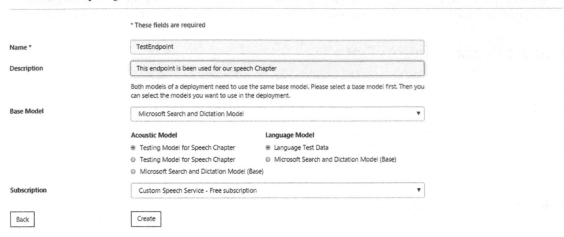

* These fields are required

Name *	TestEndpoint
Description	This endpoint is been used for our speech Chapter

Both models of a deployment need to use the same base model. Please select a base model first. Then you can select the models you want to use in the deployment.

Base Model: Microsoft Search and Dictation Model

Acoustic Model
- ◉ Testing Model for Speech Chapter
- ◎ Testing Model for Speech Chapter
- ◎ Microsoft Search and Dictation Model (Base)

Language Model
- ◉ Language Test Data
- ◎ Microsoft Search and Dictation Model (Base)

Subscription: Custom Speech Service - Free subscription

[Back] [Create]

Figure 7-25. *Creating a custom endpoint for deployment*

You will be redirected to the Deployment page. Like your custom model, you will now have one record in the table that uniquely identifies your deployment. Creating a deployment endpoint takes time. Once your endpoint is ready, your status of deployment should be marked as Complete, as shown in Figure 7-26.

Deployments

[Create New]

Locale	Name	Description	Id	Created	State	Actions	
en-us	TestEndpoint	This endpoint is been used for our speech Chapter	24a8ae1b-ae88-4876-9b14-6dc8b3338d87	5/13/2017 7:16:41 PM	Complete	Delete	Details

Figure 7-26. *List of deployment endpoints*

Clicking the Details link will redirect you to a new page where you can see the URL of the custom endpoint, as shown in Figure 7-27. You will eventually see three URLs. One URL is the HTTP URL, which should be used for HTTP requests. Other two URLs are for web sockets for a short phase mode and a long phase mode. These URLs are primarily used to create a custom application using the Microsoft Cognitive Client Service library, which internally uses web sockets.

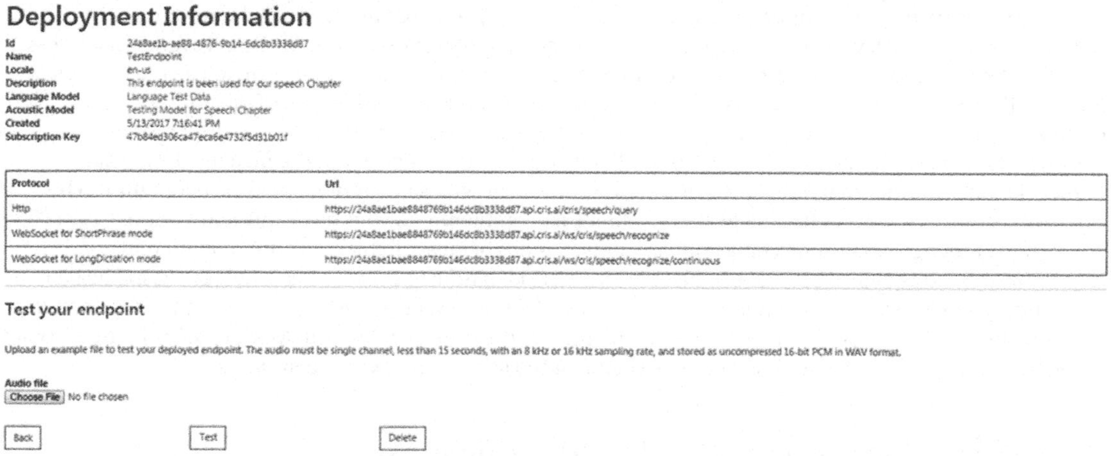

Deployment Information

Id	24a8ae1b-ae88-4876-9b14-6dc8b3338d87
Name	TestEndpoint
Locale	en-us
Description	This endpoint is been used for our speech Chapter
Language Model	Language Test Data
Acoustic Model	Testing Model for Speech Chapter
Created	5/13/2017 7:16:41 PM
Subscription Key	47b84ed306ca47eca6e4732f5d31b01f

Protocol	Url
Http	https://24a8ae1bae8848769b146dc8b3338d87.api.cris.ai/cris/speech/query
WebSocket for ShortPhrase mode	https://24a8ae1bae8848769b146dc8b3338d87.api.cris.ai/ws/cris/speech/recognize
WebSocket for LongDictation mode	https://24a8ae1bae8848769b146dc8b3338d87.api.cris.ai/ws/cris/speech/recognize/continuous

Test your endpoint

Upload an example file to test your deployed endpoint. The audio must be single channel, less than 15 seconds, with an 8 kHz or 16 kHz sampling rate, and stored as uncompressed 16-bit PCM in WAV format.

Audio file
[Choose File] No file chosen

[Back]　　　　　[Test]　　　　　[Delete]

Figure 7-27. *The deployment links of the endpoint*

As of writing the book, there was a limitation in CSS of supporting only two concurrent requests on these custom endpoints. If you scroll down the page, you will see an option to test your endpoint, as shown in Figure 7-28. You have an option to upload an audio file that follows the custom rules of the audio file, as shown in bold. As soon as you select the appropriate audio file and click Test, the custom speech engine will use your newly created custom speech to test an endpoint to recognize the audio uploaded. If the Custom Speech engine recognizes it, you will see it converted into text in the Recognition textbox, as shown in Figure 7-28.

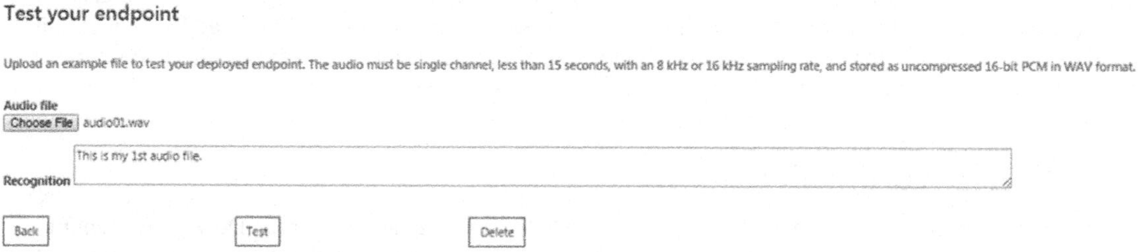

Test your endpoint

Upload an example file to test your deployed endpoint. The audio must be single channel, less than 15 seconds, with an 8 kHz or 16 kHz sampling rate, and stored as uncompressed 16-bit PCM in WAV format.

Audio file
[Choose File] audio01.wav

Recognition | This is my 1st audio file. |

[Back]　　　　　[Test]　　　　　[Delete]

Figure 7-28. *The results of testing an audio file from an endpoint*

Speaker Recognition

Now you understand speech recognition and how it's used. The Speaker Recognition APIs help to identify users and speakers from their voice. Note that there is a clear distinction between *speech recognition* and *speaker recognition*. Speech recognition is the "what" part of speech whereas speaker recognition is the "who" part of speech. In simple terms, speech recognition is the process of working with what has already been said. Speaker recognition is a method to recognize who is speaking. It's also called *voice-based biometrics*.

Any enterprise application requires validating the user. If you are familiar with the traditional ASP.NET-based model, you know terms like *authentication* and *authorization*. Authentication is a process of authenticating the user. The user can present one or more claims to announce himself as the right user. Almost all applications require the user to pass a username and password as one of the authentication mediums. Although this authentication continues to serve as a basic strong authentication model, various additional authentication models have been added to take security to the next level. One such authentication manner that the Microsoft cognitive model provides is through speaker recognition. This security can act as a second form of authentication that complements your basic authentication.

Speaker recognition is not a new concept. In fact, it has been available for more than 40 years. Historically, various algorithms have evolved over a period of time to provide accurate results in speaker recognition. It all started with frequency estimation and discrete vector quantization-based systems. In the last decade, speaker recognition systems were adapted to the Gaussian Mixture Model (GMM). The speaker recognition that Microsoft uses is based on i-Vector-based speaker recognition systems.

Speaker Verification vs. Speaker Identification

The Speaker Recognition APIs help to identify users and speakers from their voice. Using the Speaker Recognition API, you can greatly enhance the customer experience not just by verifying the user but also by helping to identify the user. Let's distinguish between *verification* and *identification*. Verification and identification are now used interchangeably but they are different. Speaker verification, also known as speaker authentication, is a process to verify the claim via one pattern or record in the repository. In speaker verification, an input voice along with a phrase is matched against an enrollment voice and phrase to certify whether they are the same or a different individual. Speaker verification works on 1:1 mapping. In real scenarios, presenting your passport or any digital identity is called authentication.

Speaker identification, on the other hand, is verifying the claim via all possible records in the repository and is primarily used to get the identity of an unknown person from a series of individuals. Speaker identification works on 1:N mapping. Before the Speaker Recognition API is used for verification or identification, it undergoes a process called enrollment. Since speaker identification is 1:N mapping, it requires more time, so speaker verification is faster than speaker identification.

Enrollment-Verification

Every voice has distinctive features that can be used to help recognize an individual. During enrollment, the speaker's voice is recorded and typically a number of features are extracted to form a voice print, such as the tone, pitch, rate, etc. Together, a combination of these features form a voice print or voice model that uniquely identifies an individual voice. As shown in Figure 7-29, the enrollment process requires an iterative approach in which each individual speaks specific phrases three times or more. Each time the user speaks the specific phrase, features are extracted. Together the extracted-features-and-phrase combination forms a unique voiceprint model for that individual. This model is then stored in Voice Print Model repository for further usage of speaker verification or identification.

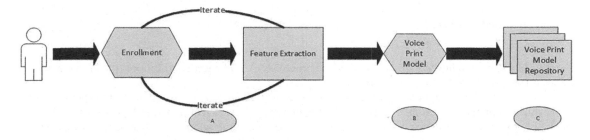

Figure 7-29. *The steps done during the enrollment process*

Enrollment verification is a three-step process:

- Creating a verification profile

- Prompting the user to speak one of the verification phrases and storing the audio

- Calling the enrollment API by passing the profile id (created in Step 1) and audio speech stream (created in Step 2)

Creating a verification profile is a straightforward, easy process. You need to use the HTTP POST API available at

```
https://westus.api.cognitive.microsoft.com/spid/v1.0/verificationProfiles
 by passing in the right locale and subscription key, like so:
```

```
POST https://westus.api.cognitive.microsoft.com/spid/v1.0/verificationProfiles HTTP/1.1
Content-Type: application/json
Host: westus.api.cognitive.microsoft.com
Ocp-Apim-Subscription-Key:••••••••••••••••••••••••••••••••
```

```
{
  "locale":"en-us",
}
```

If you call the API with an invalid subscription key, you will end up with a 401 access denied error with the message *"Access denied due to invalid subscription key. Make sure you are subscribed to an API you are trying to call and provide the right key."* While writing this book, the only locale that was supported was en-us. We do believe this list of supported locales will improve over time. If you call the API with the right subscription key, you will return a GUID called verificationProfileID, as shown:

```
Pragma: no-cache
apim-request-id: c245b8ec-2bfb-48a3-b562-cafb4b01789f
Strict-Transport-Security: max-age=31536000; includeSubDomains; preload
x-content-type-options: nosniff
Cache-Control: no-cache
Date: Sun, 14 May 2017 08:23:31 GMT
X-AspNet-Version: 4.0.30319
X-Powered-By: ASP.NET
Content-Length: 71
Content-Type: application/json; charset=utf-8
Expires: -1
```

```
{
   "verificationProfileId": "05822be0-5c41-4055-9890-6fa9219baaa6"
}
```

This id will eventually be used for creating an enrollment id. While writing this book, the individual subscription can create 1,000 verification profiles at the most.

Once you have created the `verificationProfileID`, the next step is to prompt the user to speak one of the verification phrases and store the audio. Enrollment verification is a text-dependent process. In order to speak phrases, you first need to get the list of all of the supported verification phrases. This can be achieved by calling the API as shown below, passing the right locale and subscription key:

```
GET https://westus.api.cognitive.microsoft.com/spid/v1.0/verificationPhrases?locale=en-US
HTTP/1.1
Host: westus.api.cognitive.microsoft.com
Ocp-Apim-Subscription-Key: ••••••••••••••••••••••••••••••••
```

Calling with the right subscription key and locale will return all of the phrases. As of writing, the following 10 phrases were returned by the API:

```
{ "phrase": "i am going to make him an offer he cannot refuse" },
{ "phrase": "houston we have had a problem" },
{ "phrase": "my voice is my passport verify me" },
{ "phrase": "apple juice tastes funny after toothpaste" },
{ "phrase": "you can get in without your password" },
{ "phrase": "you can activate security system now" },
{ "phrase": "my voice is stronger than passwords" },
{ "phrase": "my password is not your business" },
{ "phrase": "my name is unknown to you" },
{ "phrase": "be yourself everyone else is already taken" }
```

You can choose one of the above phrases, record it at least three times, and store in .WAV file. Let's call this an enrollment audio file for future reference. Each recording should be between 1-15 seconds long and should be PCM-encoded with a 16KHz rate and mono channel. Once you have recorded as per the above rules, you are all set to call the Verification Enrollment API by passing the recorded speech and `verificationProfileID` created in Step 1 to enroll the user. Enrollment of the user can be done by calling the API like so:

```
POST https://westus.api.cognitive.microsoft.com/spid/v1.0/verificationProfiles/05822be0-
5c41-4055-9890-6fa9219baaa6/enroll HTTP/1.1
Content-Type: multipart/form-data
Host: westus.api.cognitive.microsoft.com

[BinaryData]
```

As shown above, the `verificationProfileID` previously created is passed as a query parameter while the enrollment audio file is passed in the request body.

- Calling it with an invalid `verificationProfileID` will return 401 Access Denied.

- Calling it with a valid `verificationProfileID` and the wrong audio file will return Error 400 Bad request with the message *"Invalid Audio Format: Not a WAVE file - no RIFF header."*

- Calling with a valid `verificationProfileID` and the proper audio file will return a JSON response with the following fields:

  - `enrollmentStatus`: Specifies the enrollment status. It can be Enrolling, Training, and Enrolled.

  - `EnrollmentCounts`: Specifies speaker verification enrollment counts

  - `remainingEnrollments`: Specifies number of required enrollments

  - `Phrase`: Recognizes the phrase used in the enrollment audio file

If the speaker has been successfully enrolled by calling this enrollment API at least three times, the `enrollmentStatus` will be set as Enrolled. Once the `enrollmentStatus` is set as Enrolled, it can be used in verification scenarios. If the speaker has just called it once, the status return will be Enrolling, `EnrollmentCounts` will be set as 1, and `remainingEnrollments` should be set to 2.

Speaker Verification

Speaker verification is a text-dependent process. This means the same phrase is used for enrollment and verification. The verification process is similar to the enrollment process. You should use the same verification phrase that you recorded for enrollment. Like the enrollment process, you should call the API with the recorded speech and `verificationProfileID` as follows:

```
POST https://westus.api.cognitive.microsoft.com/spid/v1.0/verify?verificationProfileId={veri
ficationProfileId} HTTP/1.1
Content-Type: application/octet-stream
Host: westus.api.cognitive.microsoft.com
```

```
[BinaryData]
```

It will return a JSON response with following details:

- Result: Specifies whether verification was accepted or rejected

- Confidence: Shares the confidence level of the result. It can be Low, Normal, or High.

```
{
  "result" : "Accept",
  "confidence" : "Normal",
  "phrase": "my voice is my passport verify me"
}
```

The result has two options: Accept or Reject. Accept means that the verification has been accepted. Reject means that the verification has been rejected. Confidence specifies the confidence level of the verification; it can be Low, Normal, or High. It is very important to rely on a combination of results and confidence scores. If a result is marked as Accept with a low confidence score, you may want to train it more. The confidence score should at least be Normal or High. In the above example, the result was accepted with a Normal confidence score, which is ok to proceed further.

Enrollment–Identification

Similar to the enrollment–verification first step, the user first needs to create an identification profile. URLs for calling enrolment-identification are different from enrollment-verification. Creating an identification profile is a straightforward, easy process. You need to get the HTTP POST API available at https:// westus.api. cognitive.microsoft.com/spid/v1.0/verificationProfiles by passing the right locale and subscription key. As of writing, the identification profile supports an additional locale of Chinese Mandarin (zn-CN).

```
POST https://westus.api.cognitive.microsoft.com/spid/v1.0/identificationProfiles HTTP/1.1
Content-Type: application/json
Host: westus.api.cognitive.microsoft.com
Ocp-Apim-Subscription-Key: ••••••••••••••••••••••••••••••••

{
  "locale":"en-us",
}
```

If you call the API with the right subscription key and locale, the API will return a GUID called IdentificationProfileID. This ID uniquely identifies the speaker and will be used later to create an enrollment identification ID and then identify the speaker from group of speakers.

Speaker identification is a text-independent system. This means the user can use any text for a speech sample in enrollment and verification. This is the reason why, unlike enrollment-verification, enrollment-identification is a two-step process. There is no restriction on what the users speaks in the audio, so the step of getting all phrases is not required.

As shown below, the IdentificationProfileID is passed as a query parameter and the enrollment audio file is passed in the request body. Each recording should be between 5 seconds and 5 minutes long, and should be PCM-encoded with the 16KHz rate. After removing the silence, the minimum recommended stored speech for enrollment is about 30 seconds. You have an option to set ShortAudio to true/false depending on the length of audio you would like to submit. It instructs the service to waive the recommended amount of audio limit needed for enrollment and accordingly the profile's enrollment status is changed from Enrolling to Enrolled. When doing so you can send audio files starting at 1 second long but no longer than 5 minutes. Enrollment for identification of the user can be done by calling the API at

```
https:// westus.api.cognitive.microsoft.com/spid/v1.0/identificationProfiles/
{identificationProfileId}/enroll[?shortAudio]
Content-Type: multipart/form-data
Host: westus.api.cognitive.microsoft.com
```

```
[BinaryData]
```

- Calling it with an invalid IdentificationProfileID will return 401 Access Denied.

- Calling it with a valid IdentificationProfileID and the wrong audio file will return Error 400 Bad request with the message *"Invalid Audio Format: Not a WAVE file - no RIFF header."*

- You will get an error 500 if any error happens in the enrollment with a message of *"SpeakerInvalid."*

- Calling with a valid IdentificationProfileID and a proper audio file will return a JSON response with the following fields:

  - Accepted: Service has successfully accepted the request.

  - Operation URL: Used to retrieve result status later with the Operation API.

Speaker Recognition-Identification

As mentioned earlier, speaker recognition-identification helps you recognize and identify an individual from a group of speakers. Once you have registered all the speakers and have an Accepted response for all of them, you can recognize one of the speakers from a group by calling the Speaker Recognition-Identification API as follows:

```
https:// westus.api.cognitive.microsoft.com/spid/v1.0/identify?identificationProfileIds=
{identificationProfileIds}[&shortAudio]
Content-Type: multipart/form-data
Host: westus.api.cognitive.microsoft.com

[BinaryData]
```

As shown above, you need to pass all identification profiles (created earlier) as comma-separated values. Similar to enrollment-identification, you need to pass audio in the body and set the optional shortAudio field to true/false depending on the audio length. You will get the result returned with operationalURL, which you can use to track operation status.

Operation Status

Now you understand how to create identification profiles. There will be times when you will want to check the exact status of the operation. For example, you may want to check the status of the operation or enrollment status of the speaker identification profile a later time. You may want to check whether the enrollment has succeeded or is still in training mode. Microsoft Speaker Recognition makes it very easy to handle any operation task; all of this can be done by a single call to operation URL:

```
GET https://westus.api.cognitive.microsoft.com/spid/v1.0/operations/{operationID} HTTP/1.1
Host: westus.api.cognitive.microsoft.com
```

Calling the above API with the right operationID and subscription key will return a JSON response. The operationID mentioned here is available either by calling create enrollment for an identification profile or by speaker recognition-identification, which we will cover later. The following code shows the JSON response if the enrollment status is successful:

```
{
"status": "succeeded",// [notstarted|running|failed|succeeded]
  "createdDateTime":   "2017-01-13T01:28:23Z",
  "lastActionDateTime": "2017-01-15T01:37:23Z",
  "processingResult":
  {
    "enrollmentStatus" : "Enrolled", // [Enrolled|Enrolling|Training]
    "remainingEnrollmentSpeechTime" : 0.0,
    "speechTime" : 0.0,
    "enrollmentSpeechTime":0.0
  }
}
```

Once you get the JSON response, you need to first check the status. It can be one of the following:

- Not Started

- Running

- Failed

- Succeeded

If the status is Succeeded, look at the processing result JSON object as shown above. If the status is anything other than Succeeded, you may need to check the other field options. For example, if the status is Failed, check the message field to see the reason for the failure. There are other operational tasks that you can do as well; see Table 7-2 for some information.

Table 7-2. *Other Operational Tasks*

API Name	Description
Delete Profile	DELETE https:// westus.api.cognitive.microsoft.com/spid/v1.0/ identificationProfiles/{identificationProfileId}
	Deletes all speaker identification profiles along with all associated enrollment permanently from the service.
Get All Profiles	GET https:// westus.api.cognitive.microsoft.com/spid/v1.0/ identificationProfiles
	Gets all speaker identification profiles within a subscription. It will return JSON response all identification profile within a subscription with additional details like enrollment status, locale, number of seconds used for identification, number of seconds remaining for successful enrolment, etc.
Get Specific Profile	GET https:// westus.api.cognitive.microsoft.com/spid/v1.0/ identificationProfiles/{identificationProfileId}
	Passes the URL with specific identification profile id to give you the speaker identification profile associated with the id. You call this API to get the enrollment status of the identification profile.
Delete All Enrollments	POST https:// westus.api.cognitive.microsoft.com/spid/v1.0/ identificationProfiles/{identificationProfileId}/reset
	Deletes all enrollments associated with the given speaker identification profile permanently from the service.

Summary

In this chapter, you learned how to use the Bing Speech API to get speech-to-text and text-to-speech functionality. This chapter also covered in detail the need for the Custom Speech Service (previously known as CRIS). At the end of the chapter, you also explored the Speaker Recognition API and learned how to use it to do speaker identification, verification, and enrollment. The next chapter will take you on the amazing journey of using Bing Search and other various flavors of search.

CHAPTER 8

■ ■ ■

Applying Search Offerings

Imagine a life without search engines. Every time you need an answer, you automatically go to sites like Google and Bing. Over last decade or so, search has come a long way. Gone are the days when search results were restricted to picking data from a database. With the increasing amount of data getting generated every second and new algorithms getting invented, search has moved beyond the text box. Search has moved from the era of postback to partial postbacks to even now auto-suggest. Search has also moved from just giving textual results and links to images and now videos, news, and contextual search. Search has also moved from reactive to proactive. Search has also moved from generalized search to a personalized experience. Google has certainly provided a new dimension to the entire search engine. From knowing the weather for the coming weekend to a cricket score to the latest news, videos, or anything else you want to know, your first stop has been Google for the last decade or so.

You may wonder why are we discussing Google search when the topic is Microsoft Cognitive Search. Well, Google is a giant in the search arena. Comparing competitors to Google regarding search might raise some goose bumps for many of you. Google is an impressively great company, having the finest team of data scientist and engineers working for them. However, Microsoft has certainly made great progress in search by bringing Bing to the platform. Microsoft Search, which is based on Bing, provides an alternative option to Google. One of the missions of the Bing Search API is to go against the Google monopoly and provide an alternative. Bing is currently the second most powerful search engine after Google. Have you ever thought of implementing the capabilities of Google or Microsoft Bing in your enterprise application? In this chapter, you will learn about new offerings from Bing Search. At the end of this chapter, you will have learned following about Search:

- History and evolution of Microsoft Bing

- How Bing is as a competitor to Google

- The three Ps of Search

- The offerings from Bing Search

- How to leverage Bing Search offerings in your application

Search Is Everywhere

Search is everywhere. We use search from our desktops and mobiles. We use web search to do routine stuff in our daily lives. With new connected devices emerging every day, the need for smarter search has become increasing important. In a latest report, 50 billion connected devices are expected to be available by the end of 2020 and each of them requires a connected search. Search has certainly become an integral part of choosing our favorite applications as well. Think about online shopping. You probably go often to Amazon.

© Nishith Pathak 2017
N. Pathak, *Artificial Intelligence for .NET: Speech, Language, and Search*, DOI 10.1007/978-1-4842-2949-1_8

com, not just because it offers so many products but because a search on Amazon is very elegant compared to its competitors. This is exactly the same reason why Stackoverflow.com has been one of the go-to sites for a search on technical queries. Search is broadly classified into two types:

- Explicit search
- Implicit search

An explicit search is when you type something in the search box and get the results. An implicit search is an advanced form of search in which an application implicitly makes the proactive and predictive search for you. For example, whenever you select any product on Amazon, you also get a list of products similar to the selected product. You also get a list of products that other users navigated to when they browsed the selected product; see Figure 8-1. This means sometimes search is more proactive and doesn't require you to do a specific search.

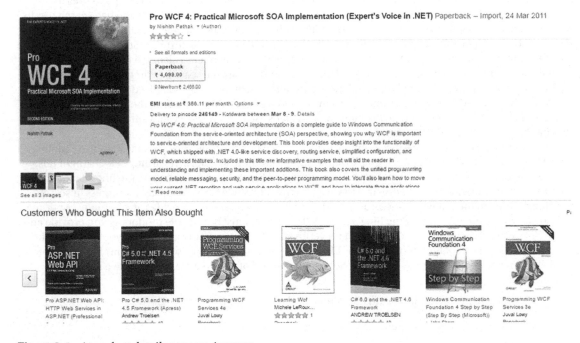

Figure 8-1. *A product details page on Amazon*

Almost all enterprise and social applications have one thing in common and it is search. Imagine a few years back when you typed in a search text box and your ASP.NET applications did some postback (maybe partial) to return some results. Search is made up of three aspects:

1. Pervasive (everywhere on any device)
2. Predictive
3. Proactive

Pervasive, Predictive, Proactive (The Three Ps of Search)

Technology is increasingly available to everyone, anytime, anywhere, and on any device. You have access to the Internet through a phone. Your phone is never more than a couple of feet away from you. It is interesting that most of us check our phones a couple of hundred times in a day. Search needs to be available anywhere, anytime, and on any device.

Predictive is the process through which a system can anticipate what's going to happen in future. This can happen by integrating search with more data. Predictive is very close to proactive; in fact, it works hand-in-hand. If we are able to predict, it helps us to do it proactively. *Proactive* means using search to provide answers before the question is asked or even thought of. Searches on these enterprise applications have given more dimensions to the search.

Wouldn't it would be great if we got recommendations and implicit searches in our search engines like Google or Bing. As of now, Google doesn't have any way to do an implicit search in its search engine other than providing autosuggest data based on historic data. Google search is primarily based on contextual search, so your search data is dependent on what you have searched for in the past.

Now let's consider Bing. If you are using Bing in Windows 10 or above, open the cognitive home page, select computer vision text, right-click, and choose "ask Cortana," as shown in Figure 8-2.

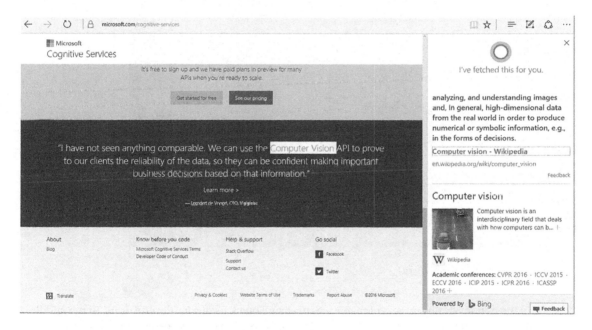

Figure 8-2. *The info Cortana shows upon selecting text in the Edge browser*

The results show you not only the definition but all information related to the academic conference, courses, people, etc. This is a classic example of a predictive and proactive search in Microsoft Bing. So now you know one of the easy tricks available in Bing. Now try this in Google. You need to open Google, type the search keyword, and get these results in various search links. Isn't the implicit, proactive search better? Microsoft wants to ensure that Bing search moves ahead in the direction of being more predictive and pervasive.

■ **Note**   Cortana is a search intelligence and digital assistant that helps you get your tasks done in Windows. It started with Windows 10 but now is available from various devices like phone, tablets, and Windows machines. In the future, you will see Cortana integrated with other smarter devices like HoloLens, Xbox, etc., which will ensure that Cortana as an intelligence search tool will be available everywhere. This is a classic example of search being pervasive.

History of Bing

We believe that best way to understand any technology is to know its origin. Let's understand the *why* of Bing first. Microsoft has been dominant in creating GUI-based OSes for the past two/three decades. During the late 1990s Microsoft released its first search engine called MSN Search, as shown in Figure 8-3. MSN Search initially started by getting results from other companies like Inktomi and AltaVista before it started using Microsoft's own search engine. During this tenure, Microsoft was still relying on third parties to return image results.

Figure 8-3. *The MSN Search (beta)*

One of the notions during this era of search was to ensure quick results for the end users. In the middle of 2006, Microsoft made a major leap in search by replacing its version of MSN Search with Windows Live Search. This allowed Search to be part of Windows Live. Windows Live Search provided additional options like news search, music, and desktop search, to name a few. One radical change that Windows Live Search brought was to use an in-house Microsoft search engine and algorithms to return the results. There were major radical changes in moving some of the Microsoft Live offerings.

Microsoft realized that search was going to be one of the emerging markets for the next decade. However, in spite of providing so many offerings, Microsoft Live Search was way behind the likes of Google and Yahoo. In fact, Microsoft's share of search was steadily declining during this time. After a lot of discussions, meetings, and branding research, Microsoft removed the word "live" from Search and then came up with a new brand name: Bing (see Figure 8-4).

Figure 8-4. *Initial Bing logo*

2009 was a cornerstone year for Microsoft in terms of search. Not only did it release Bing, but it also signed up for a ten-year deal with Yahoo to replace the Yahoo search engine with Bing on the Yahoo site. Since the adoption of the name "Bing," Microsoft search has not looked back and has started to provide more offerings.

■ **Note** During the search for a new name, various names were discussed. Out of those, Bang was the closest competitor to Bing. Bing was chosen as the final name because the name was small, one syllable, and easy to spell and recognize.

Microsoft's early mission was to have desktop computers in every home. Recently Microsoft revised its mission to one of *"empowering every person and every organization on the planet to achieve more."* This mission is more human-centric. This mission has a lot of caveats to provide a lot of services anywhere and everywhere. Bringing the Bing Search API to common people and making some of the services available in terms of RESTful APIs is one of the ways to achieve the new Microsoft mission. Now that you understand some of the history behind Bing, let's look at some of the unique features of Bing Search.

What's So Unique About Bing?

Bing is currently the web search engine from Microsoft. Certainly, for some Microsoft geeks, Bing is more than the search bar. There are certainly features of Bing that make it quite unique. Although this chapter is more focused on the Cognitive API, sharing these features are important because this can help you understand some of the Bing APIs that Microsoft may release in the future.

Both Bing and Google offer contextual search but there are some unique features of Bing as well. For example, Bing allows the user to see video previews before the user actually clicks on the video. This can save time by ensuring that the user opens the right video. In order to see it, simply hover over the video on the videos search in Bing. Quite often we search on popular personalities and want to know their history. Bing offers a unique feature of a timeline for these famous people. Bing also offers rewards. For now, this is only available to some regions along with the US. If you happened to be part of this region, don't forget to visit Bing.com/rewards for rewards on your Bing searches. You can also save bookmarks on Bing by visiting Bing.com/saves. One of the areas where Bing excels over Google is the extensive Cognitive APIs for end users.

Search APIs

The Bing Search APIs are one of the five pillars of Cognitive Services exposed by Microsoft. The Bing Search APIs help you leverage some of the searching power of Bing. They are

- Bing Autosuggest API
- Bing Image Search API
- Bing News Search API

- Bing Video Search API

- Bing Web Search API

Let's take a deep dive into each of these APIs now.

Bing Autosuggest API

The Bing Autosuggest API helps the user to type less and accomplish more. As the name suggests, the Autosuggest API provides your application's search with intelligent type-ahead and search suggestions, directly from Bing Search, when a user is parallel typing inside the search box. You typically access this API when you want to enable autosuggest in the search textbox of your application. As a user types in the search text box, your application calls the API to show some list of options for the user to select. The user has the option to select the option as well. Figure 8-5 shows different autosuggest options based on what the user typed in the text box. In an ideal scenario, you would be calling the Autosuggest API as a user typed in each character in the search box. Based on each character entered, the Bing Autosuggest API would bring up different relevant search results. Internally, this is achieved by passing a partial search query to Bing and getting results. This result is a combination of contextual search with what other users have searched in the past.

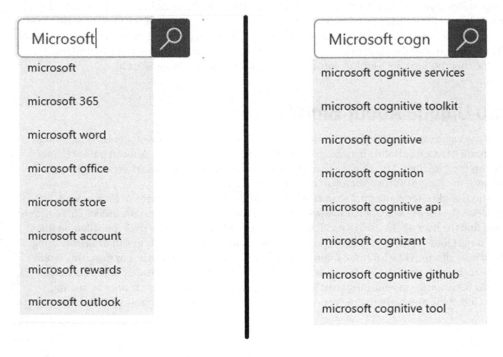

Figure 8-5. *Different results based on what the user types*

How to Consume the Bing Autosuggest API

All Bing APIs require a subscription key before consuming the access. For now, we will assume you have a subscription key handy. If you have directly jumped to this chapter or want to know the steps for creating a subscription key, refer to Chapter 2.

Consuming the Bing Autosuggest API is an easy process; you need to call a GET request to `https://api.cognitive.microsoft.com/Bing/v5.0/suggestions`, passing the search query as a parameter and the subscription key in the header with the header as `Ocp-Apim-Subscription-Key`. For example, if you want to search for Microsoft, your query should show something like this:

```
GET https://api.cognitive.microsoft.com/bing/v5.0/suggestions/?q=Microsoft HTTP/1.1
Host: api.cognitive.microsoft.com
Ocp-Apim-Subscription-Key: ••••••••••••••••••••••••••••••
```

Note that the above URL uses HTTPS. HTTP calls are certainly not supported for any of the cognitive service calls. Also, look at the version provided in the URL. While writing this book, the latest version of the Autosuggest API is V5.0. It is important to know that Microsoft will keep on releasing new versions of these APIs. Microsoft certainly reserves the right to break changes on V6.0 or later, so be sure of what version you are consuming. Having said that, Microsoft will support existing version of the API, so if you happened to grab the book after V7.0 has been released, you can still call and consume V5.0 API without any breaking changes. Also note that the search keyword is passed through parameter q.

Assuming your subscription key is correct, you will get a JSON response. The following code shows the subset of the JSON response received on searching the keyword Microsoft:

```
{
  "_type": "Suggestions",
  "queryContext": {
    "originalQuery": "microsoft"
  },
  "suggestionGroups": [
    {
      "name": "Web",
      "searchSuggestions": [
        {
          "url": "https://www.bing.com/cr?IG=D267DC92EC52478D86A10652DCDE2015&CID=297FEC8A4
          2866B4712E1E6F743636A98&rd=1&h=VmqXfTXdctZsDb12vh_sGN9LXP9iKyoAWgw5oqUAf60&v=1&r=
          https%3a%2f%2fwww.bing.com%2fsearch%3fq%3dmicrosoft%2baccount%26FORM%3dUSBAPI&p=
          DevEx,5003.1",
          "displayText": "microsoft account",
          "query": "microsoft account",
          "searchKind": "WebSearch"
        },
        {
          "url": "https://www.bing.com/cr?IG=D267DC92EC52478D86A10652DCDE2015&CID=29
          7FEC8A42866B4712E1E6F743636A98&rd=1&h=oEkAB-ob-fIDhkOiJU7ekQdYucx-voM5hWz_
          ZtijbFQ&v=1&r=https%3a%2f%2fwww.bing.com%2fsearch%3fq%3dmicrosoft%26FORM%3dUSBAPI
          &p=DevEx,5004.1",
          "displayText": "microsoft",
          "query": "microsoft",
          "searchKind": "WebSearch"
        },
```

```
{
    "url": "https://www.bing.com/cr?IG=D267DC92EC52478D86A10652DCDE2015&CID=297F
    EC8A42866B4712E1E6F743636A98&rd=1&h=l_OyDf4fwfCsVS6TzqIT1Vz-IX8Z15JKxJF3YVL-
    z48&v=1&r=https%3a%2f%2fwww.bing.com%2fsearch%3fq%3dmicrosoft%2b365%26FORM%3dUSBA
    PI&p=DevEx,5005.1",
    "displayText": "microsoft 365",
    "query": "microsoft 365",
    "searchKind": "WebSearch"
}
```

If you observe the JSON result, each of the search suggestions is an object that doesn't just contain the search result but also a URL. Typically, you take the result as is and show these search results as hyperlinks. Clicking any of the display text will redirect you to the actual Bing search with this keyword. Also note that the entire search suggestions are grouped under an object called SearchSuggestions. At the top, you see the queryContext object, which stores the query string that Bing used for the search. Let's explore how you can make your search results more relevant by adding some optional parameters and headers.

1. mkt is the query parameter that you would ideally be using most of the time. It represents the market from where results will come. You represent the market as a language code (hyphen) followed by a country code. A classic example is en-US. The market code is case insensitive. Use this parameter if your results are pointing to a specific country and a single language. There is a predefined list of market codes available for Bing. To learn more about it, go online because more codes keep getting added all the time. If the mkt parameter mentioned does not match the defined list of market codes or if the results for that market are not available, Bing intelligently returns the closest match and specifies the market being used in the response header BingAPIs-Market. You should review this header in the return result to ensure that the results are accurate. Figure 8-6 shows different results returned on the same keyword. On your left are the results for market en-us. On right side are results for market ja-jp.

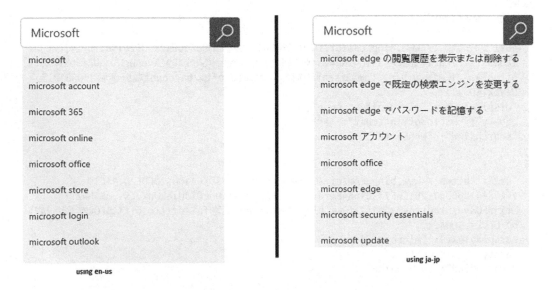

Figure 8-6. Different results in different markets with the same keywords

2. cc is query parameter that represents a two-character country code. Use this parameter to represent results coming from a specific country. Don't get it confused with the mkt parameter. In fact, cc and mkt are mutually exclusive. You should use the mkt parameter if you are working with a country and single language. If a single country has multiple languages, then you should use the cc parameter. Pass the list of languages as comma-separated values in the Accept-Language header parameter. Be specific in the order of preference of the language; the list should be in decreasing order.

3. The setLang query parameter usually works with the mkt parameter to specify the language. Typically you should set the language with the different language specified in the mkt parameter when you want your page UI to be displayed in a different language.

4. There are times when the request may be correct but doesn't return the result. If that's the case, the response from Bing will contain BingAPI-traceID, which contains the log entry of the request. Send this trace id to the Bing contact support team to get additional details.

5. Retry-After shows up in the response header only when someone exceeded the number of queries allowed per second (QPS) or per month (QPM). This is numeric and contains the number of seconds the user needs to wait before sending another request.

6. You can use user-Agent as a request header to tell Bing about the device and OS from which you are sending the request. This will allow Bing to understand the request resource and to optimize results.

7. By default, any request to Bing API is treated as unique, even if you pass it with same subscription key. While Bing sends the response, it generates new client id. This has sometimes led the user to a different experience on subsequent calls or results coming from Bing. Bing allows the user to pass the same client id during a request to understand that it's coming from the same person. You can pass the client id by adding it with a header as X-MSEdge-ClientID. The only time you should not pass the client id is on the first request, when Bing generates a unique id. Subsequent calls should pass the client id generated in the first response to Bing.

■ **Tip** Some of the headers and parameters are common to most of the Bing Cognitive API. It is important for you to get a grasp on this. We won't be going into a deep dive, but you should always point to these parameters.

---

8. There are a lot of scenarios wherein you want to get content local to the place being searched. Bing allows you to pass on an IP address of the client device, which can be used to identify the location. Bing then returns the response with relevant local content. In order to send an IP address, use the optional response header X-Search-ClientIP. If you don't have the IP address but do have a geolocation, you can pass geolocation as key-value pair through header X-Search-Location.

■ **Note** If you happen to use a lot of autosuggest, you will start noticing the difference between Google and Bing. As of the writing of this book, Microsoft Bing supports eight autosuggest options compared to four options supported by Google

---

Like all other cognitive services, the Microsoft Autosuggest API also has the free and paid tiers. At the time of writing, the free tier allows 10K calls per month and is available for three months. The paid tier has three plans: S1, S2, and S3. S1, S2, and S3 allow 10K, 100K, and 1M calls per month, respectively. S1 is available with a minimal cost of $3 and has no overage charges. S2 is available for $30, and S3 is available for $270 per month. Both of them have an overage charge of $30 for an additional 100K transactions.

The Bing Image Search API

Image search has been very prevalent over the last decade or more. The Bing Image Search API provides developers an opportunity to get a similar experience as Bing.com/images into their application. One thing to note here is you should only use the Bing Image Search API when the returns are just images. The Bing Image Search API not only provide an option to get image-based search results but also provides various options in terms of passing query parameters as well as through the header to customize the results as per your needs. One of the reasons for the popularity of image-based search nowadays is that it's more expressive in nature and thereby more effective. One can visualize the results easily by looking at image content rather than textual content. Figure 8-7 shows a sample demonstration of image results returned from the same keyword but different parameters.

Image based search on keyword Cute Animal

Image based search on keyword Cute Animal with Image type as Line

Figure 8-7. *Different image results with same query but different parameters*

How to Consume the Bing Image Search API

Similar to the Bing Autosuggest API, in order to consume the Bing Image Search API, you send a GET request to https://api.cognitive.microsoft.com/Bing/v5.0/images/search, passing a keyword to get image insights as a query parameter q and a subscription key in the header with header key as Ocp-Apim-Subscription-Key. For example, if you want to get images for Microsoft, your generalized query should look like the following:

```
POST https://api.cognitive.microsoft.com/bing/v5.0/images/search?q=Microsoft HTTP/1.1
Host: api.cognitive.microsoft.com
Ocp-Apim-Subscription-Key: ••••••••••••••••••••••••••••••
```

Similar to Autosuggest, note the URL using HTTPS and the version of V5.0. The parameter on which the query needs to be searched is also same. The only difference is in the URL being called. If the subscription key is correct, a call similar to above will end with the following JSON response subset:

```
{
  "_type": "Images",
  "instrumentation": {
    "pageLoadPingUrl": "https://www.bingapis.com/api/ping/pageload?IG=2662ED1019ED4D41990A8A
    C61216DB7E&CID=28C0E7D43623671417E9EDA937C66659&Type=Event.CPT&DATA=0"
  },
  "readLink": "https://api.cognitive.microsoft.com/api/v5/images/search?q=Microsoft",
  "webSearchUrl": "https://www.bing.com/cr?IG=2662ED1019ED4D41990A8AC61216DB7E&CID=28C0E7D43
  623671417E9EDA937C66659&rd=1&h=sfoMVpg6zTfPpJcZkSlNz-bTguuGOuLuDscR5I iHjNc&v-1&r=https%3a%
  2f%2fwww.bing.com%2fimages%2fsearch%3fq%3dMicrosoft%26FORM%3dOIIARP&p=DevEx,5245.1",
  "totalEstimatedMatches": 926,
  "value": [
    {
      "name": "Microsoft - Stretch",
      "webSearchUrl": "https://www.bing.com/cr?IG=2662ED1019ED4D41990A8AC61216DB7F&CID
      =28C0E7D43623671417E9EDA937C66659&rd=1&h=iniLs-zQ90gF1Mx35V-3tPiQh-6x2qK90ka3Qi_
      AkRE&v=1&r=https%3a%2f%2fwww.bing.com%2fimages%2fsearch%3fview%3ddetailv2%26FORM%
      3dOIIRPO%26q%3dMicrosoft%26id%3dDA06857EE5270F0FA81C85FC6A432E3F1F7FD020%26simid%
      3d608003027952795739&p=DevEx,5006.1",
      "thumbnailUrl": "https://tse3.mm.bing.net/th?id=OIP.4gTvU2SEGrWNTzuaOoa_
      nQEsCb&pid=Api",
      "datePublished": "2017-04-08T03:34:00",
      "contentUrl": "http://www.bing.com/cr?IG=2662ED1019ED4D41990A8AC61216DB7E&CID=28C0E7
      D43623671417E9EDA937C66659&rd=1&h=PPUkxm_E77Odpe1mCL2fURxcgvAfrFB6aUbZq9Zy3uc&v=1&r=
      http%3a%2f%2fwww.stretch.se%2fwp-content%2fuploads%2f2014%2f03%2fmicrosoft-logo-NYA.
      jpg&p=DevEx,5008.1",
      "hostPageUrl": "http://www.bing.com/cr?IG=2662ED1019ED4D41990A8AC61216DB7E&CID=2
      8C0E7D43623671417E9EDA937C66659&rd=1&h=_gC_9Zf6pOBB4P1CqByS7Vjss-hnVGyZSf1sXeSh-
      HU&v=1&r=http%3a%2f%2fwww.stretch.nu%2fpartners%2fmicrosoft-3%2f&p=DevEx,5007.1",
      "contentSize": "29128 B",
      "encodingFormat": "jpeg",
      "hostPageDisplayUrl": "www.stretch.nu/partners/microsoft-3",
      "width": 1242,
      "height": 643,
      "thumbnail": {
        "width": 300,
```

```
      "height": 155
    },
    "imageInsightsToken": "ccid_4gTvU2SE*mid_DA06857EE5270F0FA81C85FC6A432E3E1E7FD020*sim
    id_608003027952795739",
    "insightsSourcesSummary": {
      "shoppingSourcesCount": 0,
      "recipeSourcesCount": 0
    },
    "imageId": "DA06857EE5270F0FA81C85FC6A432E3E1E7FD020",
    "accentColor": "CB9200"
  },
  {
    "name": "All Logos: Microsoft Logo",
    "webSearchUrl": "https://www.bing.com/cr?IG=2662ED1019ED4D41990A8AC61216DB7E&CID=28C0
    E7D43623671417E9EDA937C66659&rd=1&h=_1rpMWtcxKVUrOMEAuXyC8ZRefIfVDWdPvwt8JnrwaO&v=1&r
    =https%3a%2f%2fwww.bing.com%2fimages%2fsearch%3fview%3ddetailv2%26FORM%3dOIIRPO%26q%3
    dMicrosoft%26id%3d0BD9C219266D3C08C71B244E90DB86EA1AE2675D%26simid%3d608001382978096-
    683&p=DevEx,5012.1",
    "thumbnailUrl": "https://tse1.mm.bing.net/th?id=OIP.JdXWz-
    9R1LRCPBVmGjFtvwEsDh&pid=Api",
    "datePublished": "2014-06-02T20:55:00",
    "contentUrl": "http://www.bing.com/cr?IG=2662ED1019ED4D41990A8AC61216DB7E&CID=28
    C0E7D43623671417E9EDA937C66659&rd=1&h=dOmMvwOwoksCSWQdMnQi6CqVOuHsVBej2UHj8JB4-
    pQ&v=1&r=http%3a%2f%2f1.bp.blogspot.com%2f-goOyfq407Hg%2fURx8Dz6asmI%2fAAAAAAAAAUw%2fT
    yaM8lhH-DY%2fs1600%2fNew-Microsoft-Logo-PPT-Backgrounds.jpg&p=DevEx,5014.1",
    "hostPageUrl": "http://www.bing.com/cr?IG=2662ED1019ED4D41990A8AC61216DB7E&CID=28C0E7D
    43623671417E9EDA937C66659&rd=1&h=zdMBhSwmMJmtYEP6txoc6PwR2qeQsJBXvOooRxAbqvM&v=1&r=htt
    p%3a%2f%2falllogos7.blogspot.com%2f2013%2f02%2fmicrosoft-logo.html&p=DevEx,5013.1",
    "contentSize": "78238 B",
    "encodingFormat": "jpeg",
    "hostPageDisplayUrl": "alllogos7.blogspot.com/2013/02/microsoft-logo.html",
    "width": 1600,
    "height": 1200,
    "thumbnail": {
      "width": 300,
      "height": 225
    },
    "imageInsightsToken": "ccid_JdXWz+9R*mid_0BD9C219266D3C08C71B244E90DB86EA1AE2675D*
    simid_608001382978096683",
    "insightsSourcesSummary": {
      "shoppingSourcesCount": 0,
      "recipeSourcesCount": 0
    },
```

Let's dig a little bit deeper to understand some key items in the JSON response. The JSON result is contained in an object called Images. Apart from containing the image response, it also contains one vital field called totalEstimateMatches, which, as the name suggests, is a count of all images relevant to the query being searched.

Another object to look at in the JSON response is the image object, as it contains all information about the particular image. Let's look at some of the important properties of the image object that you would use in your application. See Table 8-1.

Table 8-1. *Fields of the image Object*

Name	Description
Imageid	Uniquely identifies the image
imageInsightsToken	Use this token if you need additional information about the image not provided in the default response such as the shopping source. You need to take this id and pass it to the insightstoken query parameter
contentSize	Specifies the file size of the image. You may find it useful to filter the response based on the size of the image.
insightsSourcesSummary	Shows the number of sources where you can do actions like shopping count. This would be used in a B2C application. For example, if you got an image of a bag, this will show you a list of sites that offer a similar bag.
thumbnailUrl	URL of a thumbnail image
Thumbnail	Width and height of the thumbnail image
Height	Height of the source image in pixels
Width	Width of the source image in pixels
encodingFormat	Image type of an image such as png
contentUrl	URL of the image on the source site
datePublished	Date and time when Bing discovered it
hostPageUrl	Contains the URL of the page that hosts the image

Having a good understanding of a JSON response is important to ensure that results can be filtered before showing on the front end. You can play around with these fields once you get the response. The Bing Image API also provides a filter query parameter that allows you to filter and get response results for only those images that satisfy the criteria. Some of the parameters, like cc, mkt, q, setlang, and id, have been covered as part of the Autosuggest API but are applicable to Image Search. We are not going into their details since we covered them earlier, but it is important for you to know that these parameters can be applied to the Image Search API as well. Let's understand some of the new filter parameters for proactive filtering; see Table 8-2.

Table 8-2. *Filtered Query Parameters*

Name	Description
Count	Number of images that get returned in response.
moduleRequested	Provides additional insights on image requests that are available by default. For example, you can add a shoppingSources module to get a list of all traders that offer the product shown in an image. The moduleRequested info should be passed as comma-separated values.
Offset	Specifies the number of images to skip to return the result. This is best used in conjunction with a count for a pagination request.
SafeSearch	As the name suggests, it is used to filter adult content images. Options supported are Off, Strict, and Moderate. Strict does not return any adult images. Off returns images with adult content. The default is Moderate, which does not return adult content but will return adult content in the Search API with the thumbnail being vague.
Aspect	You can filter images by aspect ratio using this filter. The options are Square, Tall, Wide, and All. All is the default, which means no aspect ratio is specified.
Color	Use this option to filter images by color. Twelve main colors are supported, plus the option of monochrome, which just return black and white images.
Freshness	Use this option if you want images to get filtered based on when Bing discovered those images. The options are Day, Week, and Month.
Height	Filter images based on a height.
Width	Filter images based on a width.
imageType	If you want to filter images based on image type. The options are AnimatedGIF, Clipart, Line, Photo, or Shopping.
License	Used to filter images based on the license applied. This one is a personal favorite for us; we used this to get unlicensed images that can be referenced in our books and publication.
Size	Use this to filter image by size. Options included are Small, Medium, Large, Wallpaper, and All. These options are based on pixels. For example, Small returns images that are less than 200x200 pixels.

The Bing Image API also provides an option to get deep insights for the specific image. In that case, you need to pass a POST request to https://api.cognitive.microsoft.com/Bing/v5.0/images/search, passing the image sent in the POST Body. Image insights are used when you need more information, such as captions that are machine generated, getting an image of a similar type, etc.

Apart from getting insights of an image and getting images based on a certain filter, Bing can also search currently trending images based on searches made by other users. To get the trending image search, you need to call the GET API at https://api.cognitive.microsoft.com/Bing/v5.0/images/trending, like so:

```
GET https://api.cognitive.microsoft.com/bing/v5.0/images/trending HTTP/1.1
Host: api.cognitive.microsoft.com
Ocp-Apim-Subscription-Key: ••••••••••••••••••••••••••••••••
```

Once you call the API, you will get the following JSON response:

```json
{
  "_type": "TrendingImages",
  "instrumentation": {
    "pageLoadPingUrl": "https://www.bingapis.com/api/ping/pageload?IG=524A0BEF27844894B8CDA1
    900FA3A6C1&CID=39A93253FBFC66811D0F382EFA1967FC&Type=Event.CPT&DATA=0"
  },
  "categories": [
    {
      "title": "Popular people searches",
      "tiles": [
        {
          "query": {
            "text": "Nicki Minaj",
            "displayText": "Nicki Minaj",
            "webSearchUrl": "https://www.bing.com/cr?IG=524A0BEF27844894B8CDA1900FA3A6C1&CID
            =39A93253FBFC66811D0F382EFA1967FC&rid=1&h=hgzU1-YGXx61W8XxJcBbdmSRH_XABJ028PovVG6
            i118&v=1&r=https%3a%2f%2fwww.bing.com%2fimages%2fsearch%3fq%3dNicki%2bMinaj%26FO
            RM%3dISTRTH%26id%3dE9B866C2A8AE6043DAE307D0490386AA278BB419%26cat%3dPopular%2520
            people%2520searches%26lpversion%3d&p=DevEx,5000.1"
          },
          "image": {
            "thumbnailUrl": "https://tse3.mm.bing.net/th?id=OET.796b8441539c4ad0af4875cf911
            eb824&pid=Api",
            "contentUrl": "http://ime.ulximg.com/image/300x300/artist/1330095247_6dc51f
            bfeddedd01d0e78650d286e2f0.png/ce576f26cc31f554fa906b8ba115802e/1330095247_
            nickiminaj2.png",
            "thumbnail": {
              "width": 300,
              "height": 300
            },
            "imageId": "E9B866C2A8AE6043DAE307D0490386AA278BB419"
          }
        },
```

One interesting thing about the above JSON response is that the search has been divided into various categories, like a popular people search, popular animal search, popular nature search, etc.

Interestingly, Bing not only does a search on the text specified but it also smartly suggests options to narrow down the original search. For example, if you search for the keyword "Microsoft search," Bing smartly breaks this into various options like "Microsoft Desktop search," "Microsoft Windows Search," and "Microsoft search 4.0". You have an option to choose one of the query expansions and get search results. This same experience can also be had with Bing.com/images, as shown in Figure 8-8.

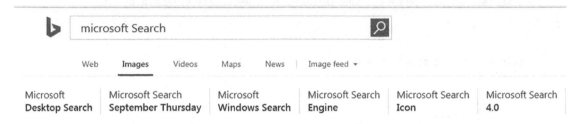

Figure 8-8. *Query expansion of Microsoft search*

Similarly, Bing also tends to break the original query into various segments called pivots to show what other users searched. This is particularly useful in giving suggestion to the user. Overall, the Bing Search API provides an extensive set of properties and query parameters to get customized image search.

The Bing Image Search API has both a free and paid tier. The free tier subscription allows you to make 1,000 calls per month and is free for three months. In terms of paid tier subscriptions, Bing Image API has seven standard plans from S1 to S6. Depending on the volume, you can opt for S1, for 1000 searches per month, to S6, which allows 10M calls per month. Apart from S1, the other standard paid versions incur overage expenses.

Bing News Search API

Bing also acts as a news aggregator that aggregates, consolidates, and categorizes news from thousands of newspapers and news articles across the world. This feature is available through Bing.com/news. The Bing News Search API offers a comparable experience so you can create a news aggregator in your application. At a high level, the Bing News Search API allows you to get top news articles/headlines based on a specific category, returns news articles based on a user's search, or allows news topics to be returned that are trending on a social network. Let's take a deep dive into the Bing News Search API now. As with the other two APIs discussed earlier, you need to call

https://api.cognitive.microsoft.com/Bing/v5.0/news/ via a GET request, passing a subscription key in the Ocp-Apim-Subscription-key header as shown:

```
GET https://api.cognitive.microsoft.com/bing/v5.0/news/search HTTP/1.1
Host: api.cognitive.microsoft.com
Ocp-Apim-Subscription-Key: •••••••••••••••••••••••••••••••
```

Unlike the Autosuggest and Image Search APIs, you can call the Bing News API by passing any parameter and it will return a top news articles in each category. You can see a subset of the JSON response returned when calling the News API without any parameter. By default, the response will include up to 12 headline articles and up to 4 articles per news category. You always have the option to use the headlineCount query parameter to change the number of headline articles to be returned.

```
{
  "_type": "News",
  "readLink": "https://api.cognitive.microsoft.com/api/v5/news/search?q=",
  "value": [
    {
      "name": "Kapil Mishra to lodge FIR , hand over 'evidences' against Kejriwal to CBI",
      "url": "http://www.bing.com/cr?IG=67AEC659B7A646BC95C49DF8347532E5&CID=3C649CB66ABA67
        FE16BF96CB6B5F6610&rd=1&h=Q_PKXZziVhM9IhE50ocONWr3e2OWBebE1RWOSuuFxxg&v=1&r=http%3a%
        2f%2ftimesofindia.indiatimes.com%2findia%2fin-letter-to-guru-kapil-mishra-says-will-
        file-an-fir-against-kejriwal%2farticleshow%2f58587624.cms&p=DevEx,5006.1",
      "image": {
        "thumbnail": {
          "contentUrl": "https://www.bing.com/th?id=ON.4B95481C9E5C3BB13058E8D39DB3BFCA&pid
            =News",
          "width": 700,
          "height": 525
        }
      },
      "description": "NEW DELHI: The war within AAP intensified on Tuesday with sacked Delhi
        minister Kapil Mishra meeting CBI officials to file FIR against Arvind Kejriwal. Kapil
        Mishra will also handed over three packets of \"evidences\" against Kejriwal to the
        CBI officials.",
      "about": [
        {
          "readLink": "https://api.cognitive.microsoft.com/api/v5/entities/03ee339a-5811-
            c624-d751-de0c2b8aaa9f",
          "name": "Kapil Mishra"
        },
        {
          "readLink": "https://api.cognitive.microsoft.com/api/v5/entities/54ac3847-14fa-
            4877-bbea-8428099abf2d",
          "name": "School of International Relations, University of Economics in Prague"
        },
        {
          "readLink": "https://api.cognitive.microsoft.com/api/v5/entities/a00227e3-ffd7-
            b1d1-b5e1-0d69bafbfa37",
          "name": "India News"
        }
      ],
      "provider": [
        {
          "_type": "Organization",
          "name": "Times of India"
        }
      ],
      "datePublished": "2017-05-09T07:31:00",
      "category": "Politics",
      "headline": true
    },
```

Let's first understand the JSON response. Table 8-3 shows some of the fields that you would use in a news article.

Table 8-3. *Fields of the Article Object*

Name	Description
Name	Name of the article
Headline	A Boolean value that tells whether news is a headline or not
Category	Specifies the category to which the news item belongs
Id	Uniquely identifies the news article
Image	Contains all images from this news article. It just contains thumbnail fields.
Description	Contains a brief description of the news article
Provider	List of organizations that ran the article
Date published	Date and time when Bing discovered it
clusteredArticle	List of news articles of similar type
URL	URL of the article

By default, news returns are of the generic market and might not be relevant. In order to get appropriate and effective news response, we encourage you to use the mkt parameter to specify the market. The following URL will return top headlines news from India:

https://api.cognitive.microsoft.com/Bing/v5.0/news/?mkt=en-in

One of the parameters you will often use is category. Bing provides a list of categories based on each market. Almost all news items are under some category or other. The following URL will return sports-related news for India:

https://api.cognitive.microsoft.com/Bing/v5.0/news/?mkt=en-in&category=sports

Not all categories are tied with each market so it is important to know the accepted list of categories in each market. For example, if you searched on a health category with India, you would get 400Bad request with the following JSON response:

```
{
  "_type": "ErrorResponse",
  "errors": [
    {
      "code": "RequestParameterInvalidValue",
      "message": "Parameter has invalid value.The category parameter is invalid.",
      "parameter": "category",
      "value": "health"
    }
  ]
}
```

In order to search for news based on some specified keyword, use the q parameter. The following URL will search for Microsoft-related news:

```
https://api.cognitive.microsoft.com/Bing/v5.0/news/search?q=microsoft
```

Just note a change in the URL; now the URL is appended with /search apart from the q parameter. If you happened to go to the Bing.com home page, you would see a list of news appear in a banner in the bottom of the page, as shown in Figure 8-9.

Figure 8-9. *Trending news in the banner of the Bing home page*

You can get list of same trending news by calling the following URL:

```
https://api.cognitive.microsoft.com/Bing/v5.0/news/trendingtopics
```

As you can see, the Bing News Search API provides an immersive news experience and is the easiest way to create a news portal experience in a matter of few lines of code. The Bing News Search API has free and paid tiers, similar to the Image Search API; refer to the last section on the Image Search API to understand the free and paid plans. Now let's do a video-based search.

Bing Video Search API

Bing video search is one of the most exciting features of Bing. The Bing Video Search API and Bing.com/videos both provide many exciting features which makes Bing video search one of our personal favorites. Features like video previews and playing a video without leaving the Bing site are popular with users. The Bing Video Search API provides a similar feature to Bing.com/videos. Figure 8-10 shows you some of the features available in Bing.com/videos.

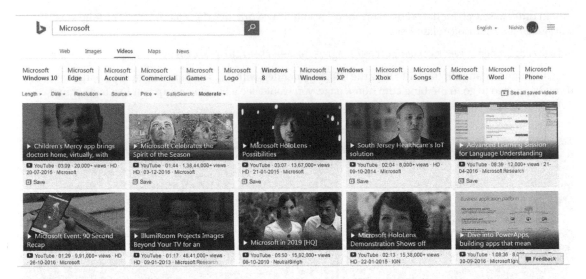

Figure 8-10. *A snapshot of Bing.com/videos*

At a high level, the Bing Video Search API allows you to get videos based on a various filters such as keywords, resolutions, etc. to return more insight about a particular video or show videos that are trending in a social network. Let's get a deep dive into the Bing Video Search API now.

How to Consume the Bing Video Search API

Like most other Bing APIs, you need to call `https://api.cognitive.microsoft.com/Bing/v5.0/videos/` `search` via a GET request, passing a subscription key in the `Ocp-Apim-Subscription-key` header and video to be searched as q parameter, like so:

```
GET https://api.cognitive.microsoft.com/bing/v5.0/videos/search?q=Microsoft HTTP/1.1
Host: api.cognitive.microsoft.com
Ocp-Apim-Subscription-Key: •••••••••••••••••••••••••••••••
```

You also have options to pass additional query parameters to refine your video search. The following code refines a video search by passing additional pa

```
GET https://api.cognitive.microsoft.com/bing/v5.0/videos/search?q=microsoft&count=50&offset=0&mkt=en-us&safeSear
ch=Moderate HTTP/1.1
Host: api.cognitive.microsoft.com
Ocp-Apim-Subscription-Key: •••••••••••••••••••••••••••••••
```

The following is a subset of the JSON response returned while calling the Video Search API:

```json
{
  "_type": "Videos",
  "instrumentation": {
    "pageLoadPingUrl": "https://www.bingapis.com/api/ping/pageload?IG=80D340D10D4A4986ACFCAE
D8781E1011&CID=079C1AB0315763FF32D110CD30B262B8&Type=Event.CPT&DATA=0"
  },
  "readLink": "https://api.cognitive.microsoft.com/api/v5/videos/search?q=Microsoft",
  "webSearchUrl": "https://www.bing.com/cr?IG=80D340D10D4A4986ACFCAED8781E1011&CID=079C1AB03
15763FF32D110CD30B262B8&rd=1&h=efHRlYPwMufONAYRYlm_kL65gvQMXF9zel8xU8F9KUw&v=1&r=https%3a%
2f%2fwww.bing.com%2fvideos%2fsearch%3fq%3dMicrosoft&p=DevEx,5387.1",
  "totalEstimatedMatches": 1000,
  "value": [
    {
      "name": "Çekinmeyin, web'e dokunun",
      "description": "Βρείτε απαντήσεις στις απορίες σας στο φόρουμ του Internet Explorer.",
      "webSearchUrl": "https://www.bing.com/cr?IG=80D340D10D4A4986ACFCAED8781E1011&CID=079C1
AB0315763FF32D110CD30B262B8&rd=1&h=qhXQDtX7quHIvkKPnI5mprr_VB03vcOBKeFLP9oPMkE&v=1&r=h
ttps%3a%2f%2fwww.bing.com%2fvideos%2fsearch%3fq%3dMicrosoft%26view%3ddetail%26mid%3d32
CCEE6E00380AACAB9E32CCEE6E00380AACAB9E&p=DevEx,5388.1",
      "thumbnailUrl": "https://tse2.mm.bing.net/th?id=OVP.bs8aHGNwEODVJFtjIsJEWQDIDI&pid=Api",
      "publisher": [
        {
          "name": "Microsoft"
        }
      ],
      "contentUrl": "https://support.microsoft.com/en-us/products/internet-explorer",
      "hostPageUrl": "https://www.bing.com/cr?IG=80D340D10D4A4986ACFCAED8781E1011&CID
=079C1AB0315763FF32D110CD30B262B8&rd=1&h=gzFge4ilBwpOcF9UunOfrqf-oD-ZRBhUexJflr
ydPT8&v=1&r=https%3a%2f%2fsupport.microsoft.com%2fen-us%2fproducts%2finternet-
explorer&p=DevEx,5011.1",
      "encodingFormat": "",
      "hostPageDisplayUrl": "https://support.microsoft.com/en-us/products/internet-explorer",
      "width": 200,
      "height": 200,
      "allowHttpsEmbed": false,
      "thumbnail": {
        "width": 200,
        "height": 200
      },
      "videoId": "32CCEE6E00380AACAB9E32CCEE6E00380AACAB9E",
      "allowMobileEmbed": false,
      "isSuperfresh": false
    },
```

Let's first understand the JSON response. At the top is the Videos object, which contains all of the videos in the form of an array in the Video object. Table 8-4 shows some of the fields that you can use in a Video object.

Table 8-4. *Fields of Video Object*

Name	Description
Name	Name of the video
Description	Short description of the video
thumbnailUrl	URL of the thumbnail image of the video
Publisher	Name of the publisher of the video
videoId	Uniquely identifies the video
contentURL	URL of the video in the site that hosts the video
encodingFormat	Specify the encoding format (e.g h264)
Width	Width of the video
Height	Height of the video
allowHTTPsEmbed	Boolean value that determines whether the video can be embedded in an HTML page or not
allowMobileEmbed	Boolean value that determines whether the video can be embedded in mobile devices or not
isSuperFresh	Boolean value that determines whether the video was recently discovered by Bing or not
viewCount	Number of times the video has been watched from source count

This table shares some of the basic fields of a Video object. There are more properties that may sound a little confusing unless we explain them. One such field is the id of the Video object. Each Video object has two fields, videoID and ID. Both of these fields uniquely identify the video. Ideally, videoID is the field that uniquely identifies the video. You also have the option to set the value of the videoID field to ID to play around with the video.

By default, the Bing Video Search API returns all kinds of videos that are relevant to your query. Some parameters you used earlier like mkt, count, freshness, offset, safesearch, and setlang can be applied to video search as well. There following are additional new query parameters that can be used to refine search results:

- Use the pricing query parameter to filter videos based on the pricing. Options available are Free, Paid, and All. All is the default.

- You also have an option to get videos based on resolutions by setting the resolution query parameter. Options available are 480p, 720p, 1080p, and All. Any options chosen will display images with a higher resolution than the option selected. For example, if the option selected is set to 720p, this means only videos with 720p or higher will be returned. By default, images are not filtered by any resolution and have the option as All.

- You can return videos based on the length of the video by setting the videoLength parameter. Options available are Short, Medium, Long, and All. Short means videos under 5 minutes. Medium means videos from 5 and 20 minutes. Long returns videos longer than 20 minutes. All is a default option that has no restriction on length.

In the above discussion, you saw that videoId uniquely identifies each video. This videoId can further be utilized to get more details and insight into the specific video, beyond what was available on normal Bing video search. In an order to get more insight, you need to call another video search API and set the id parameter to the id in videoId and modulesRequested to All as sh

```
GET https://api.cognitive.microsoft.com/bing/v5.0/videos/details?id=42656D8BF511F16E9CFD42656D8BF511F16E9CFD&mod
ulesRequested=All HTTP/1.1
Host: api.cognitive.microsoft.com
Ocp-Apim-Subscription-Key: ••••••••••••••••••••••••••••••
```

If you look at this code, you can see that you are calling a different Bing API with a URL of https://api.cognitive.microsoft.com/Bing/v5.0/videos/details. Both the videoID and modulesRequested query parameters are mandatory to get insights. modulesRequested is the specific parameter that supports a comma-delimited list of one or more insight requested. All, as shown above, will bring all the insights. You also have an option to set the option as RelatedVideos and VideoResult. RelatedVideos will list of all the videos related to the video specified by id parameter. VideoResult returns the video that you are requesting insight into. There can be a situation where you ask for insights and Bing doesn't have any; if so, the response object will not include that field.

Just like trending images, you can get list of trending videos by calling the following URL:

https://api.cognitive.microsoft.com/Bing/v5.0/videos/trending

As you can see, the Bing News Video API provides immersive video searching capabilities and is the easiest way to create a video-based portal experience with just a few API calls. The Bing Video Search API has free and paid tiers, similar to Image Search. Refer to the last section on Image Search to understand the free and paid plans.

Bing Web Search API

You are now familiar with various Bing APIs. Each of these APIs specializes in giving specific information. For example, you use the Bing Image API if you only need image results. Similarly, you use the News API if you need news results. There are quite a lot of scenarios wherein you would require a combination of results of images and videos together in the result set. This is similar to Bing.com/search where you get results that include images, videos, and more. The Bing Web Search API provides a solution for these scenarios.

How to Consume the Bing Web Search API

Like most of the other Bing APIs, you need to call https://api.cognitive.microsoft.com/Bing/v5.0/
search via a GET request, passing a subscription key in the Ocp-Apim-Subscription-key header and video
to be searched as q parameter:

```
GET https://api.cognitive.microsoft.com/bing/v5.0/search?q=Cognitive service HTTP/1.1
Host: api.cognitive.microsoft.com
Ocp-Apim-Subscription-Key: ••••••••••••••••••••••••••••••••
```

The following is a subset of the JSON response that comes when you call Bing Web Search API:

```
{
  "_type": "SearchResponse",
  "webPages": {
    "webSearchUrl": "https://www.bing.com/cr?IG=73EEE703FDE24263A07FA788B5251242&CID=2711158
    76DD9657922A81FFA6C3C645D&rd=1&h=QVjaswr8AICWOSzfYCfLtx3gSvGUR5zF6Uxs9z8U3OM&v=1&r=https
    %3a%2f%2fwww.bing.com%2fsearch%3fq%3dCognitive&p=DevEx,5363.1",
    "totalEstimatedMatches": 14000000,
    "value": [
      {
        "id": "https://api.cognitive.microsoft.com/api/v5/#WebPages.0",
        "name": "Cognition - Wikipedia",
        "url": "https://www.bing.com/cr?IG=73EEE703FDE24263A07FA788B5251242&CID=271115876DD9
        657922A81FFA6C3C645D&rd=1&h=-FncTcyJrdq3ayy4aX4tTYV7OwIX1zUpPtkDMfxBcCw&v=1&r=https%
        3a%2f%2fen.wikipedia.org%2fwiki%2fCognition&p=DevEx,5077.1",
        "about": [
          {
            "name": "Cognition"
          }
        ],
        "displayUrl": "Wikipedia › wiki › Cognition",
        "snippet": "The sort of mental processes described as cognitive are largely
        influenced by research which has successfully used this paradigm in the past, likely
        starting with Thomas Aquinas, who divided the study of behavior into two broad
        categories: cognitive (how we know the world), and affective (how we understand the
        world via feelings and emotions) [disputed - discuss]",
        "snippetAttribution": {
          "license": {
            "name": "CC-BY-SA",
            "url": "http://www.bing.com/cr?IG=73EEE703FDE24263A07FA788B5251242&CID=271115876
            DD9657922A81FFA6C3C645D&rd=1&h=tJYnHtBaEymlKo_fRlOwo_ZHu4dAaCwVMH_BvcixOgM&v=1&r
            =http%3a%2f%2fcreativecommons.org%2flicenses%2fby-sa%2f3.0%2f&p=DevEx,5362.1"
          },
          "licenseNotice": "Text under CC-BY-SA license"
        },
```

```
      "deepLinks": [
        {
          "name": "Load a Random Article",
          "url": "https://www.bing.com/cr?IG=73EEE703FDE24263A07FA788B5251242&CID=271
          115876DD9657922A81FFA6C3C645D&rd=1&h=q1Bn_OG8fm7uQkimqCtaj19x7I491UAUAQPmz-
          rYtjo&v=1&r=https%3a%2f%2fen.wikipedia.org%2fwiki%2fSpecial%3aRandom&p=Dev
          Ex,5067.1"
        },
        {
          "name": "Contact Page",
          "url": "https://www.bing.com/cr?IG=73EEE703FDE24263A07FA788B5251242&CID=27111587
          6DD9657922A81FFA6C3C645D&rd=1&h=6WyXHuw6VvpEvlqirdvJB9bZ8g86C42gTpWTmaeXGM8&v=1&
          r=https%3a%2f%2fen.wikipedia.org%2fwiki%2fWikipedia%3aContact_us&p=DevEx,5068.1"
        },
        {
          "name": "Citation Needed",
          "url": "https://www.bing.com/cr?IG=73EEE703FDE24263A07FA788B5251242&CID=271
          115876DD9657922A81FFA6C3C645D&rd=1&h=-OHnjXTBDcLsXjIzd1Ve7Ogmwak7KfLaJJFman
          iZcPBo&v=1&r=https%3a%2f%2fen.wikipedia.org%2fwiki%2fWikipedia%3aCitation_
          needed&p=DevEx,5069.1"
        }, {
  "_type": "SearchResponse",
  "webPages": {
    "webSearchUrl": "https://www.bing.com/cr?IG=73EEE703FDE24263A07FA788B5251242&CID=2711158
    76DD9657922A81FFA6C3C645D&rd=1&h=QVjaswr8AICWoSzfYCfLtx3gSvGUR5zF6Uxs9z8U3OM&v=1&r=https
    %3a%2f%2fwww.bing.com%2fsearch%3fq%3dCognitive&p=DevEx,5363.1",
    "totalEstimatedMatches": 14000000,
    "value": [
      {
        "id": "https://api.cognitive.microsoft.com/api/v5/#WebPages.0",
        "name": "Cognition - Wikipedia",
        "url": "https://www.bing.com/cr?IG=73EEE703FDE24263A07FA788B5251242&CID=2711158 76DD9
        657922A81FFA6C3C645D&rd=1&h=-FncTcyTrdq3ayy4aX4tTYV7OwIX1zUpPtkDMfxBcCw&v=1&r=https%
        3a%2f%2fen.wikipedia.org%2fwiki%2fCognition&p=DevEx,5077.1",
        "about": [
          {
            "name": "Cognition"
          }
        ],
```

As you can see, the Bing Web Search API will not only try to retrieve the relevant search results for all the Bing APIs such as Images, News, and Videos, which eventually will have separate endpoints, but it will retrieve results like related searches and spell suggestion, which don't have a separate endpoint. As mentioned earlier, you should only call the Bing Web Search API when you need to retrieve multiple sets of content; otherwise, call the individual APIs. You always have the option to filter and get the only subset of the APIs by passing them as comma-separated values in a responseFilter query parameter, as shown:

```
GET https://api.cognitive.microsoft.com/bing/v5.0/search?q=cognitive services&responseFilter=computation,images
  HTTP/1.1
Host: api.cognitive.microsoft.com
Ocp-Apim-Subscription-Key: •••••••••••••••••••••••••••••••
```

One of the interesting things that the Bing Web Search API provides in a response is ranking, as available in the `rankingResponse` parameter. Ideally, you should display your search results based on the ranking given. This will give you the user experience of any search results page. It has three options (`mainline`, `pole`, and `sidebar`). Mainline and sidebar, as the names suggest, display results in the main line and sidebar, respectively. Pole displays the search result above the main line and sidebar. Given any other scenarios, if you don't want to follow the ranking, do ensure that you give the mainline content more visibility than the sidebar.

As it's a web search, the user may ask any type of queries ranging from mathematical expression to time zone related queries. The Bing Search API provides objects for handling such responses. For any computational and conversion related queries, the response would include a `computation` object, as shown:

```
GET https://api.cognitive.microsoft.com/bing/v5.0/search?q=How many meters in a mile HTTP/1.1
Host: api.cognitive.microsoft.com
Ocp-Apim-Subscription-Key: ••••••••••••••••••••••••••••••••
```

The user asked how many meters are in a mile. If you look at the JSON response, it has one `computation` object:

```
"computation": {
    "id": "https://api.cognitive.microsoft.com/api/v5/#Computation",
    "expression": "1 mile",
    "value": "1609.344 meters"
  },
  "rankingResponse": {
    "mainline": {
      "items": [
        {
          "
```

It shows two items in the object, `expression` and `value`. The `expression` contains an expression of the query asked. If the query is of conversion, just like ours, it would show the from units in the expression, and the value would contain an actual response of expression or to the unit. As shown in above example, `value` shows actual conversion value. You also can ask queries related to time zones. For the time in the EST zone, the code would be the following:

```
GET https://api.cognitive.microsoft.com/bing/v5.0/search?q=time in EST zone HTTP/1.1
Host: api.cognitive.microsoft.com
Ocp-Apim-Subscription-Key: ••••••••••••••••••••••••••••••••
```

Asking queries like the one above will have a `timeZone` object in the JSON response, which will contain stuff like ID and the primary city name, along with the actual time and date:

```
"timeZone": {
    "id": "https://api.cognitive.microsoft.com/api/v5/#TimeZone",
    "primaryCityTime": {
      "location": "Eastern Time Zone",
      "time": "2017-05-09T04:09:00.9896042Z",
      "utcOffset": "UTC-4"
    }
```

Bing also provides RelatedSearchAnswer, QueryContext, and SpellSuggestions objects depending on the query being asked. The RelatedSearchAnswer object shows the most popular related queries made by other users. The querycontext response is used when a specified query being asked has some spelling mistakes. Bing itself corrects the mistakes and shows not just the original query but also the corrected query in the QueryContext object. You might also get a SpellSuggestions object if the Bing API finds some spelling suggestions.

Summary

To recap, in this chapter you learned about Bing and its associated APIs. You also learned how to call each API, and customized and filter search results based on query parameters and headers. You also got deep insights into understanding the JSON responses for each of the APIs, which will help you customize results as per your requirements. In the **next chapter**, you will learn about the internals of the Recommendation API of Microsoft Cognitive Services.

CHAPTER 9

■ ■ ■

Working with Recommendations

Machine learning is everywhere and so are its usages. Many of us are using machine learning a lot more than we know in our daily life. One of the classic uses and a great applicability of machine learning is a recommendation system. We see recommendations everywhere on the Internet. These recommendation systems have been heavily integrated into some of the top sites in the world. Let's first see some of the examples where you have been using recommendation systems:

- YouTube uses a recommender system to recommend videos.

- Netflix uses a recommender system to recommend interesting videos/stories.

- Amazon is not just using recommendations for showing product results but also for recommending products to sell to their end users.

- Google is not just using recommendation systems to rank the web links but is suggesting web and news links for you.

- News sites like the New York Times provide recommendations for news you should watch/read.

- Facebook provides recommendations for not just status updates but also people you may know.

- Twitter shows you recommended results and suggestions on whom to follow.

Any sites that involve user traction have a recommendation engine. As seen above, recommender systems are used extensively across application domains. The power of recommendations has been a tremendous boost for some successful companies. In fact, a classic example of using recommendations is Netflix, one of the most popular entertainment companies. According to a recent post, around 80% of its streaming content is been viewed through recommendations and personalization; the other 20% through the search. This is very impactful data because these recommendations not only helped the end users for streaming but also helped the company save a good amount of money. The Netflix recommendation engine is core to its business. If you have been following Netflix for the past 10 years, you may remember the million dollar challenge when they invited teams to improve the recommendation engine called Cinematch by 10%. It is the power of the recommendation engine has taken Netflix from 6 million US users in 2006 to 83 million users in more than 190 countries. Take another case: Amazon. Amazon says that nearly 30% of its sales are through recommendations. Note that most of today's successful companies have recommendation system as the core of their business. They keep on investing, researching, and innovating their recommendation system to improve it and provide more personalized experience to the end user.

© Nishith Pathak 2017
N. Pathak, *Artificial Intelligence for .NET: Speech, Language, and Search*, DOI 10.1007/978-1-4842-2949-1_9

Creating recommending systems is not easy, and companies have heavily invested not just in terms of resources but time too. It requires the deep expertise of data science to create a recommendation system. Microsoft provides two ways for creating a recommendation system:

- Recommendations through Azure ML via Matchbox recommender
- The Recommendations API of Microsoft Cognitive Service

Each serve a different purpose and are different in terms of functionality. Covering the Azure ML via Matchbox recommender would require a separate chapter. However, it is important to understand the key difference. Matchbox recommender offers rating-based recommendations while the Recommendations API is more transaction based. The Microsoft Recommendation API identifies transaction patterns in your data to provide recommendations. Using the Recommendation API, you can create your custom recommendations with few lines of code, improve customer experience, and thereby increase sales of your products. At the end of this chapter, you will have learned the following about recommendations:

- The need for recommendations
- The power of the Microsoft Recommendations API
- The various recommendation options provided by the Recommendations API
- The model management of the Microsoft Recommendation API
- Some best practices of using Microsoft Recommendations API
- How to use the Recommendation UI

Understanding the Basics

By now, you already know one of the systems that is running behind some of the top sites to show products that you are most likely to buy. You can think of recommendations as a way of navigation. You are mostly likely to buy a product that you see, and most of these companies only show you their product through the recommendation. This means that the recommendation system is essentially easing out navigation for that custom product. One thing you need to also understand that the Microsoft Recommendations API is not the solution for all types of recommendation. As mentioned earlier, it deals mostly with transaction-related recommendations. The Microsoft Recommendations API at a high level supports three kinds of recommendation, as shown in Figure 9-1.

Frequently Brought Together (FBT) Recommendations	Item-to-Item Recommendations	Recommendations based on past activity

Figure 9-1. *The types of recommendations supported by the Recommendations API*

Let's understand each of these types, one at a time.

Frequent Brought Together (FBT) Recommendations

Visit Amazon.com. Look up "War and Peace by Leo Tolstoy," one of my favorite books. You will see other recommendations by Amazon, as shown in Figure 9-2. These items were also bought with *War and Peace*.

Frequently bought together

Total price: $32.26

[Add all three to Cart]

[Add all three to List]

☑ **This item:** War and Peace (Vintage Classics) by Leo Tolstoy Paperback $12.19

☑ Crime and Punishment by Fyodor Dostoyevsky Paperback $5.50

☑ The Brothers Karamazov by Fyodor Dostoevsky Paperback $14.57

Figure 9-2. FBT recommendations example from Amazon

The FBT Recommendations API recommends items that are frequent bought or used in combination with each other. Normally, an underlying algorithm does an analysis of all the items that are brought together with the item you are looking for (most likely as part of the same transaction) before providing the recommendations as FBT. Take another example: if you are a fan of Apple products, you may have purchased the iPhone 7. But when you buy such a high-priced phone, would you buy it without a screen protector? Of course not!! Figure 9-3 shows recommendations from Amazon.

Frequently bought together

Total price: $822.48

[Add both to Cart]

[Add both to List]

☑ **This item:** Apple iPhone 7 Unlocked Phone 128 GB - US Version (Black) $814.49

☑ iPhone 7 6S 6 Screen Protector Glass, amFilm iPhone 7 Tempered Glass Screen Protector for Apple... $7.99

Figure 9-3. FBT items recommendations when buying iPhone 7

To your delight, Amazon recommends screen protector glass as part of its Frequent Brought Together plugin. These recommendations are creating wow discoveries of products for retail companies. FBT recommendations are an integral part for some retail sites. Normally, most of the products ordered as part of FBT are complementary products and hence the end user normally buys them together. Let's look at the item-to-item recommendations.

Item-to-Item Recommendations

Item-to-item recommendations, also popularly known as collaborative filtering, are another way of providing recommendations of items to the end user. Take the case of *War and Peace*. Wouldn't you like to see books brought by people who brought *War and Peace*? Tis might give you easy insights to books that might interest you. Amazon.com does this in a section called "Customers who bought this item also bought…", as shown in Figure 9-4.

Customers who bought this item also bought

Anna Karenina (Modern Library Classics)
› Leo Tolstoy
⭐⭐⭐⭐☆ 2,584
Paperback
$9.62 ✓Prime

Crime and Punishment
› Fyodor Dostoyevsky
⭐⭐⭐⭐☆ 1,546
Paperback
$5.50 ✓Prime

The Brothers Karamazov
Fyodor Dostoevsky
⭐⭐⭐⭐½ 1,160
Paperback
$14.57 ✓Prime

Anna Karenina
› Leo Tolstoy
⭐⭐⭐⭐☆ 2,584
Paperback
$9.99 ✓Prime

The Idiot (Vintage Classics)
Fyodor Dostoevsky
⭐⭐⭐⭐☆ 538
Paperback
$12.05 ✓Prime

Figure 9-4. More purchase ideas

Take our iPhone example. If you brought an iPhone, you probably want to buy other accessories (not just a screen protector) like a headphone jack adapter, wallet cover case, etc. Sooner or later, you will buy some of these. Amazon brings all of these item recommendations and shows them in one section. One benefit of these recommendations is that you don't need to navigate to other sites to search for these products. These products are available on the same page and certainly offer great user satisfaction and ease.

Recommendations Based on Past History

Recommendation based on past history, also known as customer-to-item recommendations, is another way to provide a recommendation of an item to an end user. Back to our previous examples, I would certainly be interested in knowing when a new book is released by Leo Tolstoy or if a new version of the iPhone is available. Normally these recommendations are available passively. For example, certain companies drop an email to inform the user about new product arrivals that might be of interest. Another option is to show these products as fresh arrivals on the home page. By now, you should have a fair understanding of ways that the Microsoft Recommendations API can be helpful.

Let's learn more about the Recommendations API. Like all other Cognitive Services, the first thing that you need to do is sign up for the Recommendations API. Signing up for the Recommendations API is the same as for other Cognitive APIs. Flip back to Chapters 2 and 3 for examples of how to sign up. Moving forward, we assume that you have already signed up for the Recommendations API and have the primary and secondary keys.

How Do These Recommendations Work?

By now, you are familiar with most of the machine learning and AI jargon. Essentially, the goal of machine learning is learning to program by taking the input of historical and past data, analyzing the patterns, and using those patterns to solve some specific problems. The key important stuff to understand is the essence of historic and past data. Back in Chapters 4 and 5, we laid out the importance of models and historic data.

First, you must create a *model*. Model as a term has a different context for the Recommendations API. For the Recommendations API, model is nothing but a container for your usage data, recommendations model, and catalog. Usage data is history transactional data. Catalog, as the name suggest, is a dataset about your items. The term model that we have used in the previous chapter(s) is referred here as a recommendation model. In our honest opinion, it should have a better name just to avoid confusion but let's go ahead with this word. In order to create model (aka container), call the API https://westus.api. cognitive.microsoft.com/recommendations/v4.0/models through POST by passing a subscription key in the header and a model name and its description in the body, as shown:

```
POST https://westus.api.cognitive.microsoft.com/recommendations/v4.0/models HTTP/1.1
Content-Type: application/json
Host: westus.api.cognitive.microsoft.com
Ocp-Apim-Subscription-Key: ••••••••••••••••••••••••••••••

{
  "modelName": "BookModel",
  "description": "This is a demo model for our chapter"
}
```

If your subscription key is valid, you will quickly create your model named BookModel and you will get the following JSON response:

```
{
"id": "6db5116c-977c-4a6d-b1d0-e7b968a8901f",
"name": "BookModel",
"description": "This is a demo model for our chapter",
"createdDateTime": "2017-04-21T09:59:00Z",
 "activeBuildId": -1
 }
```

For any unused model, you always have an option to delete the model by calling the same API using Delete and passing the model id, as shown:

```
DELETE https://westus.api.cognitive.microsoft.com/recommendations/v4.0/models/6db5116c-977c-
4a6d-b1d0-e7b968a8901f HTTP/1.1
Host: westus.api.cognitive.microsoft.com
Ocp-Apim-Subscription-Key: ••••••••••••••••••••••••••••••
```

In total, for any given subscription, you can create up to 10 models. Any time you want to get a list of all the models, call the same API using GET, passing the subscription key as shown:

```
GET https://westus.api.cognitive.microsoft.com/recommendations/v4.0/models HTTP/1.1
Host: westus.api.cognitive.microsoft.com
Ocp-Apim-Subscription-Key: ••••••••••••••••••••••••••••••••••••••••••••••••••••••••••••••••••
```

As discussed earlier, the Recommendations API is based on historic data. The more accurate your historic data, the more accurate your recommendations. As our Recommendations API is transaction based, in order to create a recommendation model (irrespective of the options you choose), you essentially end up providing two types of historic data:

- Product-related data

- Previous transaction data

Product-related data, also known as a *catalog*, is a data set about your item(s). Treat it as a list of items that you are offering to your end users. It not just contains the list of the items but also metadata and some other key information like itemid, description, category (if any), etc. Your catalog file can be as simple as three items separated by a comma. For example, the following code saved as CSV can be used as a catalog file:

```
itemid,item name,Category
P1001,Monitor,Laptop
P1002,Samsung Galaxy S,Phone
P1003,CPU,PC
P1004,iPhone 7,Phone
```

In fact, for a basic catalog file to work, you need to have it in the format shown in Figure 9-5.

Figure 9-5. *The basic format of the catalog file*

Such types of catalog files that only have three fields are known as catalog files without features. Catalog files without features can be used for demos and pilots, but in an actual production environment, catalog files without features may not work, essentially because of less information about the product. A catalog file can be made more substantial and useful by adding a feature list. In order to add a feature, you need to follow the format shown in Figure 9-6.

> Item ID, Item Name, Category, Description, Feature List

Figure 9-6. *Format of a catalog with features*

Adding features and optional descriptions makes your catalog meatier and very useful. Internally, the Recommendation API creates the statistical model based on the catalog data. Flip back to Chapter 4 if you would like to know more about the statistical model. More features in a catalog and more records mean a better statistical model for recommendations. Based on the format, your catalog sample would look something like the following:

P1001,Monitor,Laptop,,"Color=Black, availability =US/UK, Size =15.6""""

P1002,Samsung Galaxy S,Phone,,"Color-Gray, availability=All, Screen size=5"" , RAM=4 GB"

P1003,CPU,PC,,"Color=While, availability=APAC"

P1004,iPhone 7,Phone,,"Color-Gray, availability=US, Screen size=5""", RAM=16GB"

Another advantage to looking on the feature list is to recommend fresh, newly added items to the end users. Once you have features, you can compare them with the end user's interest and see if some of the newly added products have some features similar to a product that end user bought in the past before offering them to him. Also, look at the above code; we have not added any description fields in the above sample and hence after item name you see two commas. As of the writing of this book, the catalog has some limitations:

1. You can have as many as 20 features.

2. The file size of a catalog file should not be more than 200 MB.

3. The maximum number of items in a catalog file is 100K.

■ **Note** If you have a very heavy catalog file with more than 20 features, try putting a rank on those features so the model can take only those features that are ranked higher. Ideally, your usage data would determine the recommendation in an actual sense. However, adding more features would also bring cold items for recommendations. A *cold item* is a term used for those items that are not bought often and have very few transactions in the past.

In order to upload a catalog file, call the API at `https://westus.api.cognitive.microsoft.com/recommendations/v4.0/models/`, passing the model id created earlier and the catalog display name with the file to be uploaded in the body as binary file, as shown:

```
POST https://westus.api.cognitive.microsoft.com/recommendations/v4.0/models/6db5116c-977c-
4a6d-b1d0-e7b968a8901f/catalog?catalogDisplayName=BookCatalog HTTP/1.1
Content-Type: application/octet-stream
Host: westus.api.cognitive.microsoft.com
Ocp-Apim-Subscription-Key: •••••••••••••••••••••••••••••••
```

Assuming your model id and subscription key are correct and the catalog file passed is in the right format and in binary form, you will end up getting a response something like the following with status 201-Created:

```
{
  "processedLineCount": 5,
  "errorLineCount": 0,
  "importedLineCount": 5,
  "errorSummary": [],
  "sampleErrorDetails": []
}
```

As mentioned earlier, apart from the catalog file, another thing required is historic data or previous usage data. Usage data plays an important role in creating a statistical analysis model because it provides good insights about the interest of the users. It shows the historic interactions of the end user with the catalog items. Like your catalog file, usage file creation is also an easy process: you just have the four fields shown in Figure 9-7.

User ID, Item Id, Timestamp, Event(optional)

Figure 9-7. The basic format for the usage file

The first three fields are mandatory. Out of them, item id is the field that needs to be one of those item ids in the catalog file. Your simple usage file would look like

```
User1001,P1001,2017/08/04T11:02:52
User1005,P1002,2017/08/04T09:02:52
User1001,P1003,2017/08/01T11:01:10
User1003,P1004,2017/08/04T08:02:52
```

Each row in the usage file can be treated as a single interaction between the user and the item. We can call it a transaction as well. Event is an optional field and can have one of the below values where Purchase is a default value:

- Click

- RecommendationClick

- AddShopCart

- RemoveShopCart

- Purchase

The usage file needs at least 10-20 records even if you are using it for a demo. You will end up getting an error that the *"associated model does have the usage file uploaded"* **if your usage file has a lesser number of records**. Also, while writing this book, there is a cap of 200 MB data for the usage file to be uploaded on one

POST event. Also, it is prerequisite to upload the catalog file first before uploading your usage file. If you have more usage data than that, split it into multiple CSV files with each CSV not more than 200 MB. Your API call to associate your usage file with a model should have HTTP request as shown:

```
POST https://westus.api.cognitive.microsoft.com/recommendations/v4.0/models/6db5116c-977c-
4a6d-b1d0-e7b968a8901f//usage?usageDisplayName=BookUsage HTTP/1.1
Content-Type: application/octet-stream
Host: westus.api.cognitive.microsoft.com
Ocp-Apim-Subscription-Key: ●●●●●●●●●●●●●●●●●●●●●●●●●●●●●●●●●●●●●●●●●●●●●●●●●●●●●●●●
```

If your model id and subscription key are valid and your usage file is as per defined guidelines, you will end up creating your usage file with the status of 201 created response. So far you have seen how to create a model, and add a catalog file and usage file to it. The next step is to use these three items to create a machine learning-based recommendation model. Before we delve into the actual creation of a recommendation model, let's understand the various types of recommendation models supported by the Microsoft Cognitive Recommendation API.

Recommendation Models and Types

In order to create a recommendation machine learning model, you need to trigger a build. Internally, Microsoft uses it like a training process to come up with the ML-based recommendation model. The only prerequisite for triggering a build is that you should have created a model (aka container), and uploaded your catalog and usage file. The entire build process of triggering a model is an asynchronous process and it may take a couple of minutes to a couple of hours depending on the load of catalog and usage file. Before we go into the internals of how to trigger a build, let's understand more about the types of builds supported by the Microsoft Recommendations API. For creating or triggering a build, you need to make a POST call to https://westus.api.cognitive.microsoft.com/recommendations/v4.0/models/, passing modelid as a query parameter and the subscription key in the header. There are two basic parameters that need to be part of any build:

- Description

- Build type

The description is the basic description of the build. You can treat it as a name of the build as well. For now, it is important to understand that while triggering a build, you need to understand which type of recommendation build needs to be created. Currently there are four types of recommendations builds supported:

- Recommendation Build

- Frequent Bought Together Build

- Rank Build

- Smart Adaptive Recommendation (SAR) build

You need to set one of the above as the build type. Other info like associated parameters for that build part need to be part of the request body of the message. Each build type has some unique parameters. Let's go through and understand each one of them.

Recommendation Build

Recommendation build is used when you want to do either item-to-item recommendations or user-to-item recommendations. We have already covered the fundamentals of what each one of them meant but if you wish to refresh your memory, see the previous sections of this chapter. Recommendation build supports quite a number of unique parameters, which are detailed below:

1. While training on these builds, Microsoft recommendation, by default, goes through 20 iterations on the model. The higher the number of iterations, the longer the computing time but the better the accuracy of the model. If you want to change the number of iterations, set the parameter `NumberOfModelIterations` to a specific number. You can have any integer value between 10 and 50.

2. During training, the model will try to find 20 features within your data. In most scenarios, this value is fine and shouldn't be modified. You can always change the value by setting the parameter `NumberOfModelDimensions` between 10 and 50. Increasing the number will allow better fine-tuning but will compromise finding correlations between items. Mark this value as unchanged unless you have strong reasons for fine-tuning your results.

3. You also can change the minimum and maximum number of usage points required to be considered in the model by changing the value of `ItemCutOffLowerBound` and `ItemCutOffUpperBound`, respectively. The value should be between 0 and 30. `ItemCutOffLowerBound` has a default value of 20.

4. You also can change the minimum and maximum number of transactions the user must have performed to be considered in the model by changing the value of `UserCutOffLowerBound` and `UserCutOffUpperBound`, respectively. The value should be between 0 and 10. `UserCutOffLowerBound` has a default value of 2.

5. Most of the time, usage data is a key factor in deciding the recommendation. You can also decide whether features can be used to enhance the model by setting the value of `UseFeaturesInModel`. By default, it is set to `True`. Don't change this value unless you have a strong reason for your model being already very promising. You can also suggest features be used for the recommendation model by specifying features names as comma-separated value in `ModelingFeatureList`. Specifying features names are important because the recommendation model won't take any feature unless the list is not empty.

6. You can also decide whether the recommendation model should show cold items when showing similar items by setting `AllowColdItemPlacement` to `True`.

7. Set `EnableFeaturesCorrelation` to `True` if you want features to be used for reasoning. If you set `EnableFeaturesCorrelation` to `True`, specify the feature names as comma-separated values in `ReasoningFeatureList` to be used for reasoning.

8. By default, the recommendation model will show the item-to-item recommendation. Set `EnableU2I` to `True` to get the user-to-item recommendation.

A sample POST request for the recommendation model using some of the build parameters would be something like

POST https://westus.api.cognitive.microsoft.com/recommendations/v4.0/models/6db5116c-977c-4a6d-b1d0-e7b968a8901f/builds HTTP/1.1

```
Content-Type: application/json
Host: westus.api.cognitive.microsoft.com
Ocp-Apim-Subscription-Key: ●●●●●●●●●●●●●●●●●●●●●●●●●●●●●●●

{

"description": "Simple recomendations build",

"buildType": "recommendation",

"buildParameters": {

    "recommendation": {

      "numberOfModelIterations": 25,

      "itemCutOffLowerBound": 1,

      "userCutOffLowerBound": 0,

      "userCutOffUpperBound": 0,

      "enableModelingInsights": false,

      "useFeaturesInModel": false,

      "modelingFeatureList": "string",

      "allowColdItemPlacement": false,

      "enableFeatureCorrelation": true,

      "reasoningFeatureList": "string",

      "enableU2I": true

    }

  }

}
```

As triggering a build is an asynchronous operation, executing the above statement would return a 202 Accepted status with the response as follows:

```
Pragma: no-cache
Transfer-Encoding: chunked
Operation-Location: https://westus.api.cognitive.microsoft.com/recommendations/v4.0/
operations/1623835
x-ms-request-id: f1e5bcb5-660c-4489-b72c-4197fa5d7969
X-Frame-Options: deny
X-Content-Type-Options: nosniff
Strict-Transport-Security: max-age=31536000; includeSubDomains; preload
apim-request-id: 587594af-b0c4-473b-baa3-09fe75a12313
Cache-Control: no-store, no-cache
Date: Sun, 23 Apr 2017 04:56:08 GMT
Location: https://westus.api.cognitive.microsoft.com/recommendations/v4.0/operations/1623835
Content-Type: application/json; charset=utf-8
Expires: -1

{
  "buildId": 1623835
}
```

Note the operationsid mentioned in the header status. In the above code, the operationsid is 1623835. You need this operationsid to track or cancel the build. It is also handy just in case you accidently created the operation and want to delete the existing build. In order to track the status of the build, call https://westus.api.cognitive.microsoft.com/recommendations/v4.0/operations/ through GET and pass operationsid as a query parameter and the subscription key in the header. A valid operationsid request would look something like the following:

```
GET https://westus.api.cognitive.microsoft.com/recommendations/v4.0/operations/1623835
HTTP/1.1
Host: westus.api.cognitive.microsoft.com
Ocp-Apim-Subscription-Key: ••••••••••••••••••••••••••••••••
```

Calling the same API with Delete will cancel the operation. A successful HTTP request for tracking the status will return an HTTP response, as shown:

```
Pragma: no-cache
Transfer-Encoding: chunked
x-ms-request-id: 1bc423b1-8942-4fb6-a047-cda7a535ad4e
X-Frame-Options: deny
X-Content-Type-Options: nosniff
Strict-Transport-Security: max-age=31536000; includeSubDomains; preload
apim-request-id: a1861134-4ee7-4ef8-91a9-6d63a5955fdf
Cache-Control: no-store, no-cache
Date: Mon, 24 Apr 2017 13:07:51 GMT
Content-Type: application/json; charset=utf-8
Expires: -1

{
  "type": "BuildModel",
  "status": "Succeeded",
```

```
  "createdDateTime": "2017-04-23T04:56:09",
  "percentComplete": 0,
  "resourceLocation": "https://westus.api.cognitive.microsoft.com/recommendations/v4.0/opera
  tions/1623835?buildId=1623835",
  "result": {
    "id": 1623835,
    "type": "Recommendation",
    "modelName": "BookModel",
    "modelId": "6db5116c-977c-4a6d-b1d0-e7b968a8901f",
    "status": "Succeeded",
    "startDateTime": "2017-04-23T04:56:09",
    "endDateTime": "2017-04-23T04:57:55"
  }
}
```

As you can see, the HTTP response clearly specifies the name of the model, its type, modelId, status, and when it was created and completed.

Sometimes your parameters may be incorrect. For example, setting NumberOfModelIterations to less than 10 will result in a 401 message. If you end up in such circumstance, ensure that you read the JSON message properly. Normally, the innerError message is descriptive enough to suggest possible reasons for the error. In our example, NumberOfxModelIterations less than 10 would result in the following JSON response:

```
Pragma: no-cache
Transfer-Encoding: chunked
x-ms-request-id: ed216733-9634-4abc-bd6d-ad3d077499ee
X-Frame-Options: deny
X-Content-Type-Options: nosniff
Strict-Transport-Security: max-age=31536000; includeSubDomains; preload
apim-request-id: 94c53473-f078-45bd-a3ea-3294519f2e99
Cache-Control: no-store, no-cache
Date: Sun, 23 Apr 2017 05:01:14 GMT
Content-Type: application/json; charset=utf-8
Expires: -1

{
  "error": {
    "code": "BadArgument",
    "message": "(EXT-0108) Passed argument is invalid.",
    "innerError": {
      "code": "EXT-0310",
      "message": "Failed to trigger build for model 6db5116c-977c-4a6d-b1d0-e7b968a8901f.
      Invalid build parameter.",
      "innerError": {
        "code": "EXT-0046",
        "message": "Build parameter 'NumberOfModelIterations' has invalid value '5'.
        ModelId: 6db5116c-977c-4a6d-b1d0-e7b968a8901f"
      }
    }
  }
}
```

Frequent Brought Together (FBT) Build

FBT, in essence, recommends items that are frequent bought or used in combination with each other. This is possible by doing an analysis of the usage data to see what items co-occurred together in a purchase and then use similarity analysis through Jaccard, Lift, or co-occurence. Table 9-1 shows examples of co-occurence.

Table 9-1. *The Co-occurence Metrics Between the Items*

	Item001	Item002	Item003	Item004	item005
Item001	3	7	1	2	6
Item002	7	7	5	4	3
Item003	1	5	6	5	1
Item004	2	4	5	1	1
Item005	6	3	2	1	3

The above example is a classic way of defining similarity analysis through co-occurence. You look at the table and you can figure out how many times a specific item co-occurred. This is the easiest way of doing similarity analysis; however, it is quite predictable as well. There is a good chance that items that are the most popular will be recommended all the time. To resolve this issue of similarity, two other algorithms are supported: Lift and Jaccard.

Lift is a process of finding the item through serendipity or discovery. In Table 9-1, item 2 and item 4 have the same co-occurence with item 3 but item 4 generally occurs less frequent than item 2, so Lift would favor item 4 over item 2. Lift is the default similarity model for FBT. Co-occurence is all about predictability and Jaccard combines the best of both Lift and co-occurence. As FBT is based on the above process it the most conventional recommendation build. Since recommendations through FBT involve a user buying two items together as part of the same transaction, FBT build doesn't support personalized recommendations and cold items. FBT supports only a few types of parameters:

1. As mentioned earlier, a FBT build only recommends items when they are seen co-occurring a couple of times in the usage data. By default, a FBT build expects two items to have co-occurred at least 6 times to be considered for modeling. However, you can change this value by setting FbtSupportThreshold to any number between 3 and 50. The higher the value of FbtSupportThreshold, the more conservative your FBT build. As a good suggestion, initially this value should be marked as low as possible (say 3) for the initial data; once you have a lot of transaction data, set it to a higher value. If you set numbers other than specified value, you will get the build status as a Bad request with error as *"code": "EXT-0046", "message": "Build parameter 'FbtSupportThreshold' has invalid value '0'. ModelId: 6db5116c-977c-4a6d-b1d0-e7b968a8901f"*.

2. By default, FBT builds bind the number of items in a set as 2. This works most of the time. In certain scenarios, you may want 3 items in a set, so you can change the value of FbtMaxItemSetSize to 3. Do remember that the only values supported by FbtMaxItemSetSize are 2 and 3. Any other value set would return an inner error as *"innerError": { "code": "EXT-0046", "message": "Build parameter 'FbtMaxItemSetSize' has invalid value '0'. ModelId: 6db5116c-977c-4a6d-b1d0-e7b968a8901f"*

3. Once you have set the number of items in the frequent set, you may want to set the minimal score for this set to occur. You can set this value by setting FbtMinimalScore to any integer value. By default, it is set to 2. The higher the value, the better the recommendation, but this value needs to be set in conjunction with the amount of usage data. If the usage data is not so large, don't modify this item.

4. By default, the FBTSimilarityFunction that is applied to FBT build is Lift. If you want to change the similarity function, set the value of FbtSimilarityFunction to either Jaccard or co-occurrence.

A good FBT build successful POST would have the following HTTP request:

```
POST https://westus.api.cognitive.microsoft.com/recommendations/v4.0/models/6db5116c-977c-
4a6d-b1d0-e7b968a8901f/builds HTTP/1.1
Content-Type: application/json
Host: westus.api.cognitive.microsoft.com
Ocp-Apim-Subscription-Key: ••••••••••••••••••••••••••••••••

{

"description": "Simple frequent build",

"buildType": "fbt",

"buildParameters": {

    "fbt": {
      "supportThreshold": 4,
      "maxItemSetSize": 2,
      "minimalScore": 2,
      "similarityFunction": "Jaccard",
      "enableModelingInsights": true,
        }

  }

}
```

Once successful, you will get the proper response with operationid as shown:

```
Pragma: no-cache
Transfer-Encoding: chunked
Operation-Location: https://westus.api.cognitive.microsoft.com/recommendations/v4.0/
operations/1623876
x-ms-request-id: 4dbf70be-af6f-41ca-b849-df9c8b51c3a6
X-Frame-Options: deny
X-Content-Type-Options: nosniff
Strict-Transport-Security: max-age=31536000; includeSubDomains; preload
apim-request-id: 1ebade34-a252-4440-9e30-683cd1f9588f
```

```
Cache-Control: no-store, no-cache
Date: Sun, 23 Apr 2017 16:43:36 GMT
Location: https://westus.api.cognitive.microsoft.com/recommendations/v4.0/operations/1623876
Content-Type: application/json; charset=utf-8
Expires: -1

{
  "buildId": 1623876
}
```

Do remember that each of these build activities is an asynchronous operation. As discussed earlier, you can use operationsid to track or cancel the status of the build.

Ranking Recommendation

Ranking plays an important role in the results of a response. In fact, most of the responses returned are certainly based on a rank. We covered ranking briefly during Search but take a look at the Bing video results shown in Figure 9-8.

Figure 9-8. *Bing videos search result with an example of ranking*

The search results returned by the Bing videos are in fact rank-based with the first video having the highest rank. It goes from left to right and then top to bottom in terms of ranking. Ranking is the core of recommendations for many scenarios, such as search results, news feeds, and so on. So the next time you go to YouTube, Bing, Google, or Netflix and do a search, do remember that these search results are rank-based.

So how can ranking be done on the results? Well, the answer depends on whether your usage data is small or large. If your usage data is large, you can simply rely on creating the model based on ranking, and the Microsoft recommendation ranking model will do the honors of sharing the results. But what happens if the data is too small? That's where features play a key role. Remember you added features in the catalog data and also specified the importance of the feature. These features and their importance are taken into initial consideration if the usage data is small. Once your usage data increases, the ranking of a feature also changes accordingly.

Ranking parameters are similar to recommendation parameters and are shown below. We are not covering them because these items were already covered; if you need to refresh, flip back to the recommendation model to understand these items.

- NumberOfModelIterations

- NumberOfModelDimensions

- ItemCutOffLowerBound and ItemCutOffUpperBound

- UserCutOffLowerBound and UserCutOffUpperBound

A typical ranking build HTTP POST would look something like the following:

```
POST https://westus.api.cognitive.microsoft.com/recommendations/v4.0/models/6db5116c-977c-
4a6d-b1d0-e7b968a8901f/builds HTTP/1.1
Content-Type: application/json
Host: westus.api.cognitive.microsoft.com
Ocp-Apim-Subscription-Key: ••••••••••••••••••••••••••••••••

{

"description": "Simple Ranking build",

"buildType": "ranking",

"buildParameters": {

        "ranking": {
        "numberOfModelIterations": 15,
        "numberOfModelDimensions": 10,
        "itemCutOffLowerBound": 10,
        "itemCutOffUpperBound": 20,
        "userCutOffLowerBound": 5,
        "userCutOffUpperBound": 9
    },

  }

}
```

Like any other model build, a successful rank build would return an operationsid as shown in the following HTTP response:

```
Pragma: no-cache
Transfer-Encoding: chunked
Operation-Location: https://westus.api.cognitive.microsoft.com/recommendations/v4.0/
operations/1623950
x-ms-request-id: ca874586-a650-4422-811a-308cef8c4838
X-Frame-Options: deny
X-Content-Type-Options: nosniff
Strict-Transport-Security: max-age=31536000; includeSubDomains; preload
apim-request-id: 84a1c08b-3b80-43a5-af19-239c19138aad
Cache-Control: no-store, no-cache
Date: Mon, 24 Apr 2017 05:10:17 GMT
Location: https://westus.api.cognitive.microsoft.com/recommendations/v4.0/operations/1623950
Content-Type: application/json; charset=utf-8
Expires: -1


{
  "buildId": 1623950
}
```

SAR (Smart Adaptive Recommendations) Build

Take the earlier case of the recommendation build. Recommendation builds work well for user-to-item and item-to-item recommendations. The good thing about its model is that the response to the end user is been personalized according to the recommendation model. However, as and when new items keep on adding, the recommendation build doesn't tend to yield great responses apart from showing some cold items as part of the result. This is where the Smart Adaptive Recommendation (SAR) build comes. It's the newest addition to the recommendations supported by the Recommendation API. It's different from the recommendation build because SAR is based on user interactions with the system. SAR doesn't rely on user ratings, which are not often reliable, but relies more on user affinities with the system. Table 9-2 specifies the user-to-item matrix.

Table 9-2. *User-to-Item Matrix*

	Item001	Item002	Item003	Item004	item005
User001	2	1		4	6
User002	1		5	4	1
User003	1	2	1	1	4
User004	3	2		1	
User005	6		2		

If you look at the matrix, you can safely assume that User001 has maximum times been associated with item006, followed by Item004, and has never been associated with item003. Also, User004 has never been associated with Item005 but has maximum association with Item001. This can actually be changed based on the events when the user and item interacted. Also, each event might have a different weight; for example, an event purchase would have a maximum weight. Combining the weight with the above matrix would yield the user affinity matrix, which can then be used to provide recommendations. SAR produces two types of recommendations:

- User Recommendations

- Frequent Occurring Together (FOT) Recommendations

For user recommendations, as we saw earlier, SAR is dependent on transaction data, user affinity, and feature similarity to come up with a recommendation matrix having a score and user interaction for items. SAR acts more like a dynamic recommendation build and its scoring keeps on changing based on the user's interaction. FOT, on the other hand, is a superset of FBT and is based on item-to-item recommendations and similarity analysis. In comparison to actual FBT, Jaccard is treated as the default similarity analysis function. Based on initial experiments, SAR outperforms previous recommendation builds. We certainly encourage you to try SAR if you have been using recommendation build until now. SAR comes with a variety of parameters, some of which are common to recommendations and FBT:

1. Similar to the `FbtSupportThreshold` covered in the FBT section, you can provide the threshold number to decide on threshold co-occurrence of two items by setting `SupportThreshold` to value specified. The default value and valid values are same for both `FbtSupportThreshold` and `SupportThreshold`.

2. You can set similarity functions to be applied on SAR by setting `SimilarityFunction` to either `Jaccard`, `Lift`, or co-occurrence. `Jaccard` is the default value for SAR.

3. You can group occurrence either based on user or based on timestamp. By default, grouping is user based. You can change it to timestamp by setting `CooccurrenceUnit` to `Timestamp`.

4. By default, cold items placement is not pushed through similarity. Set `EnableColdItemPlacement` to True for setting it for feature similarity. Once done, you may optionally want to enable the cold-item-to-cold-item recommendation. This is not enabled by default. To enable it, set `EnableColdToColdRecommendations` to True.

5. Set `EnableBackfilling` to True to provide popular item recommendations when suitable recommendations are not available.

The following is a sample HTTP POST for creating a SAR build:

```
POST https://westus.api.cognitive.microsoft.com/recommendations/v4.0/models/6db5116c-977c-
4a6d-b1d0-e7b968a8901f/builds HTTP/1.1
Content-Type: application/json
Host: westus.api.cognitive.microsoft.com
Ocp-Apim-Subscription-Key: •••••••••••••••••••••••••••••

{

"description": "Simple SAR build",

"buildType": "sar",

"buildParameters": {
```

```
        "sar": {
    "supportThreshold": 5,
    "cooccurrenceUnit": "User",
    "similarityFunction": "Jaccard",
    "enableColdItemPlacement": true,
    "enableColdToColdRecommendations": true,
    "enableModelingInsights": true,
    "enableU2I": true,

  }

}
```

Like all of our builds, the above code when executed will return an operationsid in the HTTP response, as follows:

```
Pragma: no-cache
Transfer-Encoding: chunked
Operation-Location: https://westus.api.cognitive.microsoft.com/recommendations/v4.0/
operations/1624000
x-ms-request-id: 8dc96af3-a20a-46c8-a8c4-99b40e0f9580
X-Frame-Options: deny
X-Content-Type-Options: nosniff
Strict-Transport-Security: max-age=31536000; includeSubDomains; preload
apim-request-id: 9e3f69f4-b150-4431-889a-37440eada16a
Cache-Control: no-store, no-cache
Date: Mon, 24 Apr 2017 12:56:46 GMT
Location: https://westus.api.cognitive.microsoft.com/recommendations/v4.0/operations/1624000
Content-Type: application/json; charset=utf-8
Expires: -1

{
  "buildId": 1624000
}
```

Setting Rules in Build

These builds and recommendations are great but at times you might want to enforce some rules. For example, you have a new item and you want it to be featured as one of the recommendation items in all the recommendations you share or you know that one of the items in your list is not available and so you want to block that item from the recommendations. For such scenarios, business rules are created on top of the build. With the help of business rules, you can do the following:

1. Block one or more lists of items from recommendation by either name or by feature.

2. Enable item-wise blocking from a recommendation list.

3. Force the item to be part of a recommendation either by name or by feature.

A simple business rule to block one of the items from recommendation is as follows:

```
POST https://westus.api.cognitive.microsoft.com/recommendations/v4.0/models/6db5116c-977c-
4a6d-b1d0-e7b968a8901f/rules HTTP/1.1
Content-Type: application/json
Host: westus.api.cognitive.microsoft.com
Ocp-Apim-Subscription-Key: ••••••••••••••••••••••••••••••

{
  "type": "blocklist",
  "parameters": {
    "blockList": {
      "itemIds": [
        "item001"
      ]
    },
  }
}
```

Offline Evaluation

Now you have a good understanding of the types of builds and associated features. There is a good chance that you might end up taking one of the builds, which may or may not recommend the right items to the actual end user. So how can you determine the right build for your solutions? Indeed the best way is to do experiments by deploying different builds based on different models and algorithms. In this, you create a build, deploy the solution in production, and then track the conversion rate. A conversion rate has a couple of parameters and can be dependent on your business solution but normally conversation rate is measured by recommendation clicks and items purchased through recommendation click, to name a few. The higher the conversion rate, the better the build. Not all business can give you the benefit of deploying recommendations in production and then testing with actual users. You could do this experiment offline and come to some definitive initial conclusions by testing with sample data before deploying it in production. This is where offline evaluation comes into play.

Offline evaluation is a pretty straightforward process. All that is required is a good amount of usage data. Offline evaluation splits the usage data into two parts: training data and testing data. You got a glimpse of the usage of training and testing data in previous chapters. In an order to enable offline evaluation, you need to indicate during the build process that offline evaluation should be performed. This is done by setting enableModelingInsights to True. Once done, you need to decide on how the testing and training data should be split. There are three ways to decide a split:

- Random Splitter
- LastEvent Splitter
- Date Splitter

The random splitter splits the usage based on percentage and random seed values. The last event splitter splits the usage based on the last transaction for each user. The date splitter splits the usage and training data based on a specified date. Once the build is generated, you can get diversity and precision metrics by calling the metrics API as shown:

```
GET https://westus.api.cognitive.microsoft.com/recommendations/v4.0/models/6db5116c-977c-
4a6d-b1d0-e7b968a8901f/builds/1624000/metrics HTTP/1.1
Host: westus.api.cognitive.microsoft.com
Ocp-Apim-Subscription-Key: ••••••••••••••••••••••••••••••••
```

Note that observe model and build id are passed as query parameters. The HTTP response would return with metric details like precision item recommend, precision user recommend, diversity user recommend, etc.

Recommendation UI

By now, you have a good understanding of the Recommendation API and how to use it. One of the reasons we emphasized this route of concepts with code and APIs is to make sure you as a developer are aware of the internals of the application. Microsoft also came up with the Recommendation UI (in beta while writing this book) that abstracts the internals and provides an easy-to-use interface to play and test the recommendations. You can create a build, upload a catalog and usage data, and test the actual build even in offline mode through just a matter of clicks. To access the Recommendation UI, go to `https://recommendations-portal.azurewebsites.net/`. Just note that this URL might change later during launch so I highly recommend that when you need access to the portal, please go to `www.microsoft.com/cognitive-services/en-us/recommendations-api`, as shown in Figure 9-9.

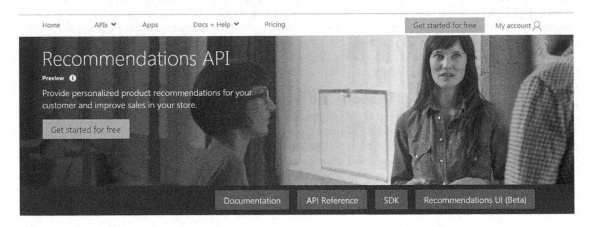

Figure 9-9. *The home page of the Recommendations API*

Once you get in the Recommendation UI, you will see the screen shown in Figure 9-10 where you provide your subscription key for recommendations.

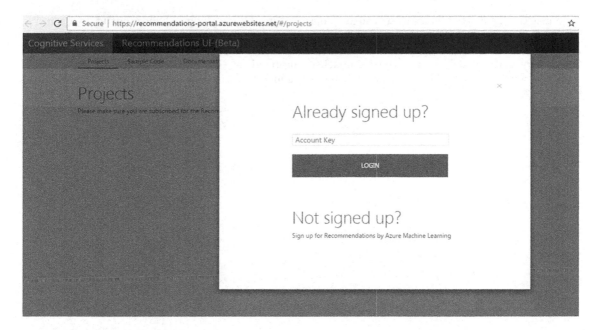

Figure 9-10. *Enter your subscription key*

Enter the subscription key and you will be redirected to the home page, shown in Figure 9-11.

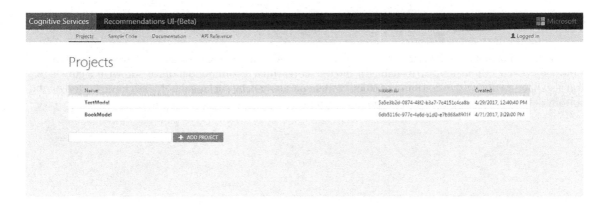

Figure 9-11. *The home page of the Recommendations UI for a logged-in user*

Once you log in, you will see a list of all the projects created by you along with the modelId. To create a new project, just specify the project name in the text box and click the Add Project button and your project will be created. Projects in this UI are nothing but a container (model). Each of these projects are clickable. Clicking one of the models will take you the model-specific build page wherein you can add a catalog file, usage file, see the list of the build along with their scores and features, and create a new build, as shown in Figure 9-12.

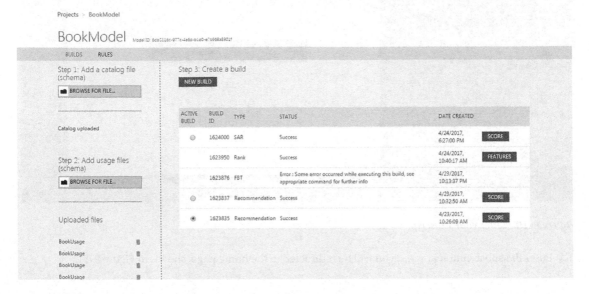

Figure 9-12. *The book model page in the Recommendations UI*

Clicking one of the build ids will take you to a build details page where you can see data statistics, build parameters used, offline metrics (if enabled), and the score with a recommendation, as shown in Figure 9-13. You also have an option to build another clone of these parameters by clicking the "Make clone" button on the bottom right of the page in the Build Parameters section.

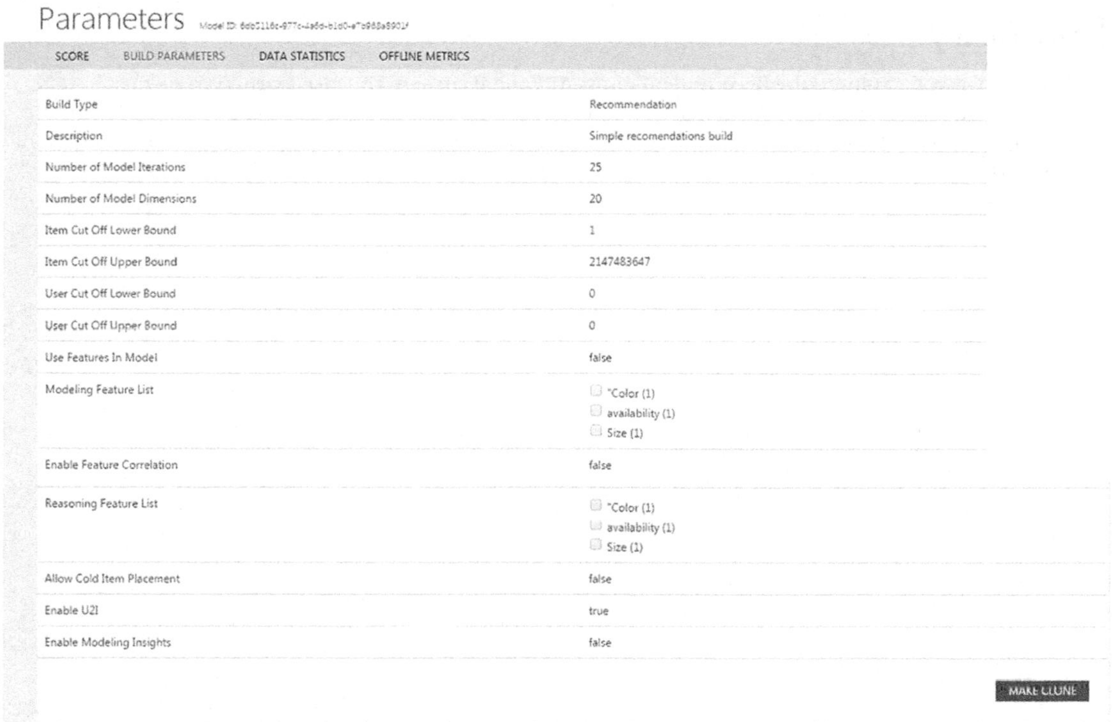

Parameters Model ID: 6db3116c-977c-4a6d-b1d0-e7b968a8901f

SCORE	BUILD PARAMETERS	DATA STATISTICS	OFFLINE METRICS

Build Type	Recommendation
Description	Simple recomendations build
Number of Model Iterations	25
Number of Model Dimensions	20
Item Cut Off Lower Bound	1
Item Cut Off Upper Bound	2147483647
User Cut Off Lower Bound	0
User Cut Off Upper Bound	0
Use Features In Model	false
Modeling Feature List	☐ *Color (1) ☐ availability (1) ☐ Size (1)
Enable Feature Correlation	false
Reasoning Feature List	☐ *Color (1) ☐ availability (1) ☐ Size (1)
Allow Cold Item Placement	false
Enable U2I	true
Enable Modeling Insights	false

MAKE CLONE

Figure 9-13. *The model details page*

You also have the option to set rules for your build by going on the Rules tab on the model's home page, as shown in Figure 9-14.

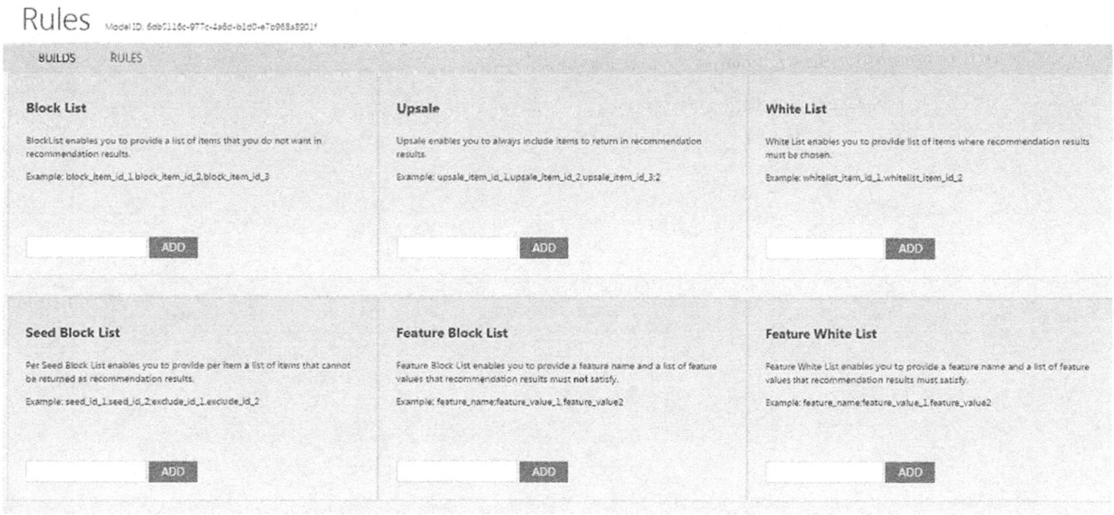

Rules Model ID: 6db3116c-977c-4a6d-b1d0-e7b968a8901f

BUILDS	RULES

Block List

BlockList enables you to provide a list of items that you do not want in recommendation results.

Example: block_item_id_1,block_item_id_2,block_item_id_3

[   ] ADD

Upsale

Upsale enables you to always include items to return in recommendation results.

Example: upsale_item_id_1,upsale_item_id_2,upsale_item_id_3:2

[   ] ADD

White List

White List enables you to provide list of items where recommendation results must be chosen.

Example: whitelist_item_id_1,whitelist_item_id_2

[   ] ADD

Seed Block List

Per Seed Block List enables you to provide per item a list of items that cannot be returned as recommendation results.

Example: seed_id_1,seed_id_2,exclude_id_1,exclude_id_2

[   ] ADD

Feature Block List

Feature Block List enables you to provide a feature name and a list of feature values that recommendation results must **not** satisfy.

Example: feature_name:feature_value_1,feature_value2

[   ] ADD

Feature White List

Feature White List enables you to provide a feature name and a list of feature values that recommendation results must satisfy.

Example: feature_name:feature_value_1,feature_value2

[   ] ADD

Figure 9-14. *The Rules page to apply rules on a specific build*

245

Summary

In this chapter, you explored the Recommendations API and its usage. You also learned some best practices for using the Recommendations API. At the end of the chapter, you learned how to work with the Recommendations UI with ease. In the next chapter, you will learn where the cognitive space is going in the future of AI.

■ ■ ■

CHAPTER 10

The Future of AI

In previous chapters, we covered some of the most powerful ways to use and consume Cognitive APIs. In Chapter 1, you started your journey into the world of artificial intelligence. In Chapters 2 and 3, you created your first AI-based project using Visual Studio and also explored the conversational user interface (CUI). The later chapters helped you understand how your application can deeply understand and interpret content on the Web or a user's machine, intelligently react to direct user interaction through speech or text, or make smart recommendations on products or services that are tailored to each individual user. You also got familiar with building applications that make intelligent use of language and user interaction to better compete in today's marketplace. Developers normally think of AI as tough task involving writing algorithms. One of the goals of this book is to remove the anxiety among you and to show you how easy it is to create amazing applications with just a few lines of code. By now you should be convinced that bringing these Cognitive APIs into your application is easy. Microsoft certainly did a great job in abstracting all the nuances of the deep neural network and complex algorithms by exposing easy-to-use REST APIs. So what's next? Where should you go from here?

I am sure some of your queries about how and when to use these API are resolved. But now you may have new questions. What's happening next? Is the AI all about consuming Cognitive Services in a RESTful manner? Is there a future where all of these cognitive applications can be integrated with devices and make them smarter? What about jobs? You may have heard that AI is going to take X% of all jobs in next few years or so. What are the existing challenges in the field of cognitive computing? This chapter attempts to resolve some of the burning misnomers and act as a guide to help you make a few decisions well ahead of time. At the end of this chapter, you will have a fair understanding about

- Misconceptions vs. actual reality on AI

- Risks and challenges behind the cognitive technologies

- The Microsoft vision on AI

- The path moving forward on AI

Why Is AI So Popular?

We covered why AI is disruptive in bits and pieces in previous chapters. It is important for us to collate and understand it under one roof because these reasons also give us clues on future innovation and direction. **Most of us are in this area of cognitive computing because of the disruption that started with the Jeopardy! match between Watson and a human being in 2011.** That match was an eye-opener; many of us saw the power of cognitive computing for the first time. Since then, a lot of innovations have been happening across the globe, every hour and every day. The rapid adoption of cognitive computing is fascinating to us because of the outcomes. Some of the consequences of cognitive computing have resulted in products and technologies that help us do things that we could not have done before.

© Nishith Pathak 2017

N. Pathak, *Artificial Intelligence for .NET: Speech, Language, and Search*, DOI 10.1007/978-1-4842-2949-1_10

AI is certainly disruptive and has crossed the line from gradually to suddenly. AI is not a new concept. Chapter 1 discussed in brief the history of AI. Before we try to resolve some of the misconception and challenges, and discuss the future, it is important to understand why AI is been so popular. It is primarily because of the following reasons:

- Improved computing power
- Improved AI algorithms
- Big data
- The Internet and the cloud

Improved Computing Power

The immense rise in computing power has been one of the critical factors for the popularity of AI. Improving computing power helps in processing a large amount of data quickly.

■ **Note** What required months of processing in the late 1980s can be done in a matter of few seconds today, even on low-end machines. The processing power of our low-end mobile phones is way higher than the supercomputers of the 1980s.

Yes, that's so true. The rise of GPUs, TPUs, and FPGA shows us that we have moved beyond the era of Moore's Law. In addition to this processing power, the cost of storage has gone down. By 2020 or earlier, it is estimated that 1GB of storage will cost less than $0.001. In addition to storage costs getting lower day by day, there are many innovations in the field of chips, offering more processing power at a low cost. There is also tremendous innovation happening in the area of new chip design. The advent of the neuromorphic chip has phenomenally changed processing power. Neuromorphic chips not only provide million times faster speed but also save the power consumption.

■ **Note** Watson's triumph over Jeopardy champions was conceivable through the use of the TrueNorth native processor. TrueNorth is based on the neuromorphic chips that mimic a brain. TrueNorth chips have a million computer "neurons" that work in parallel with millions of interneuron connections to make processing faster than ever.

Inventions in AI Algorithms

The last decade has been phenomenal in terms of innovations in AI algorithms. Flip back to Chapter 1 to learn about the rise of AI algorithms and their successful implementation across various verticals. The key innovation in the field of machine learning, especially in areas of deep learning, shallow learning, and neural networks, has already resolved some of the complex issues. For example, by using deep learning, the word error rate has seen a reduction of more than 25%. One of the changes that happened during the last decade in AI was to make machines learn based on historic data rather than programming. This fundamental approach has brought a lot of merits and revolutions in AI. Because of recent inventions in the area of AI algorithms, we are moving into the world of the conversational user interface. The rise of personal assistants like Siri, Cortana, and Google Now are some of the by-product inventions of AI algorithms.

■ **Note** Amazon Alexa and Google's Google home are giving rise to personalized CUIs. In addition, Cubic, one of the very disruptive companies on the conversational platform, is able to communicate with the user and integrate with any internet-connected device. For example, you can use Cubic to turn on the lights before you go home or get advice on how to reach your destination faster or use it to order any delivery.

We have seen the era where AI-led machines defeated some of the champions of the game, from chess to Go. Very recently, Libratus, designed by a team at Carnegie Mellon, defeated human poker champions. Poker, as you may know, requires some information to be kept hidden until a certain point of time and it is very difficult to create a model to handle such situations.

Data Is the New Currency

We cannot use processing power and AI algorithms alone. As discussed earlier, machine learning uses historical data to identify patterns. More data makes it easier to define the pattern. The rise of IOT and new devices makes fuel for data the new oil for any organization.

■ **Note** Most autonomous cars generate around 100 gigabytes per second of data. Isn't that huge? In fact, every day 2.5 quintillion bytes of data is created. The last two years have generated 90% of the data of all time. It is also expected that 25 billion such devices will be connected by 2020. Of this data, 80% is unstructured, which means normal computer systems can't process it. Consider another example of huge data: health care. Every person generates 1 million GB of health data. Some companies like IBM and Enlitic are already using deep learning tools and this data to identify patterns in health data, making the doctor more effective and also predicting about health.

With new devices coming every day or so, this data needs to be utilized with the power of AI algorithms and processing power properly to do a variety of things. Figure 10-1 shows some of the devices that can emit data.

Figure 10-1. *Some of the devices where data can be collected and used to resolved complex business problem*

The rise of the Internet of Things (IoT) and big data has helped a lot in the field of AI algorithms as well. In fact, when there was not enough data generated, human instinct used to play the tasks. In recent years, we have seen improvement in various domains especially where we have a lot of data in the forms of text, images, and speech; and using deep learning, AI researchers have replace human instinct with this data to bring more accuracy. Even now, when a domain doesn't have a lot of data, human instinct is still used.

Some of you may think that the future of cognitive may replace the human brain. Well, there are a couple of projects, like Project Nengo, which is trying to create and simulate the mind by combining large-scale neural system but most of the AI research have been inclined towards creating a system that can analyze and process data that the human mind cannot. If you really look at some of the emerging AI platforms like Watson, you can observe that they really were developed to make the system handle the huge amounts of data generated. Most of the research has been around creating new algorithms, systems, and chips to handle this massive amount of data. This data can give new insights and resolve complex problems. Think about health care data. If we are able to analyze 1 million GB of health data per person, we would presumably be able to get insights to make a person healthy all the time. Data is certainly becoming as valuable as oil and the new currency of an organization. **An organization that has data and the ability to generate insights is going to be a future leader.** Now you know why a company like Google has brought companies like YouTube (data in form of videos). Now you probably know why Facebook acquired WhatsApp. According to the metrics of company acquisition in the last five years, most of the companies that have been acquired are related to Cognitive, AI, or are the companies that have data and the ability to generate insights.

Emergence of Cloud Computing

The rise of Internet and cloud computing is the fourth pillar for the emergence of AI. Once we have a product offering, it needs to reach the common masses and needs to be available everywhere and almost on every device. This became reality with the rise of Internet and cloud computing. Cloud computing not only ensures the reaching of the common masses, it also provides a unique opportunity to process complex computation in an abstract manner. Take the case of the Microsoft Cognitive API. Thousands and thousands of Microsoft Azure cloud servers are behind the processing of each of your queries to the Cognitive API. Figure 10-2 shows that cloud computing is helping products to reach every device.

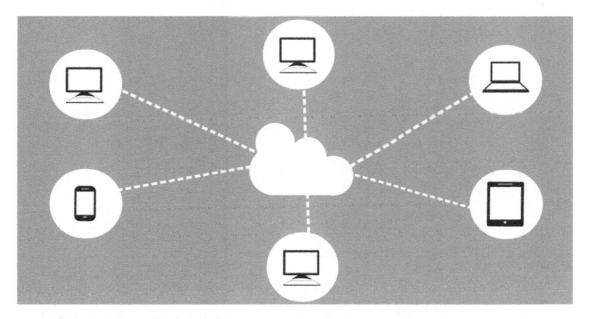

Figure 10-2. A simple diagram of using cloud computing to interact with devices

Services vs Solutions?

The Microsoft Cognitive space has been growing at a steady pace. What started with four cognitive APIs last year has grown to 29 while writing this book. Microsoft as a company has suites of product offerings. They also have a suite of cloud-based capabilities. You might wonder why Microsoft created these services rather than creating specific solutions and products. Well, the answer is no big deal. Over the last few years, Microsoft's strategy has been to create and focus on a platform rather than creating systems. These platforms and services can eventually be used by others to resolve domain-specific problems. The intent of the platform is to scale up by creating more and more offerings in the cognitive space over a period of time and giving the immersive experience of consuming it to the end users. You should not be surprised if the cognitive list of API increases to over 50 in less than a year.

Cognitive Categories

Let's now try to understand some of the challenges in the cognitive space. These challenges not only talk about existing prevailing constraints but give directions of research on each of the cognitive areas. Figure 10-3 shows the general classification of the Cognitive APIs. Almost all the APIs released by Microsoft can be categorized into one of these groups.

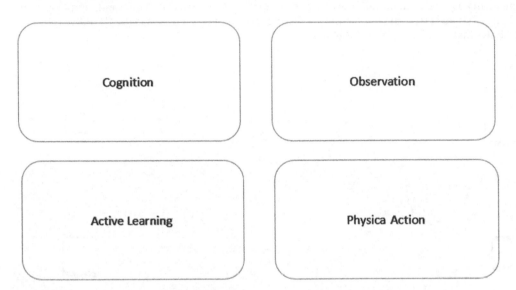

Figure 10-3. *Various categories of Cognitive APIs*

Cognition is the process of representing the information machine and using that representation to reason automatically. Observation is a category to mimic human behavior, such as interacting with speech, text, or vision like humans do. Active learning is the process of improving automatically over a period of time. A classic example of active learning is Microsoft Language Understanding Intelligent Service (LUIS), which we covered in Chapter 6 in detail. Physical action requires combining these three and using devices to interact intelligently.

Challenges and the Future of NLU

We talked extensively about natural language understanding in Chapter 4. Natural language processing and understanding can be used in a variety of scenarios such as extracting, pulling, and analyzing the context and intent of the sentence. There are quite a number of scenarios like medical, academic, or legal where there is a lot of textual content getting generated every day. This data can come from research, legal cases, and medical diagnosis, to name a few. The natural language understanding engine can help you manipulate the text but one of the core issues is understanding the right context. As detailed earlier, you can always understand syntax (grammar) and semantics (meaning) but having a deep understanding of pragmatics (context) is a real challenge. If you are familiar with NLU engines, you know that a very large amount of effort has been invested in training these engines to understand the right context. Is there a future where contextual stuff can be understood through algorithms? There is various research in this area. Some of the AI companies like Pat.ai seem to have promising recognition because they are focussed on meaning matches rather than statistical analysis. In the future, you can expect various internet-connected devices and others using NLU to understand the context and then integrate with components like speech and search to provide a more immersive experience.

Challenges and Future of Speech

As discussed back in Chapter 7, innovation in speech has come a long way. What's more interesting is the stuff coming now about natural interaction with speech. There are areas where natural interaction with speech can be seen now especially around cars and personal assistants. It still has to cover a lot of miles to ensure natural interaction is 100% applied and reliable. Take the case of a telecaller. The style is to dial 1 for balance information, dial 2 to pay a bill, etc. These telecaller automated agents get so frustrating at times that person needs to talk to a human. Wouldn't it be great if the telecaller was more interactive and asked you questions like "Tell me what you want to do today." Based on the answer, it could provide actual support. Such speech interactions would really help the user. Speech recognition needs to have unobtrusive interaction with the user. Apart from natural interactions, speech currently faces a lot of other issues like

- Accuracy
- Performance
- User responsive
- Grammatical collisions
- Background noises
- Diverse accents

Take the case of accuracy. In cars, you might lose recognition accuracy just because the audio signal quality is poor. Similarly, your agent might not be ready to listen but the user started speaking, resulting in bad user responsiveness. Speech recognition also faces challenges with performance and speed. One of the other issues with natural interaction is the ability of speech recognition to understand and work with the pace of human speech. This has been achieved up to a certain degree but still, new algorithms with the right pace need to be devised to have a seamless experience in real time. Another reason for accuracy can be related to words that are spelled alike; "bet" and "bed" seem alike to the underlying speech recognition engine.

Most of the industry titans in the field of speech, like IBM, Google, and Microsoft, are focussing on improving speech accuracy by reducing the word error rate. Google recently claimed that its word error rate has come down to 4.9%, which means it is able to predict 19 out of 20 words correctly. This is a great success but in order to make speech recognition more reliable and accurate, the word error rate needs to come down to less than 1% in the future. It is also very important to have a system wherein NLP and speech recognition work hand in hand. NLP can handle what you meant and, based on the context, inform speech recognition about the right word. Apart from such scenarios, there are other areas where speech still faces a lot of challenge. Speech recognition needs to be prudent enough to handle environments with a lot of background noise. Microsoft has come up with a custom speech service (covered extensively in Chapter 7) that tries to address this issue to a certain extent. These areas are very new and certainly need to be properly tested in an actual production environment.

A lot of companies are also trying to use speech in the automatic speech recognition (ASR) area. Take the case of Google using YouTube to do ASR along with a translation. Blame it on various accents or the Web being multilingual, but we have yet to see 100% accurate ASR. In future, you can certainly expect real-time translation to be happening very soon with high reliability.

Challenges and the Future of Search

The Microsoft Bing Search API brought a lot of credentials in API to the table. Chapter 8 extensively covered the Bing Search API and its offerings. You can not only search the Web but also news, videos, etc. Search can now provide location-based results as well. Search in the future will get more contextual. In the future, you should be able to search for devices in your home just like you search any product on the Web. This is going to be a phenomenal experience. Think about searching for your wallet via your mobile phone, as shown in Figure 10-4. Search, in order to achieve something like this, needs to be integrated with other cognitive technologies.

Figure 10-4. Finding you wallet via your phone

Challenges and the Future of Recommendations

Microsoft and other companies are already investing a lot in recommendation engines and systems. Chapter 9 covered some of the benefits and results of using recommendations. Recommendations have been key for some top companies. Most of the recommendations nowadays come from ways such as frequently brought together (FBT), user navigation, or previous history. Now think about the same customer's social data. Around 500 million tweets and 55 million Facebook updates happen every day. Everyone on an average spends five or more hours every day in watching movies and shows either on television or on a phone. Think about the future of recommendations based on social insights, channels you watch on TV, and the conversation you have on the phone.

AI First

You're by now familiar with the terms *cloud first* and *mobile first*. As technology adoption happens, each technology gets spearheaded initially. The IT industry has seen a lot of transformation in past, like having a client-server architecture, the Web, distributed computing, the cloud, and now AI. Having said that, no trend has moved as fast as AI is moving in the present era. It doesn't matter what role you are playing in your organization, or if you have your own business or a startup, one thing is for sure: AI is going to not only affect the work we do but also our day-to-day life in a big way. If you look around, every company is focusing on AI. Stuff like bots, personal assistants, conversational interfaces, and machine learning are some of the buzzwords you will see on the home pages of most companies. It is important for these companies not only to focus on offering new services in the AI space, but they also need to be focused on their people and their existing products. The reason why we emphasize *on people* is primarily that human or machines alone cannot bring transformational changes. It's the power of combining both human and machine that is going to bring miraculous changes. Organizations need to think about finding new opportunities for their existing people if their tasks are adopted by machines. **Companies who focus on AI innovation together with their people and products are the companies that will thrive in the long run.** This will allow companies to use their competitive advantage to move forward. You not only need to think about transforming your business with AI but also need to think about using AI and machine learning together with humans as the core of your business strategy.

Intelligent Edge

So far we have tried to consume APIs in the RESTFul manner. These APIs have certainly helped us resolve some complex problems that were not possible to resolve earlier. Another reason for this API-driven model is that it abstracts thousands of processors and VMs running behind the API. With the rise of technologies like IoT and sensors, there are unbelievable opportunities to automate and analyze data. Think of the personal assistants like Google Now or Cortana. Each and every request gets routed to the cloud before the actual processing happens. The reason for moving these requests to the cloud is because our mobile application doesn't have enough processing power to process complex computations. Calling the APIs back and forth certainly requires time. This model works in most situations but also creates scenarios where this model can't achieve. It is therefore required to have these models deployed on the edge rather than the cloud. Quite a lot of research is been going on these days. Apart from the neuromorphic chip that we discussed earlier in the book, many companies are designing chips to bring the power of the cloud closer to the devices. Intel recently released a chip called the Joule platform that allows you to deploy these complex models in a chip, which can be used in most IoT devices, robots, and even drones. The mobile processor is upgraded daily, and certainly the day is not very far when you will have the machine learning model directly deployed on the mobile. Google CEO Sundar Pichai during the Google I/O Summit in May 2017 revealed the new Google chip which can eventually be used to train and execute deep neural networks. Microsoft CEO Satya Nadela also announced the Intelligent edge solution with the help of various projects like Project Rome and others. Apple has also announced that it's building a secondary mobile processor to power AI. Very soon, the new pricing model for consuming these APIs on the edge are likely to be announced by Microsoft. Microsoft Graph may get a lot of attention in the future as it plans to connect all devices and application together by creating a fabric model. This model will open the next big set of opportunities and resolve problems because we can use these technologies where internet connectivity is slow, such as in the dense forest of Africa or in the remotest village in India or beneath the sea or in deepest part of the ocean.

Tasks, not Jobs, Will Be Eliminated

Gone are those days where machines are just used for repetitive, monotonous, and iterative work. Machines are getting smarter day by day. You already saw some of the examples where AI-supported machines could defeat human champions in games. AI is certainly not just restricted to games; in fact, AI is disrupting each and every domain. One of the curious and heated discussions on the Web is how AI is going to affect jobs. See Figure 10-5. Some AI experts say that half of the jobs will be replaced by AI very soon. Are you worried?

Figure 10-5. *Will a robot ever replace a human DJ?*

Think of it this way: any new thing always brings fear. Think about the first time a human planned to travel in an aircraft. There was fear. Let's go simpler. What about when cars and mobile phones were introduced? Certainly, there was some degree of fear, but we need to admit that these technologies have come to be a huge help. These technologies initially were slowly adopted and have now become part of our daily lives. They improve the human experience in insightful ways. We should also welcome the changes that AI will bring. AI changes need not be feared. These changes are going to affect not just our work but also our day-to-day life. Some of your tasks will certainly be automated and of course, benefits can be seen in the short to midterm. Here is the true reality. Machines have always helped humans get their repetitive work done. Figure 10-6 shows an example of robots carrying trolleys.

Figure 10-6. *A robot pushing a cart*

Training the machine is one of the core components of an AI-based application. How an AI application responds is dependent on how well is it trained. Think of an autonomous car. We need to train the car to drive but we also need to educate the system to understanding about bad car driving vs good car driving. The end result of how the well autonomous car is driven has more to do with a human angle on their skill in training it. At some extent, this is one of the classical examples of imbibing human values in the machine. This in AI world is also called "augmented intelligence."

■ **Note**   Take another example of customer service. Say a customer calls customer service to resolve his queries. Some of the queries are basic but a few are complex in nature. The company has employed hundreds of people as support staff just to answer those basic and complex questions. How long do you feel an employee on the support staff will be motivated and energized to respond to the same support questions with full zest? Certainly, no one likes to do a monotonous job for a large amount of time. Various surveys have revealed that the productivity of an employee gradually decreases over a period of time if they are doing the same repetitive work. Also, there is a good chance that support staff can make mistakes in responding correctly. Take the same scenario where now the basic questions are been addressed by intelligent bots. If bots are not able to answer, those complex questions are redirected for human intervention. Hundreds of support folks who were answering the basic questions are now involved more in training the bot to be more efficient and are utilized in other new opportunities that have resulted from the introduction of these AI-supported bots.

The above example is a classic example that's applied in companies. If you see the above scenario, bots have taken up the tasks of humans. Bots are addressing basic queries of customer service and the support staff is tasked with new jobs such as training, deployment, etc. By introducing a proper way of AI, you can certainly create a lot of value in any domain. This also gives a unique opportunity for the company to identify new avenues where employees can be used.

> ■ **Note** Take another example of Arizona State University (AZU), which collaborated with Knewton and Cengage Learning to offer a personalized curriculum to students. By using predictive analytics, they were able to involve instructors only when students really needed them. Initial pilot results have been phenomenal and the passing percentage of students has risen from 64 to 75 percent.

In a nutshell, introducing AI into the process has brought a lot of value. It has certainly eaten up a lot of tasks but has also given the opportunity to create new ones. Certainly, that proportion of old tasks eaten up vs new tasks creation gap can be a little wider initially but the onus is on the organization to transform at rapid leaps and bounds in order to keep up competitive advantages and bring more tasks/jobs to the table.

> ■ **Note** Take the case of Uber, which has completely disrupted the taxi market. With the usage of new technology, AI, and immersive personal experience, Uber, though operating in more than 600 cities, is the largest taxi company but doesn't own any vehicles. Just like Uber, Airbnb, which provides the largest accommodation services across the world and yet doesn't own any accommodations, uses AI for dynamic pricing of rooms based on demand in real time. Hundreds of people are working on support teams to help the processes of Uber and Airbnb run in an uninterrupted way.

Technologies in the past have quietly eliminated a number of jobs. As mentioned earlier, jobs that are more human-centric will be later or never replaced by AI. Take an example here. Can you think of a robot replacing the infamous *Rowan Atkinson* in *Mr. Bean* even in the future by any chance? Not really. If you clearly observe the process, it all started with blue collar tasks getting automated, and now some white collar tasks are getting replaced. It is very important for all of us to educate ourselves and be prepared for these changes. Practicing and upgrading skills regularly is the need of an hour. Companies and individuals will be required to adapt if events require reinventing in this era of digital disruption.

> ■ **Note** Digital disruption is everywhere. Since 2000, more than half of the Fortune 500 companies are gone. However, some of the best companies in the world today did not even exist a decade or two back. Only companies that focus on machines and humans are going to be successful in the coming years.

So Where Do We Go From Here?

In next few years, we can expect AI to be seen everywhere. AI has become the driving force for a fourth industrial revolution. The AI influence has started, and in coming years, AI will certainly affect our day-to-day life in a massive, transformative way. We as developers need to choose the right usages and certainly take the world towards augmented intelligence, contrary to artificial intelligence. Imagine a world where most of the cars are driven by machines. Imagine a world where most of the factories have more robots than humans. Imagine a retail shop where you are welcomed by a robot who understands your query and provides a customer-centric retail experience. Imagine a hospital where the initial analysis is done by robots. Imagine a refrigerator being smart enough to order vegetables when the basket is empty. Think of a world where your parcels are delivered through drones. Welcome to the dystopian world of AI, coming no later than 2020. Maybe in the next 15 years you can expect machines reproducing themselves using AI and 3D printing. You can also expect robots to play tennis matches and defeat the champions of the game. You can expect AI-based robots to perform medical surgeries. However, we still don't know if we can ever produce a machine that has the power of intuition and moral values like us.

People always ask how exactly should we utilize and sail in the disruptive era of AI. AI has already started disruption for blue-collar jobs (see Figure 10-7). They are in the process of disrupting white-collar jobs. How disruptive it will be is unknown to all of us but certainly governance-based augmented intelligence will be required soon. We tried to answer some of those questions in this chapter but it also reminds me of a famous quote by Francis of Assisi:

■ **Note** "Start doing what's necessary, then do what's possible, and suddenly you are doing the impossible."

Figure 10-7. *A robot takes stock before doing manual work*

Index

© Nishith Pathak 2017
N. Pathak, *Artificial Intelligence for .NET: Speech, Language, and Search*, DOI 10.1007/978-1-4842-2949-1

Get the eBook for only $5!

Why limit yourself?

With most of our titles available in both PDF and ePUB format, you can access your content wherever and however you wish—on your PC, phone, tablet, or reader.

Since you've purchased this print book, we are happy to offer you the eBook for just $5.

To learn more, go to http://www.apress.com/companion or contact support@apress.com.

Apress®

Made in the USA
Columbia, SC
30 August 2019